W9-ARC-442

A SYNOPTIC HARMONY OF SAMUEL, KINGS, AND CHRONICLES

A SYNOPTIC HARMONY OF SAMUEL, KINGS, AND CHRONICLES

With Related Passages from Psalms, Isaiah, Jeremiah, and Ezra

EDITED BY
JAMES D. NEWSOME, JR.

BAKER BOOK HOUSE
Grand Rapids, Michigan 49506

Contents

Section	Samuel/Kings		Chronicles	Page

Section	Samuel/Kings	Chronicles	Page

Section	Samuel/Kings	Chronicles	Page

Section	Samuel/Kings		Chronicles	Page

Foreword

Students of the Old Testament have long recognized that in the two histories of the Hebrew monarchies, Samuel/Kings and Chronicles, a literary relationship exists which is akin to that of the Synoptic Gospels of the New Testament. That is, more than one extended narrative have come down to us from antiquity, each of which exhibits distinctive characteristics, while at the same time demonstrating a more than casual relationship with the other(s). Unlike their colleagues in Synoptic Gospel studies, however, students of Samuel/Kings and Chronicles have not had easy access to English-language harmonies in which the principal texts are laid side-by-side in such a manner that comparison is facilitated not just of large blocks of text, but of individual words and phrases as well. Primus Vannutelli's fine *Libri Synoptici Veteris Testamenti* (Rome: Pontifical Biblical Institute, 1931) renders that service for those who are schooled in biblical Hebrew, and, in addition, provides references to relevant passages in the Septuagint (in Greek), the Vulgate (in Latin) and Flavius Josephus (in Greek). Vannutelli will continue to serve as an important tool for all who attempt comparative literary studies in the Hebrew texts of Samuel/Kings and Chronicles. However, it is my hope that this book will provide a similar resource for those who are interested in comparative studies of this literature, but who work in the English language. It is also expected that this harmony may be of use to those who simply wish to have brought together, for narrative purposes, the major texts dealing with the history of the Hebrew kingdoms.

The text is that of the Revised Standard Version, Samuel/Kings in the left column, Chronicles in the right (except where noted). At all times, however, the standard of reference has remained the Masoretic Text, and occasionally I have ventured to introduce minor adjustments to the RSV text in order more accurately to demonstrate the relationship between the received Hebrew text of our sources. For example, if differences between an English language (RSV) passage in Samuel/Kings and its parallel in Chronicles give the false impression that corresponding differences exist in the Hebrew of those texts, then the English texts have been reconciled with one another, usually by accommodating the reading in Chronicles to that in Samuel/Kings. A case in point is I Kings 7:47, which reads ". . . the weight of the bronze was not found out," and II Chronicles 4:18, ". . . the weight of the bronze was not ascertained." Since the Hebrew verb is identical in both cases, "ascertained" has been changed to "found out." In instances of this nature, the number of the verse which has been adjusted is enclosed with slash marks / /.

On the other hand, if similar or identical English readings conceal significant differences in the Hebrew text, at least one of the English texts in question has been altered to reflect the Hebrew, frequently by adopting the marginal RSV reading. For example, the RSV of I Kings 12:2 (following II Chronicles 10:2) reads ". . . then Jeroboam returned from Egypt." However, the RSV marginal reading, which has been adopted here, conveys the true state of the Hebrew text: ". . . then Jeroboam dwelt in Egypt." In such cases, the number of the verse in question has been marked: ⟨ ⟩.

At various points the Hebrew text has apparently been disturbed, either through scribal error or some other cause. The RSV translators have wisely elected, where possible in these instances, to rely on the parallel text to supply the "lost" reading, noting the true state of the Hebrew text in a marginal notation. Where it seemed appropriate, these marginal notations have been introduced into the main body of our text and designated by: [ ]. Example: II Samuel 6:7.

Punctuation and capitalization of letters were not, of course, features of biblical Hebrew. The RSV has been followed in this regard, except in those instances where differences in the RSV punctuation and capitalization of parallel passages would provide the false impression of differences in the Hebrew text.

With the RSV, the principal divine name in the Hebrew Scriptures, YHWH or Yahweh, is here represented by the word LORD.

Two indices have been provided for the convenience of the reader. The first of these, the Contents, lists texts in Samuel/Kings (beginning with I Samuel 31:1–13) in the order in which they appear in those Old Testament books. Thus, those who wish to identify passages parallel to a text in Samuel/Kings may consult this table for the appropriate section in this harmony where such may be found. In addition, an *Index of Passages in I and II Chronicles, Psalms, Isaiah, Jeremiah and Ezra* has been included for those whose starting point is a text in Chronicles or in one of the other Old Testament books which contain parallel texts included here.

James D. Newsome, Jr.
Columbia Theological Seminary
October 11, 1985

A Synoptic Harmony
of Samuel, Kings,
and Chronicles

Key

( ) RSV with no alterations.

/ / Differences in the English language text (RSV) between Samuel/Kings and parallel passage in Chronicles have been reconciled to reflect the state of the Hebrew text.

⟨ ⟩ Passage has been modified to reflect a significant difference between parallel Hebrew text.

[ ] Hebrew text is uncertain or has been disturbed.

1 The Death of Saul

I Samuel 31:1–13   *I Chronicles 10:1–14*

(1)Now the Philistines fought against Israel; and the men of Israel fled before the Philistines, and fell slain on Mount Gilboa. (2)And the Philistines overtook Saul and his sons; and the Philistines slew Jonathan and Abinadab and Malchishua, the sons of Saul. (3)The battle pressed hard upon Saul, and the archers found him; and he was <u>badly</u> wounded by the archers. (4)Then Saul said to his armor-bearer, "Draw your sword, and thrust me through with it, lest these uncircumcised come and <u>thrust me through, and</u> make sport of me." But his armor-bearer would not; for he feared greatly. Therefore Saul took his own sword, and fell upon it. (5)And when his armor-bearer saw that Saul was dead, he also fell upon his sword, and died <u>with him</u>. (6)Thus Saul died, and his three sons, <u>and his armor-bearer, and all his men,</u> <u>on the same day</u> together. (7)And when the men of Israel who were <u>on the other side of</u> the valley <u>and those beyond the Jordan</u> saw that <u>the men of Israel</u> had fled and that Saul and his sons were dead, they forsook their cities and fled; and the Philistines came and dwelt in them. (8)On the morrow, when the Philistines came to strip the slain, they found Saul and his <u>three</u> sons fallen on Mount Gilboa. (9)And they <u>cut off his head,</u> and <u>stripped off</u> his armor, and sent messengers throughout the land of the Philistines, to carry the good

(1)Now the Philistines fought against Israel; and the men of Israel fled before the Philistines, and fell slain on Mount Gilboa. (2)And the Philistines overtook Saul and his sons; and the Philistines slew Jonathan and Abinidab and Malchishua, the sons of Saul. (3)The battle pressed hard upon Saul, and the archers found him; and he was wounded by the archers. (4)Then Saul said to his armor-bearer, "Draw your sword, and thrust me through with it, lest these uncircumcised come and

make sport of me." But his armor-bearer would not; for he feared greatly. Therefore Saul took his own sword, and fell upon it. (5)And when his armor-bearer saw that Saul was dead, he also fell upon his sword, and died. (6)Thus Saul died; <u>he</u> and his three sons

<u>and all his house</u> died together. (7)And when all the men of Israel who were <u>in</u> the valley

saw that <u>they</u> had fled and that Saul and his sons were dead, they forsook their cities and fled; and the Philistines came and dwelt in them. (8)On the morrow, when the Philistines came to strip the slain, they found Saul and his sons fallen on Mount Gilboa. (9)And they <u>stripped him</u> and <u>took his head and</u> his armor, and sent messengers throughout the land of the Philistines, to carry the good

19

news to the house of their idols
and to the people. (10)They put
his armor in the temple of Ashtaroth;
and they fastened his body to the
wall of Beth-shan.
(11)But when the inhabitants of
Jabesh-gilead heard what the
Philistines had done to Saul, (12)all
the valiant men arose,
and went all night,
and took the body of Saul and the
bodies of his sons
from the wall of Beth-shan;
and they came to Jabesh
and burnt them there.
(13)And
they took their bones and buried them
under the tamarisk tree in Jabesh,
and fasted seven days.

news to their idols
and to the people. (10)And they put
his armor in the temple of their gods,
and fastened his head in the
temple of Dagon.
(11)But when all
Jabesh-gilead heard all that the
Philistines had done to Saul, (12)all
the valiant men arose,

and took away the body of Saul and the
bodies of his sons,

and brought them to Jabesh.

And
they buried their bones
under the oak in Jabesh,
and fasted seven days.
(13)So Saul died for his
unfaithfulness; he was unfaithful to
the LORD in that he did not keep the
command of the LORD, and also
consulted a medium, seeking guidance,
(14)and did not seek guidance from
the LORD. Therefore the LORD slew
him, and turned the kingdom over to
David the son of Jesse.

2 David's Response to Saul's Death

II Samuel 1:1–27

(1)After the death of Saul, when David had returned from the slaughter of the Amalekites, David remained two days in Ziklag; (2)and on the third day, behold, a man came from Saul's camp, with his clothes rent and earth upon his head. And when he came to David, he fell to the ground and did obeisance. (3)David said to him, "Where do you come from?" And he said to him, "I have escaped from the camp of Israel." (4)And David said to him, "How did it go? Tell me." And he answered, "The people have fled from the battle, and many of the people also have fallen and are dead; and Saul and his son Jonathan are also dead." (5)Then David said to the young man who told him, "How do you know that Saul and his son Jonathan are dead?" (6)And the young man who told him said, "By chance I happened to be on Mount Gilboa; and there was Saul leaning upon his spear; and lo, the chariots and the horsemen were close upon him. (7)And when he looked behind him, he saw me, and called to me. And I answered, 'Here I am.' (8)And he said to me, 'Who are you?' I answered him, 'I am an Amalekite.' (9)And he said to me, 'Stand beside me and slay me; for anguish has seized me, and yet my life still lingers.' (10)So I stood beside him, and slew him, because I was sure that he could not live after he had fallen; and I took the crown which was on his head and the armlet which was on his arm, and I have brought them here to my lord."

(11)Then David took hold of his clothes, and rent them; and so did all the men who were with him; (12)and they mourned and wept and fasted until evening for Saul and for Jonathan his son and for the people of the LORD and for the house of Israel, because they had fallen by the sword. (13)And David said to the young man who told him, "Where do you come from?" And he answered, "I am the son of a sojourner, an Amalekite." (14)David said to him, "How is it you were not afraid to put forth your hand to destroy the LORD's anointed?" (15)Then David called one of the young men and said, "Go, fall upon him." And he smote him so that he died. (16)And David said to him, "Your blood be upon your head; for your own mouth has testified against you, saying, 'I have slain the LORD's anointed.' "

(17)And David lamented with this lamentation over Saul and Jonathan his son, (18)and he said it should be taught to the people of Judah; behold, it is written in the Book of Jashar. He said:

> (19)"Thy glory, O Israel, is slain upon the high places!
> How are the mighty fallen!
> (20)Tell it not in Gath,
> publish it not in the streets of Ashkelon;
> lest the daughters of the Philistines rejoice,
> lest the daughters of the uncircumcised exult.
> (21)"Ye mountains of Gilboa,
> let there be no dew or rain upon you,
> nor upsurging of the deep!
> For there the shield of the mighty was defiled,
> the shield of Saul, not anointed with oil.
> (22)"From the blood of the slain,
> from the fat of the mighty,
> the bow of Jonathan turned not back,
> and the sword of Saul returned not empty.
> (23)"Saul and Jonathan, beloved and lovely!
> In life and in death they were not divided;
> they were swifter than eagles,
> they were stronger than lions.
> (24)"Ye daughters of Israel, weep over Saul,
> who clothed you daintily in scarlet,
> who put ornaments of gold upon your apparel.
> (25)"How are the mighty fallen
> in the midst of the battle!
> "Jonathan lies slain upon thy high places.
> (26) I am distressed for you, my brother Jonathan;
> very pleasant have you been to me;
> your love to me was wonderful,
> passing the love of women.
> (27)"How are the mighty fallen,
> and the weapons of war perished!"

3 David Becomes King over Judah

II Samuel 2:1–7

[1]After this David inquired of the LORD, "Shall I go up into any of the cities of Judah?" And the LORD said to him, "Go up." David said, "To which shall I go up?" And he said, "To Hebron." [2]So David went up there, and his two wives also, Ahinoam of Jezreel, and Abigail the widow of Nabal of Carmel. [3]And David brought up his men who were with him, every one with his household; and they dwelt in the towns of Hebron. [4]And the men of Judah came, and there they anointed David king over the house of Judah.

When they told David, "It was the men of Jabesh-gilead who buried Saul," [5]David sent messengers to the men of Jabesh-gilead, and said to them, "May you be blessed by the LORD, because you showed this loyalty to Saul your lord, and buried him! [6]Now may the LORD show steadfast love and faithfulness to you! And I will do good to you because you have done this thing. [7]Now therefore let your hands be strong, and be valiant; for Saul your lord is dead, and the house of Judah has anointed me king over them."

4 The Death of Asahel, Joab's Brother

II Samuel 2:8–32

[8]Now Abner the son of Ner, commander of Saul's army, had taken Ish-bosheth the son of Saul, and brought him over to Mahanaim; [9]and he made him king over Gilead and the Ashurites and Jezreel and Ephraim and Benjamin and all Israel. [10]Ish-bosheth, Saul's son, was forty years old when he began to reign over Israel, and he reigned two years. But the house of Judah followed David. [11]And the time that David was king in Hebron over the house of Judah was seven years and six months.

[12]Abner the son of Ner, and the servants of Ish-bosheth the son of Saul, went out from Mahanaim to Gibeon. [13]And Joab the son of Zeruiah, and the servants of David, went out and met them at the pool of Gibeon; and they sat down, the one on the one side of the pool, and the other on the other side of the pool. [14]And Abner said to Joab, "Let the young men arise and play before us." And Joab said, "Let them arise." [15]Then they arose and passed over by number, twelve for Benjamin and Ish-bosheth the son of Saul, and twelve of the servants of David. [16]And each caught his opponent by the head, and thrust his sword in his opponent's side; so they fell down together. Therefore that place was called Helkath-hazzurim, which is at Gibeon. [17]And the battle was very fierce that day; and Abner and the men of Israel were beaten before the servants of David.

[18]And the three sons of Zeruiah were there, Joab, Abishai, and Asahel. Now Asahel was as swift of foot as a wild gazelle; [19]and Asahel pursued Abner, and as he went he turned neither to the right hand nor to the left from following Abner. [20]Then Abner looked behind him and said, "Is it you, Asahel?" And he answered, "It is I." [21]Abner said to him, "Turn aside to your right hand or to your left, and seize one of the young men, and take his spoil." But Asahel would not turn aside from following him. [22]And Abner said again to Asahel, "Turn aside from following me; why should I smite you to

the ground? How then could I lift up my face to your brother Joab?" (23)But he refused to turn aside; therefore Abner smote him in the belly with the butt of his spear, so that the spear came out at his back; and he fell there, and died where he was. And all who came to the place where Asahel had fallen and died, stood still.

(24)But Joab and Abishai pursued Abner; and as the sun was going down they came to the hill of Ammah, which lies before Giah on the way to the wilderness of Gibeon. (25)And the Benjaminites gathered themselves together behind Abner, and became one band, and took their stand on the top of a hill. (26)Then Abner called to Joab, "Shall the sword devour for ever? Do you not know that the end will be bitter? How long will it be before you bid your people turn from the pursuit of their brethren?" (27)And Joab said, "As God lives, if you had not spoken, surely the men would have given up the pursuit of their brethren in the morning." (28)So Joab blew the trumpet; and all the men stopped, and pursued Israel no more, nor did they fight any more.

(29)And Abner and his men went all that night through the Arabah; they crossed the Jordan, and marching the whole forenoon they came to Mahanaim. (30)Joab returned from the pursuit of Abner; and when he had gathered all the people together, there were missing of David's servants nineteen men besides Asahel. (31)But the servants of David had slain of Benjamin three hundred and sixty of Abner's men. (32)And they took up Asahel, and buried him in the tomb of his father, which was at Bethlehem. And Joab and his men marched all night, and the day broke upon them at Hebron.

5 David's Sons Born at Hebron

II Samuel 3:1–5	*I Chronicles 3:1–4*
(1)There was a long war between the house of Saul and the house of David; and David grew stronger and stronger, while the house of Saul became weaker and weaker.	
(2)And sons were born to David at Hebron: his first-born was Amnon, of Ahino-am of Jezreel;	(1)These are the sons of David that were born to him in Hebron: the first-born Amnon, by Ahino-am the Jezreelitess;
(3)and his second, Chile-ab, of Abigail the widow of Nabal of Carmel;	the second Daniel, by Abigail the Carmelitess,
and the third, Absalom the son of Maacah the daughter of Talmai king of Geshur;	(2)the third Absalom, whose mother was Maacah, the daughter of Talmai, king of Geshur;
(4)and the fourth, Adonijah the son of Haggith;	the fourth Adonijah, whose mother was Haggith;
and the fifth, Shephatiah the son of Abital;	(3)the fifth Shephatiah, by Abital;
(5)and the sixth, Ithre-am of Eglah, David's wife. These were born to David in Hebron.	the sixth Ithre-am, by his wife Eglah; (4)six were born to him in Hebron, where he reigned for seven years and six months.

6 The Defection and Murder of Abner

II Samuel 3:6–39

[6]While there was war between the house of Saul and the house of David, Abner was making himself strong in the house of Saul. [7]Now Saul had a concubine, whose name was Rizpah, the daughter of Aiah; and Ish-bosheth said to Abner, "Why have you gone in to my father's concubine?" [8]Then Abner was very angry over the words of Ish-bosheth, and said, "Am I a dog's head of Judah? This day I keep showing loyalty to the house of Saul your father, to his brothers, and to his friends, and have not given you into the hand of David; and yet you charge me today with a fault concerning a woman. [9]God do so to Abner, and more also, if I do not accomplish for David what the LORD has sworn to him, [10]to transfer the kingdom from the house of Saul, and set up the throne of David over Israel and over Judah, from Dan to Beer-sheba." [11]And Ish-bosheth could not answer Abner another word, because he feared him.

[12]And Abner sent messengers to David at Hebron, saying, "To whom does the land belong? Make your covenant with me, and behold, my hand shall be with you to bring over all Israel to you." [13]And he said, "Good, I will make a covenant with you; but one thing I require of you; that is, you shall not see my face, unless you first bring Michal, Saul's daughter, when you come to see my face." [14]Then David sent messengers to Ish-bosheth Saul's son, saying, "Give me my wife Michal, whom I betrothed at the price of a hundred foreskins of the Philistines." [15]And Ish-bosheth sent, and took her from her husband Palti-el the son of Laish. [16]But her husband went with her, weeping after her all the way to Bahurim. Then Abner said to him, "Go, return"; and he returned.

[17]And Abner conferred with the elders of Israel, saying, "For some time past you have been seeking David as king over you. [18]Now then bring it about; for the LORD has promised David, saying, 'By the hand of my servant David I will save my people Israel from the hand of the Philistines, and from the hand of all their enemies.' " [19]Abner also spoke to Benjamin; and then Abner went to tell David at Hebron all that Israel and the whole house of Benjamin thought good to do.

[20]When Abner came with twenty men to David at Hebron, David made a feast for Abner and the men who were with him. [21]And Abner said to David, "I will arise and go, and will gather all Israel to my lord the king, that they may make a covenant with you, and that you may reign over all that your heart desires." So David sent Abner away; and he went in peace.

[22]Just then the servants of David arrived with Joab from a raid, bringing much spoil with them. But Abner was not with David at Hebron, for he had sent him away, and he had gone in peace. [23]When Joab and all the army that was with him came, it was told Joab, "Abner the son of Ner came to the king, and he has let him go, and he has gone in peace." [24]Then Joab went to the king and said, "What have you done? Behold, Abner came to you; why is it that you have sent him away, so that he is gone? [25]You know that Abner the son of Ner came to deceive you, and to know your going out and your coming in, and to know all that you are doing."

[26]When Joab came out from David's presence, he sent messengers after Abner, and they brought him back from the cistern of Sirah; but David did not know about it. [27]And when Abner returned to Hebron, Joab took him aside into the midst of the gate

to speak with him privately, and there he smote him in the belly, so that he died, for the blood of Asahel his brother. (28)Afterward, when David heard of it, he said, "I and my kingdom are for ever guiltless before the LORD for the blood of Abner the son of Ner. (29)May it fall upon the head of Joab, and upon all his father's house; and may the house of Joab never be without one who has a discharge, or who is leprous, or who holds a spindle, or who is slain by the sword, or who lacks bread!" (30)So Joab and Abishai his brother slew Abner, because he had killed their brother Asahel in the battle at Gibeon.

(31)Then David said to Joab and to all the people who were with him, "Rend your clothes, and gird on sackcloth, and mourn before Abner." And King David followed the bier. (32)They buried Abner at Hebron; and the king lifted up his voice and wept at the grave of Abner; and all the people wept. (33)And the king lamented for Abner, saying,

(34)Should Abner die as a fool dies?
Your hands were not bound,
    your feet were not fettered;
as one falls before the wicked
    you have fallen.

Then all the people wept again over him. (35)Then all the people came to persuade David to eat bread while it was yet day; but David swore, saying, "God do so to me and more also, if I taste bread or anything else till the sun goes down!" (36)And all the people took notice of it, and it pleased them; as everything that the king did pleased all the people. (37)So all the people and all Israel understood that day that it had not been the king's will to slay Abner the son of Ner. (38)And the king said to his servants, "Do you not know that a prince and a great man has fallen this day in Israel? (39)And I am this day weak, though anointed king; these men the sons of Zeruiah are too hard for me. The LORD requite the evildoer according to his wickedness!"

7 The Murder of Ish-bosheth

II Samuel 4:1–12

(1)When Ish-bosheth, Saul's son, heard that Abner had died at Hebron, his courage failed, and all Israel was dismayed. (2)Now Saul's son had two men who were captains of raiding bands; the name of the one was Baanah, and the name of the other Rechab, sons of Rimmon a man of Benjamin from Be-eroth (for Be-eroth also is reckoned to Benjamin; (3)the Be-erothites fled to Gittaim, and have been sojourners there to this day).

(4)Jonathan, the son of Saul, had a son who was crippled in his feet. He was five years old when the news about Saul and Jonathan came from Jezreel; and his nurse took him up, and fled; and, as she fled in her haste, he fell, and became lame. And his name was Mephibosheth.

(5)Now the sons of Rimmon the Be-erothite, Rechab and Baanah, set out, and about the heat of the day they came to the house of Ish-bosheth, as he was taking his noonday rest. (6)And behold, the doorkeeper of the house had been cleaning wheat, but she grew drowsy and slept; so Rechab and Baanah his brother slipped in. (7)When they came into the house, as he lay on his bed in his bedchamber, they smote him, and slew him, and beheaded him. They took his head, and went by the way of the Arabah all night, (8)and brought the head of Ish-bosheth to David at Hebron. And they said to the king, "Here is the head of Ish-bosheth, the son of Saul, your enemy, who sought your life; the LORD has avenged my lord the king this day on Saul and his offspring." (9)But David answered Rechab and Baanah his brother, the sons of Rimmon the Be-erothite, "As the LORD lives, who has redeemed my life out of every adversity, (10)when one told me, 'Behold, Saul is dead,' and thought he was bringing good news, I seized him and slew him at Ziklag, which was the reward I gave him for his news. (11)How much more, when wicked men have slain a righteous man in his own house upon his bed, shall I not now require his blood at your hand, and destroy you from the earth?" (12)And David commanded his young men, and they killed them, and cut off their hands and feet, and hanged them beside the pool at Hebron. But they took the head of Ish-bosheth, and buried it in the tomb of Abner at Hebron.

8 David Becomes King over Israel

II Samuel 5:1–5

(1)Then all the tribes of Israel came to David at Hebron, and said, "Behold, we are your bone and flesh. (2)In times past, when Saul was king over us, it was you that led out and brought in Israel; and the LORD said to you, 'You shall be shepherd of my people Israel, and you shall be prince over Israel.' " (3)So all the elders of Israel came to the king at Hebron; and King David made a covenant with them at Hebron before the LORD, and they anointed David king over Israel.

(4)David was thirty years old when he began to reign, and he reigned forty years. (5)At Hebron he reigned over Judah seven years and six months; and at Jerusalem he reigned over all Israel and Judah thirty-three years.

I Chronicles 11:1–3

(1)Then all Israel gathered together to David at Hebron, and said, "Behold, we are your bone and flesh. (2)In times past, even when Saul was king, it was you that led out and brought in Israel; and the LORD your God said to you, 'You shall be shepherd of my people Israel, and you shall be prince over my people Israel.' " (3)So all the elders of Israel came to the king at Hebron; and David made a covenant with them at Hebron before the LORD, and they anointed David king over Israel, according to the word of the LORD by Samuel.

26

9 David Captures Jerusalem

II Samuel 5:6–10

⁽⁶⁾And the king and his men went
to Jerusalem
against the Jebusites,
the inhabitants of the land,
who
said to David,
"You will not come in here,
but the blind and the lame will ward
you off"—thinking, "David cannot
come in here."
⁽⁷⁾Nevertheless David took the
stronghold of Zion, that is, the city
of David. ⁽⁸⁾And David said
on that day,
"Whoever would smite the Jebusites,

let him get up the water shaft to
attack the lame and the blind, who
are hated by David's soul."
Therefore it is said, "The blind and
the lame shall not come into the
house."

⁽⁹⁾And David dwelt in the stronghold,
and called it the city of
David. And David built the city
round about from the Millo
inward.

⁽¹⁰⁾And David became greater and
greater, for the LORD,
the God of hosts was with him.

I Chronicles 11:4–9

⁽⁴⁾And David and all Israel went
to Jerusalem, that is Jebus,
where the Jebusites were,
the inhabitants of the land.
⁽⁵⁾The inhabitants of Jebus
said to David,
"You will not come in here."

Nevertheless David took the
stronghold of Zion, that is, the city
of David. ⁽⁶⁾David said,

"Whoever shall smite the Jebusites
first shall be chief and commander."

And Joab the son of Zeruiah went up
first, so he became chief.
⁽⁷⁾And David dwelt in the stronghold;
therefore it was called the city of
David. ⁽⁸⁾And he built the city
round about from the Millo
in complete circuit; and
Joab repaired the rest of the city.
⁽⁹⁾And David became greater and
greater, for the LORD
of hosts was with him.

10 David Consolidates His Kingdom

II Samuel 5:11–25

⁽¹¹⁾And Hiram king of Tyre sent
messengers to David, and cedar trees,
also carpenters and masons who built
David a house. ⁽¹²⁾And David
perceived that the LORD had

I Chronicles 14:1–17

⁽¹⁾And Hiram king of Tyre sent
messengers to David, and cedar trees,
also masons and carpenters to build
a house for him. ⁽²⁾And David
perceived that the LORD had

27

established him king over Israel, and
that he had exalted his kingdom
for the sake of his people Israel.
(13)And David took more
concubines and wives from Jerusalem,
after he came from Hebron;
and more sons and daughters
were born to David.
(14)And these are the names of those
who were born to him in Jerusalem:
Shammu-a, Shobab, Nathan, Solomon,
(15)Ibhar, Elishu-a,

Nepheg, Japhia, (16)Elishama,
Eliada, and Eliphelet.
(17)When the Philistines heard
that David had been anointed king
over Israel, all the Philistines
went up in search of David; but
David heard of it and
went down to the stronghold.
(18)Now the Philistines had come and
spread out in the valley of Rephaim.
(19)And David inquired of the LORD,
"Shall I go up against the
Philistines? Wilt thou give them
into my hand?" And the LORD said to
David, "Go up; for I will certainly
give the Philistines into your hand."
(20)And David came to Baal-perazim,
and David defeated them there; and
he said, "The LORD has broken through
my enemies before me, like a bursting
flood." Therefore the name of that
place is called Baal-perazim.
(21)And the Philistines left their
idols there, and David and his men
carried them away.
(22)And the Philistines came up
yet again, and spread out
in the valley of Rephaim. (23)And
when David inquired of the LORD,
he said, "You shall not go up;
go around to their rear, and come
upon them opposite the balsam trees.
(24)And when you hear the sound of
marching in the tops of the balsam

established him king over Israel, and
that his kingdom was highly exhalted
for the sake of his people Israel.
(3)And David took more
wives in Jerusalem,
and David begot
more sons and daughters.

/4/And these are the names of the children whom he had in Jerusalem:
Shammu-a, Shobab, Nathan, Solomon,
(5)Ibhar, Elishu-a,
Elpelet, (6)Nogah,
Nepheg, Japhia, (7)Elishama,
Beeliada, and Eliphelet.
(8)When the Philistines heard
that David had been anointed king
over all Israel, all the Philistines
went up in search of David; and
David heard of it and
went out against them.
(9)Now the Philistines had come and
made a raid in the valley of Rephaim.
(10)And David inquired of God,
"Shall I go up against the
Philistines? Wilt thou give them
into my hand?" And the LORD said to
him, "Go up, and I will
give them into your hand."
(11)And he went up to Baal-perazim,
and David defeated them there; and
David said, "God has broken through
my enemies by my hand, like a bursting
flood." Therefore the name of that
place is called Baal-perazim.
(12)And they left their
gods there, and David
gave command, and they were burned.
(13)And the Philistines
yet again made a raid
in the valley. (14)And
when David again inquired of God,
God said to him, "You shall not go up
after them; go around and come
upon them opposite the balsam trees.
(15)And when you hear the sound of
marching in the tops of the balsam

trees, then bestir yourself; for
then the LORD has gone out before you to
smite the army of the Philistines."
(25)And David did as the LORD
commanded him, and smote the
Philistines from Geba to Gezer.

trees, then go out to battle; for
God has gone out before you to
smite the army of the Philistines."
(16)And David did as God
commanded him, and they smote the
Philistine army from Gibeon to Gezer.
(17)And the fame of David went out
into all lands, and the LORD brought
the fear of him upon all nations.

11 The Death of Uzzah

II Samuel 6:1–11

I Chronicles 13:1–14

(1)David consulted with the
commanders of thousands and of
hundreds, with every leader. (2)And
David said to all the assembly of
Israel, "If it seems good to you, and
if it is the will of the LORD our God,
let us send abroad to our brethren who
remain in all the land of Israel, and
with them to the priests and Levites
in the cities that have pasture lands,
that they may come together to us.
(3)Then let us bring again the ark of
our God to us; for we neglected it in
the days of Saul." (4)All the
assembly agreed to do so, for the
thing was right in the eyes of all the
people.

(1)David again gathered
all the chosen men of Israel,
thirty thousand.

(5)So David assembled
all Israel

from the Shihor of Egypt to the
entrance of Hamath, to bring the ark
of God from Kiriath-jearim.

(2)And David arose
and went with all the people
who were with him from Baale-judah,

(6)And David
and all Israel went up
to Baalah, that is, to Kiriath-jearim
which belongs to Judah,

to bring up from there the ark of God,
which is called by the name of the
LORD of hosts who sits enthroned
on the cherubim. (3)And they
carried the ark of God upon a new

to bring up from there the ark of God,
which is called by the name of the
LORD who sits enthroned
above the cherubim. (7)And they
carried the ark of God upon a new

29

cart, and brought it out of the house of
Abinadab which was on the hill; and
Uzzah and Ahio, the sons of Abinadab,
were driving the new cart,
and brought it out of the house of
Abinadab which was on the hill
(4)with the ark of God; and Ahio
went before the ark.
(5)And David and all the house of
Israel were making merry before
the LORD with all their might, with
fir-trees and lyres and harps and
tambourines and castanets
and cymbals.
   (6)And when they came to the
threshing floor of Nacon, Uzzah
put out his hand to the ark
of God and took hold of it,
for the oxen stumbled. (7)And the
anger of the LORD was kindled against
Uzzah; and God smote him there
. . . (*)

and he died there
beside the ark of God.
/8/And David was angry because
the LORD had broken forth upon Uzzah;
and that place is called Perez-uzzah
to this day. (9)And David was afraid
of the LORD that day; and he said,
"How can the ark of the LORD
come to me?"
(10)So David was not willing
to take the ark of the LORD
into the city of David; but
David took it aside to the house of
Obed-edom the Gittite. (11)And the
ark of the LORD remained in the house
of Obed-edom the Gittite three
months; and the LORD blessed
Obed-edom and all his household.

cart, from the house of
Abinadab, and
Uzzah and Ahio
were driving the cart.

(8)And David and all
Israel were making merry before
God with all their might, with
song and lyres and harps and
tambourines and cymbals
and trumpets.
   (9)And when they came to the
threshing floor of Chidon, Uzzah
put out his hand to hold the ark,

for the oxen stumbled. (10)And the
anger of the LORD was kindled against
Uzzah; and he smote him
because he put forth
his hand to the ark;
and he died there
before God.
(11)And David was angry because
the LORD had broken forth upon Uzzah;
and that place is called Perez-uzza
to this day. (12)And David was afraid
of God that day; and he said,
"How can I bring the ark of God
home to me?"
(13)So David did not
take the ark home
into the city of David, but
took it aside to the house of
Obed-edom the Gittite. (14)And the
ark of God remained with the household
of Obed-edom in his house three
months; and the LORD blessed
the household of Obed-edom and all
that he had.

*Hebrew is uncertain.

30

12 The Ark Is Brought to Jerusalem (Beginning)

— *II Samuel 6:12–19a; I Chronicles 15:1–16:3*

I Chronicles 15:1–24

(1)David built houses for himself in the city of David; and he prepared a place for the ark of God, and pitched a tent for it. (2)Then David said, "No one but the Levites may carry the ark of God, for the LORD chose them to carry the ark of the LORD and to minister to him for ever." (3)And David assembled all Israel at Jerusalem, to bring up the ark of the LORD to its place, which he had prepared for it. (4)And David gathered together the sons of Aaron and the Levites: (5)of the sons of Kohath, Uriel the chief, with a hundred and twenty of his brethren; (6)of the sons of Merari, Asaiah the chief, with two hundred and twenty of his brethren; (7)of the sons of Gershom, Joel the chief, with a hundred and thirty of his brethren; (8)of the sons of Elizaphan, Shemaiah the chief, with two hundred of his brethren; (9)of the sons of Hebron, Eliel the chief, with eighty of his brethren; (10)of the sons of Uzziel, Amminadab the chief, with a hundred and twelve of his brethren. (11)Then David summoned the priests Zadok and Abiathar, and the Levites Uriel, Asaiah, Joel, Shemaiah, Eliel, and Amminadab, (12)and said to them, "You are the heads of the fathers' houses of the Levites; sanctify yourselves, you and your brethren, so that you may bring up the ark of the LORD, the God of Israel, to the place that I have prepared for it. (13)Because you did not carry it the first time, the LORD our God broke forth upon us, because we did not care for it in the way that is ordained." (14)So the priests and the Levites sanctified themselves to bring up the ark of the LORD, the God of Israel. (15)And the Levites carried the ark of God upon their shoulders with the poles, as Moses had commanded according to the word of the LORD.

(16)David also commanded the chiefs of the Levites to appoint their brethren as the singers who should play loudly on musical instruments, on harps and lyres and cymbals, to raise sounds of joy. (17)So the Levites appointed Heman the son of Joel; and of his brethren Asaph the son of Berechiah; and of the sons of Merari, their brethren, Ethan the son of Kushaiah; (18)and with them their brethren of the second order, Zechariah, Ja-aziel, Shemiramoth, Jehiel, Unni, Eliab, Benaiah, Maaseiah, Mattithiah, Eliphelehu, and Mikneiah, and the gatekeepers Obed-edom and Je-iel. (19)The singers, Heman, Asaph, and Ethan, were to sound bronze cymbals; (20)Zechariah, Azi-el, Shemiramoth, Jehiel, Unni, Eliab, Maaseiah, and Benaiah were to play harps according to Alamoth; (21)but Mattithiah, Eliphelehu, Mikneiah, Obed-edom, Je-iel, and Azaziah were to lead with lyres according to the Sheminith. (22)Chenaniah, leader of the Levites in music, should direct the music, for he understood it. (23)Berechiah and Elkanah were to be gatekeepers for the ark. (24)Shebaniah, Joshaphat, Nethanel, Amasai, Zechariah, Benaiah, and Eliezer, the priests, should blow the trumpets before the ark of God. Obed-edom and Jehiah also were to be gatekeepers for the ark.

II Samuel 6:12–19a	*I Chronicles 15:25–16:3*
(12)And it was told King David, "The LORD has blessed the household of Obed-edom and all that belongs to him, because of the ark of God." So David	(25)So David and the elders of Israel, and the commanders of thousands,

31

went and brought up the ark
of God
from the house of Obed-edom
to the city of David with rejoicing;
(13)and when those who bore the ark
of the LORD had gone six paces,

he sacrificed an ox and
a fatling.
(14)And David danced before the LORD
with all his might;

and David was girded with
a linen ephod.
(15)So David and
all the house of Israel brought up
the ark of the LORD
with shouting,
and with the sound of the horn.

(16)As the ark of
the LORD
came into the city of David,
Michal the daughter of Saul
looked out of the window,
and saw King David
leaping and dancing before the LORD;
and she despised him in her heart.
(17)And they brought in
the ark of the LORD,
and set it
in its place,
inside the tent which David had
pitched for it; and
David offered burnt offerings and
peace offerings before the LORD.
(18)And when David had finished
offering the burnt offerings and
the peace offerings, he blessed
the people in the name of

went to bring up the ark
of the covenant of the LORD
from the house of Obed-edom
with rejoicing.

(26)And because God helped the
Levites who were carrying the ark
of the covenant of the LORD,
they sacrificed seven bulls and
seven rams.

(27)David was clothed with a robe of
fine linen, as also were all the
Levites who were carrying the ark, and
the singers, and Chenaniah the leader
of the music of the singers;
and David wore
a linen ephod.
(28)So
all Israel brought up
the ark of the covenant of the LORD
with shouting,
to the sound of the horn,
trumpets, and cymbals, and made loud
music on harps and lyres.
(29)And as the ark of
the covenant of the LORD
came to the city of David,
Michal the daughter of Saul
looked out of the window,
and saw King David
dancing and making merry;
and she despised him in her heart.
(16:1)And they brought in
the ark of God,
and set it

inside the tent which David had
pitched for it; and
they offered burnt offerings and
peace offerings before God.
(2)And when David had finished
offering the burnt offerings and
the peace offerings, he blessed
the people in the name of

the LORD of hosts,
(19)and distributed among all
the people,
the whole multitude of Israel,
both men and women,
to each a cake of bread,
a portion of meat, and
a cake of raisins.

the LORD,
(3)and distributed to all

Israel,
both men and women,
to each a loaf of bread,
a portion of meat, and
a cake of raisins.

13 Levites Minister Before the Ark

Psalms 105:1–15; 96:1–13; 106:1, 47–48; I Chronicles 16:4–42

I Chronicles 16:4–42

(4)Moreover he appointed certain
of the Levites as ministers before the
ark of the LORD, to invoke, to thank,
and to praise the LORD, the God of
Israel. (5)Asaph was the chief, and
second to him were Zechariah, Je-iel,
Shemiramoth, Jehiel, Mattithiah,
Eliab, Benaiah, Obed-edom, and
Je-iel, who were to play harps and
lyres; Asaph was to sound the cymbals,
(6)and Benaiah and Jahaziel the
priests were to blow trumpets
continually, before the ark of the
covenant of God.

(7)Then on that day David first
appointed that thanksgiving be sung to
the LORD by Asaph and his brethren.

Psalm 105:1–15

(1)O give thanks to the LORD, call
　　on his name,
　　　make known his deeds among
　　　the peoples!
(2)Sing to him, sing praises to him,
　　tell of all his wonderful works!
(3)Glory in his holy name;
　　let the hearts of those who
　　seek the LORD rejoice!
(4)Seek the LORD and his strength,
　　seek his presence continually!

(8)O give thanks to the LORD, call
　　on his name,
　　　make known his deeds among
　　　the peoples!
(9)Sing to him, sing praises to him,
　　tell of all his wonderful works!
(10)Glory in his holy name;
　　let the hearts of those who
　　seek the LORD rejoice!
(11)Seek the LORD and his strength,
　　seek his presence continually!

33

(5)Remember the wonderful works that
    he has done,
      his miracles, and the
      judgments he uttered,
(6)O offspring of Abraham his
    servant,
      sons of Jacob, his chosen ones!

(7)He is the LORD our God;
    his judgments are in all the
      earth.
(8)He is mindful of his covenant
    for ever,
      of the word that he commanded,
      for a thousand generations,
(9)the covenant which he made with
    Abraham,
      his sworn promise to Isaac,
(10)which he confirmed to Jacob as
    a statute,
      to Israel as an everlasting
      covenant,
/11/saying, "To you I will give
    the land of Canaan,
      as your portion for an
      inheritance."

(12)When they were few in number,
    of little account, and
      sojourners in it,
(13)wandering from nation to nation,
    from one kingdom to another
      people,
(14)he allowed no one to oppress
    them;
      he rebuked kings on their
      account,
(15)saying, "Touch not my
    anointed ones,
      do my prophets no harm!"

Psalm 96:1–13

(1)O sing to the LORD a new song;
    sing to the LORD, all the earth!
(2)Sing to the LORD, bless his name;
    tell of his salvation from day
      to day.

(12)Remember the wonderful works that
    he has done,
      the wonders he wrought, the
      judgments he uttered,
(13)O offspring of Abraham his
    servant,
      sons of Jacob, his chosen ones!

(14)He is the LORD our God;
    his judgments are in all the
      earth.
(15)He is mindful of his covenant
    for ever,
      of the word that he commanded,
      for a thousand generations,
(16)the covenant which he made with
    Abraham,
      his sworn promise to Isaac,
/17/which he confirmed to Jacob as
    a statute,
      to Israel as an everlasting
      covenant,
(18)saying, "To you I will give
    the land of Canaan,
      as your portion for an
      inheritance."

/19/When you were few in number,
    of little account, and
      sojourners in it,
(20)wandering from nation to nation,
    from one kingdom to another
      people,
(21)he allowed no one to oppress
    them;
      he rebuked kings on their
      account,
(22)saying, "Touch not my
    anointed ones,
      do my prophets no harm!"

(23)Sing to the LORD, all the earth!

    Tell of his salvation from day
      to day.

(3) Declare his glory among the
    nations,
    his marvelous works among all
      the peoples!
(4) For great is the LORD, and
    greatly to be praised;
    he is to be feared above
      all gods.
(5) For all the gods of the peoples
    are idols;
    but the LORD made the heavens.
(6) Honor and majesty are before him;
    strength and beauty are in
      his sanctuary.

(7) Ascribe to the LORD, O families
    of the peoples,
    ascribe to the LORD glory and
      strength!
(8) Ascribe to the LORD the glory
    due his name;
    bring an offering, and come
      into his courts!
(9) Worship the LORD in holy array;
    tremble before him, all
      the earth!

(10) Say among the nations, "The LORD
    reigns!
    Yea, the world is established,
    it shall never be moved;
    he will judge the peoples
      with equity."
(11) Let the heavens be glad, and
    let the earth rejoice;

    let the sea roar, and all that
      fills it;
(12)   let the field exult, and
    everything in it!
    Then shall all the trees of the
      wood sing for joy
(13)   before the LORD, for he comes,
    for he comes to judge
      the earth.
    He will judge the world with
      righteousness,
    and the peoples with his truth.

(24) Declare his glory among the
    nations,
    his marvelous works among all
      the peoples!
/25/ For great is the LORD, and
    greatly to be praised,
    and he is to be feared above
      all gods.
(26) For all the gods of the peoples
    are idols;
    but the LORD made the heavens.
(27) Honor and majesty are before him;
    strength and joy are in
      his place.

(28) Ascribe to the LORD, O families
    of the peoples,
    ascribe to the LORD glory and
      strength!
(29) Ascribe to the LORD the glory
    due his name;
    bring an offering, and come
      before him!
    Worship the LORD in holy array;
/30/   tremble before him, all
      the earth;

    yea, the world is established,
    it shall never be moved.

(31) Let the heavens be glad, and
    let the earth rejoice,
    and let them say among the
      nations, "The LORD reigns!"
(32) Let the sea roar, and all that
    fills it,
    let the field exult, and
    everything in it!
(33) Then shall the trees of the
    wood sing for joy
    before the LORD,
    for he comes to judge
      the earth.

35

Psalm 106:1, 47–48

(1)Praise the LORD!
O give thanks to the LORD, for
he is good;
for his steadfast love endures
for ever!

/47/ Save us, O LORD our God,
and gather us
from among the nations,
that we may give thanks to thy
holy name,
and glory in thy praise.
(48)Blessed be the LORD, the
God of Israel,
from everlasting to
everlasting!
And let all the people say,
"Amen!"
Praise the LORD!

(34)O give thanks to the LORD, for
he is good;
for his steadfast love endures
for ever!
/35/ Say also:
Save us, O God of our salvation,
and gather and save us
from among the nations,
that we may give thanks to thy
holy name,
and glory in thy praise.
(36)Blessed be the LORD, the
God of Israel,
from everlasting to
everlasting!
Then all the people said
"Amen!" and
praised the LORD.
(37)So David left Asaph and his
brethren there before the ark of the
covenant of the LORD to minister
continually before the ark as each day
required, (38)and also Obed-edom and
his sixty-eight brethren; while
Obed-edom, the son of Jeduthun, and
Hosah were to be gatekeepers. (39)And
he left Zadok the priest and his
brethren the priests before the
tabernacle of the LORD in the high
place that was at Gibeon, (40)to
offer burnt offerings to the LORD upon
the altar of burnt offering
continually morning and evening,
according to all that is written in
the law of the LORD which he commanded
Israel. (41)With them were Heman and
Jeduthun, and the rest of those chosen
and expressly named to give thanks to
the LORD, for his steadfast love
endures for ever.* (42)Heman and
Jeduthun had trumpets and cymbals for
the music and instruments for sacred
song. The sons of Jeduthun were
appointed to the gate.

*Cf. Ps. 136.

36

14 The Ark Is Brought to Jerusalem (Conclusion)

II Samuel 6:19b–23

(19b)Then all the people departed, each to his house.
(20)And David returned to bless his household.
But Michal the daughter of Saul came out to meet David, and said, "How the king of Israel honored himself today, uncovering himself today before the eyes of his servants' maids, as one of the vulgar fellows shamelessly uncovers himself!"
(21)And David said to Michal, "It was before the LORD, who chose me above your father, and above all his house, to appoint me as prince over Israel, the people of the LORD—and I will make merry before the LORD.
(22)I will make myself yet more contemptible than this, and I will be abased in your eyes; but by the maids of whom you have spoken, by them I shall be held in honor."
(23)And Michal the daughter of Saul had no child to the day of her death.

I Chronicles 16:43

(43)Then all the people departed each to his house,
and David went home to bless his household.

15 The Divine Promise to David

II Samuel 7:1–29

(1)Now when the king dwelt in his house,
and the LORD had given him rest from all his enemies round about,
(2)the king said to Nathan the prophet, "See now, I dwell in a house of cedar, but
the ark of God
dwells in a tent."
/3/And Nathan said to the king,
"Go, do all that is in your heart, for the LORD is with you."

I Chronicles 17:1–27

(1)Now when David dwelt in his house,

David said to Nathan the prophet, "Behold, I dwell in a house of cedar, but
the ark of the covenant of the LORD
is under a tent."
(2)And Nathan said to David,
"Do all that is in your heart, for God is with you."

37

(4)But that same night the word
of the LORD came to Nathan, (5)"Go
and tell my servant David,
'Thus says the LORD: Would you
build me a house to dwell in?
(6)I have not dwelt in a
house since the day
I brought up the people of Israel
from Egypt
to this day,
but I have been moving about
in a tent
for my dwelling.
(7)In all places where I have moved
with all the people of Israel,
did I speak a word with any of the
tribes of Israel, whom I commanded
to shepherd my people Israel, saying,
"Why have you not built me a house of
cedar?" ' (8)Now therefore thus you
shall say to my servant David, 'Thus
says the LORD of hosts, I took you
from the pasture, from following the
sheep, that you should be prince over
my people Israel; (9)and I have been
with you wherever you went, and have
cut off all your enemies from before
you; and I will make for you a great
name, like the name of the great ones
of the earth. (10)And I will appoint
a place for my people Israel, and
will plant them, that they may dwell
in their own place, and be disturbed
no more; and violent men shall
afflict them no more, as formerly,
(11)from the time that I appointed
judges over my people Israel; and
I will give you rest from
all your enemies. Moreover the LORD
declares to you that the LORD will
make you a house. (12)When your
days are fulfilled and you
lie down with your fathers, I will
raise up your offspring after you,
who shall come forth from your body,
and I will establish his kingdom.
(13)He shall build a house for

(3)But that same night the word
of the LORD came to Nathan, (4)"Go
and tell my servant David,
'Thus says the LORD: You shall not
build me a house to dwell in.
(5)For I have not dwelt in a
house since the day
I led up Israel

to this day,
but I have gone
from tent to tent
and from dwelling to dwelling.
(6)In all places where I have moved
with all Israel,
did I speak a word with any of the
judges of Israel, whom I commanded
to shepherd my people, saying,
"Why have you not built me a house of
cedar?" ' /7/Now therefore thus you
shall say to my servant David, 'Thus
says the LORD of hosts, I took you
from the pasture, from following the
sheep, that you should be prince over
my people Israel; (8)and I have been
with you wherever you went, and have
cut off all your enemies from before
you; and I will make for you a
name, like the name of the great ones
of the earth. (9)And I will appoint
a place for my people Israel, and
will plant them, that they may dwell
in their own place, and be disturbed
no more; and violent men shall
waste them no more, as formerly,
(10)from the time that I appointed
judges over my people Israel; and
I will subdue
all your enemies. Moreover I
declare to you that the LORD will
build you a house. (11)When your
days are fulfilled
to go to be with your fathers, I will
raise up your offspring after you,
one of your own sons,
and I will establish his kingdom.
(12)He shall build a house for

my name, and I will establish
the throne of his kingdom for ever.
(14)I will be his father, and
he shall be my son.
When he commits iniquity, I will
chasten him with the rod of men,
with the stripes of the sons of men;
(15)but my steadfast love shall not
depart from him,
as I took it from Saul,
whom I put away from before you.
(16)And your house
and your kingdom shall be made sure
for ever before me;
your throne shall be established
for ever.' " (17)In accordance with
all these words, and in accordance
with all this vision, Nathan spoke
to David.
   (18)Then King David went in and
sat before the LORD, and said, "Who
am I, O Lord GOD, and what is my
house, that thou hast brought me thus
far? (19)And yet this was a small
thing in thy eyes, O Lord GOD; thou
hast spoken also of thy servant's
house for a great while to come,
and this is the law for man,
O Lord GOD! (20)And what
more can David say to thee?

For thou knowest thy servant,
O Lord GOD!
(21)Because of thy promise,
and according to thy own heart,
thou hast wrought all this greatness,
to make thy servant know it.

(22)Therefore thou art great,
O LORD God;
for there is none like thee,
and there is no God besides thee,
according to all that we have heard
with our ears. (23)What one nation
on earth is like thy people Israel,
whom God went to redeem to be his

me, and I will establish
his throne for ever.
(13)I will be his father, and
he shall be my son;

I will not take my steadfast love
from him,
as I took it from him
who was before you,
(14)but I will confirm him in my house
and in my kingdom
for ever
and his throne shall be established
for ever.' " (15)In accordance with
all these words, and in accordance
with all this vision, Nathan spoke
to David.
   (16)Then King David went in and
sat before the LORD, and said, "Who
am I, O LORD God, and what is my
house, that thou hast brought me thus
far? (17)And this was a small
thing in thy eyes, O God; thou
hast also spoken of thy servant's
house for a great while to come,*

O LORD God! (18)And what
more can David say to thee
for honoring thy servant?
For thou knowest thy servant.

(19)For thy servant's sake, O LORD,
and according to thy own heart,
thou hast wrought all this greatness,
in making known
all these great things.

(20)There is none like thee, O LORD,
and there is no God besides thee,
according to all that we have heard
with our ears. (21)What one nation
on earth is like thy people Israel,
whom God went to redeem to be his

*The Hebrew text is defective.

people, making himself a name,
and doing for you
great and terrible things
for thy land,
before thy people,
whom thou didst redeem for thyself
from Egypt,
nations and its gods?
(24)And thou didst establish
for thyself thy people Israel
to be thy people for ever;
and thou, O LORD, didst
become their God. (25)And now,
O LORD God, confirm for ever the
word which thou hast spoken
concerning thy servant and
concerning his house,

and do as thou hast spoken; (26)and
thy name will be
magnified for ever, saying,
'The LORD of hosts
is God over Israel,'
and the house of thy servant David
will be established before thee.
(27)For thou, O LORD of hosts,
the God of Israel,
hast made this revelation
to thy servant,
saying, 'I will build you a house';
therefore thy servant has found
courage to pray this prayer to thee.
(28)And now, O Lord GOD,
thou art God, and
thy words are true, and
thou hast promised this good thing
to thy servant; (29)now therefore
may it please thee to bless the house
of thy servant, that it may continue
for ever before thee; for
thou, O Lord GOD, hast spoken,
and with thy blessing
shall the house of thy servant
be blessed for ever."

people, making for thyself a name

for great and terrible things,
in driving out nations
before thy people
whom thou didst redeem
from Egypt?

(22)And thou didst make
thy people Israel
to be thy people for ever;
and thou, O LORD, didst
become their God. (23)And now,
O LORD, let the
word which thou hast spoken
concerning thy servant and
concerning his house
be established for ever,
and do as thou hast spoken; (24)and
thy name will be established and
magnified for ever, saying,
'The LORD of hosts, the God of Israel,
is Israel's God,'
and the house of thy servant David
will be established before thee.
(25)For thou, my God,

hast revealed
to thy servant
that thou wilt build a house for him;
therefore thy servant has found
courage to pray before thee.
(26)And now, O LORD,
thou art God, and

thou hast promised this good thing
to thy servant; (27)now therefore
may it please thee to bless the house
of thy servant, that it may continue
for ever before thee; for
what thou, O LORD, hast blessed

is blessed for ever."

16 David's Foreign Wars

II Samuel 8:1 –18

(1)After this David defeated the
Philistines and subdued them, and
David took Metheg-ammah out of
the hand of the Philistines.
(2)And he defeated Moab,
and measured them with a line, making
them lie down on the ground; two lines
he measured to be put to death, and
one full line to be spared.
And the Moabites became servants to
David and brought tribute.
(3)David also defeated
Hadadezer
the son of Rehob,
king of Zobah,
as he went to restore his power at
the river Euphrates. (4)And David
took from him a thousand and
seven hundred horsemen,
and twenty thousand foot soldiers;
and David hamstrung all the chariot
horses, but left enough for a hundred
chariots. (5)And when the Syrians of
Damascus came to help Hadadezer king
of Zobah, David slew twenty-two
thousand men of the Syrians. /6/Then
David put garrisons
in Syria of Damascus; and the Syrians
became servants to David and brought
tribute. And the LORD gave victory
to David wherever he went. (7)And
David took the shields of gold which
were carried by the servants of
Hadadezer, and brought them to
Jerusalem. (8)And from Betah and
from Berothai, cities of Hadadezer,
King David took very much bronze.

(9)When Toi king of Hamath heard

I Chronicles 18:1 –17

(1)After this David defeated the
Philistines and subdued them, and
he took Gath and its villages out of
the hand of the Philistines.
(2)And he defeated Moab,

and the Moabites became servants to
David and brought tribute.
(3)David also defeated
Hadadezer

king of Zobah, toward Hamath,
as he went to set up his monument at
the river Euphrates. (4)And David
took from him a thousand chariots,
seven thousand horsemen,
and twenty thousand foot soldiers;
and David hamstrung all the chariot
horses, but left enough for a hundred
chariots. (5)And when the Syrians of
Damascus came to help Hadadezer king
of Zobah, David slew twenty-two
thousand men of the Syrians. [6]Then
David put*
in Syria of Damascus; and the Syrians
became servants to David and brought
tribute. And the LORD gave victory
to David wherever he went. (7)And
David took the shields of gold which
were carried by the servants of
Hadadezer, and brought them to
Jerusalem. (8)And from Tibhath and
from Cun, cities of Hadadezer,
David took very much bronze;
with it Solomon made the bronze sea
and the pillars and the vessels of
bronze.
(9)When Tou king of Hamath heard

*Hebrew lacks "garrisons."

41

II Samuel 8:9–18	I Chronicles 18:9–17
that David had defeated the whole army of Hadadezer,	that David had defeated the whole army of Hadadezer, king of Zobah,
⁽¹⁰⁾Toi sent his son Joram to King David, to greet him, and to congratulate him because he had fought against Hadadezer and defeated him; for Hadadezer had often been at war with Toi. And Joram brought with him articles of silver, of gold, and of bronze; ⁽¹¹⁾these also King David dedicated to the LORD, together with the silver and gold which he dedicated from all the nations he subdued,	⁽¹⁰⁾he sent his son Hadoram to King David, to greet him, and to congratulate him because he had fought against Hadadezer and defeated him; for Hadadezer had often been at war with Tou. And he sent all sorts of articles of gold, of silver, and of bronze; ⁽¹¹⁾these also King David dedicated to the LORD, together with the silver and gold which he had carried off from all the nations,
⁽¹²⁾from Edom, Moab, the Ammonites, the Philistines, Amalek, and from the spoil of Hadadezer the son of Rehob, king of Zobah.	from Edom, Moab, the Ammonites, the Philistines, and Amalek.
⁽¹³⁾And David won a name for himself when he returned from	
smiting eighteen thousand Syrians in the Valley of Salt. ⁽¹⁴⁾And he put garrisons in Edom; throughout all Edom he put garrisons, and all the Edomites became David's servants. And the LORD gave victory to David wherever he went.	⁽¹²⁾And Abishai, the son of Zeruiah, slew eighteen thousand Edomites in the Valley of Salt. ⁽¹³⁾And he put garrisons in Edom; and all the Edomites became David's servants. And the LORD gave victory to David wherever he went.
⁽¹⁵⁾So David reigned over all Israel; and David administered justice and equity to all his people. ⁽¹⁶⁾And Joab the son of Zeruiah was over the army; and Jehoshaphat the son of Ahilud was recorder; ⁽¹⁷⁾and Zadok the son of Ahitub and Ahimelech the son of Abiathar were priests; and Seraiah was secretary; ⁽¹⁸⁾and Benaiah the son of Jehoiada the Cherethites and the Pelethites; and David's sons were priests.*	⁽¹⁴⁾So David reigned over all Israel; and he administered justice and equity to all his people. ⁽¹⁵⁾And Joab the son of Zeruiah was over the army, and Jehoshaphat the son of Ahilud was recorder; ⁽¹⁶⁾and Zadok the son of Ahitub and Ahimelech the son of Abiathar were priests; and Shavsha was secretary; ⁽¹⁷⁾and Benaiah the son of Jehoiada was over the Cherethites and the Pelethites; and David's sons were the chief officials in the service of the king.

*The Hebrew text is defective.

17 David's Kindness Toward Mephibosheth

II Samuel 9:1–13

(1)And David said, "Is there still any one left of the house of Saul, that I may show him kindness for Jonathan's sake?" (2)Now there was a servant of the house of Saul whose name was Ziba, and they called him to David; and the king said to him, "Are you Ziba?" And he said, "Your servant is he." (3)And the king said, "Is there not still some one of the house of Saul, that I may show the kindness of God to him?" Ziba said to the king, "There is still a son of Jonathan; he is crippled in his feet." (4)The king said to him, "Where is he?" And Ziba said to the king, "He is in the house of Machir the son of Ammiel, at Lo-debar." (5)Then King David sent and brought him from the house of Machir the son of Ammiel, at Lo-debar. (6)And Mephibosheth the son of Jonathan, son of Saul, came to David, and fell on his face and did obeisance. And David said, "Mephibosheth!" And he answered, "Behold, your servant." (7)And David said to him, "Do not fear; for I will show you kindness for the sake of your father Jonathan, and I will restore to you all the land of Saul your father; and you shall eat at my table always." (8)And he did obeisance, and said, "What is your servant, that you should look upon a dead dog such as I?"

(9)Then the king called Ziba, Saul's servant, and said to him, "All that belonged to Saul and to all his house I have given to your master's son. (10)And you and your sons and your servants shall till the land for him, and shall bring in the produce, that your master's son may have bread to eat; but Mephibosheth your master's son shall always eat at my table." Now Ziba had fifteen sons and twenty servants. (11)Then Ziba said to the king, "According to all that my lord the king commands his servant, so will your servant do." So Mephibosheth ate at David's table, like one of the king's sons. (12)And Mephibosheth had a young son, whose name was Mica. And all who dwelt in Ziba's house became Mephibosheth's servants. (13)So Mephibosheth dwelt in Jerusalem; for he ate always at the king's table. Now he was lame in both his feet.

18 Further Foreign Wars

II Samuel 10:1–19	*I Chronicles 19:1–19*
(1)After this the king of the Ammonites died, and Hanun his son reigned in his stead. (2)And David said, "I will deal loyally with Hanun the son of Nahash, as his father dealt loyally with me." So David sent by his servants to console him concerning his father. And David's servants came into the land of the Ammonites.	/1/After this Nahash the king of the Ammonites died, and his son reigned in his stead. (2)And David said, "I will deal loyally with Hanun the son of Nahash, for his father dealt loyally with me." So David sent messengers to console him concerning his father. And David's servants came to Hanun in the land of the Ammonites, to console him.
(3)But the princes of the Ammonites said to Hanun their lord,	(3)But the princes of the Ammonites said to Hanun,

"Do you think, because David has sent
comforters to you, that he
is honoring your father?
Has not David sent his servants
to you to search the city, and

to spy it out,
and to overthrow it?"
(4)So Hanun took David's servants,
and shaved off half the beard of each,
and cut off their garments in the
middle, at their hips, and sent
them away.

(5)When it was told David,

he sent to meet them, for the men were
greatly ashamed. And the king said,
"Remain at Jericho until your beards
have grown, and then return."
(6)When the Ammonites saw that
they had become odious
to David,
the Ammonites sent
and hired

the Syrians of Beth-rehob,
and the Syrians of Zobah,

twenty thousand foot soldiers,
and the king of Maacah with
a thousand men,

and the men of Tob,
twelve thousand men.

(7)And when David heard of it,
he sent Joab and all the host
of the mighty men. (8)And the
Ammonites came out and drew up in
battle array at the entrance of the
gate; and the
Syrians of Zobah and of Rehob,
and the men of Tob and Maacah,
were by themselves in the
open country.

"Do you think, because David has sent
comforters to you, that he
is honoring your father?
Have not his servants come
to you to search and
to overthrow and
to spy out the land?"

(4)So Hanun took David's servants,
and shaved them,
and cut off their garments in the
middle, at their hips, and sent
them away;
(5)and they departed.
When David was told
concerning the men,

he sent to meet them, for the men were
greatly ashamed. And the king said,
"Remain at Jericho until your beards
have grown, and then return."
(6)When the Ammonites saw that
they had made themselves odious
to David,
Hanun and the Ammonites sent
a thousand talents of silver to hire
chariots and horsemen from
Mesopotamia, from Aram-maacah,

and from Zobah.
(7)they hired
thirty-two thousand chariots
and the king of Maacah with
his army,
who came and encamped before Medeba.

And the Ammonites were mustered from
their cities and came to battle.
/8/And when David heard of it,
he sent Joab and all the host
of the mighty men. (9)And the
Ammonites came out and drew up in
battle array at the entrance of the
city, and the
kings who had come

were by themselves in the
open country.

(9)When Joab saw that the battle
was set against him both in front and
in the rear, he chose some of the
picked men of Israel, and arrayed them
against the Syrians; (10)the rest of
his men he put in the charge of
Abishai his brother, and he
arrayed them against the Ammonites.
(11)And he said, "If the Syrians
are too strong for me, then you shall
help me; but if the Ammonites are too
strong for you, then I will come and
help you. (12)Be of good courage,
and let us play the man for our
people, and for the cities of our
God; and may the LORD do what seems
good to him." (13)So Joab and the
people who were with him drew near
to battle against the Syrians;
and they fled before him. (14)And
when the Ammonites saw that the
Syrians fled, they likewise fled
before Abishai,
and entered the city. Then Joab
returned from fighting against
the Ammonites,
and came to Jerusalem.
(15)But when the Syrians saw
that they had been defeated by
Israel, they gathered themselves
together.
(16)And Hadadezer sent, and brought
out the Syrians who were beyond
the Euphrates;
and they came to Helam,
with Shobach the commander of the
army of Hadadezer at their head.
(17)And when it was told David, he
gathered all Israel together, and
crossed the Jordan, and came to Helam.

And the Syrians arrayed themselves
against David,
and fought with him. (18)And the
Syrians fled before Israel; and David
slew of the Syrians the men of
seven hundred chariots, and

(10)When Joab saw that the battle
was set against him both in front and
in the rear, he chose some of the
picked men of Israel, and arrayed them
against the Syrians; (11)the rest of
his men he put in the charge of
Abishai his brother, and they were
arrayed against the Ammonites.
(12)And he said, "If the Syrians
are too strong for me, then you shall
help me; but if the Ammonites are too
strong for you, then I will
help you. (13)Be of good courage,
and let us play the man for our
people, and for the cities of our
God; and may the LORD do what seems
good to him." (14)So Joab and the
people who were with him drew near
before the Syrians for battle;
and they fled before him. (15)And
when the Ammonites saw that the
Syrians fled, they likewise fled
before Abishai, Joab's brother,
and entered the city. Then Joab

came to Jerusalem.
(16)But when the Syrians saw
that they had been defeated by
Israel,

they sent messengers and brought
out the Syrians who were beyond
the Euphrates,

with Shophach the commander of the
army of Hadadezer at their head.
(17)And when it was told David, he
gathered all Israel together, and
crossed the Jordan, and came to them,
and drew up his forces against them.
And when David set the battle in array
against the Syrians,
they fought with him. (18)And the
Syrians fled before Israel; and David
slew of the Syrians the men of
seven thousand chariots, and

forty thousand <u>horsemen</u>, and <u>wounded</u> Shobach the commander of their army, <u>so that he died there.</u> ⁽¹⁹⁾And when <u>all the kings who were</u> servants of Hadadezer saw that they had been defeated by Israel, they made peace with <u>Israel,</u> and became subject to them. So the Syrians <u>feared</u> to help the Ammonites any more.	forty thousand <u>foot soldiers</u>, and <u>killed also</u> Shophach the commander of their army. ⁽¹⁹⁾And when <u>the</u> servants of Hadadezer saw that they had been defeated by Israel, they made peace with <u>David,</u> and became subject to him. So the Syrians <u>were not willing</u> to help the Ammonites any more.

19 The Capture of Rabbah (Beginning)

II Samuel 11:1	*I Chronicles 20:1a*
⁽¹⁾In the spring of the year, the time when kings go forth to battle, <u>David sent</u> Joab, <u>and his servants with him,</u> <u>and all Israel;</u> and <u>they</u> ravaged the Ammonites, and besieged Rabbah. But David remained at Jerusalem.	⁽¹⁾In the spring of the year, the time when kings go forth to battle, Joab <u>led out the army,</u> and ravaged the <u>country</u> <u>of the</u> Ammonites, <u>and came</u> and besieged Rabbah. But David remained at Jerusalem.

20 David Loves Bathsheba and Murders Uriah

II Samuel 11:2–27

⁽²⁾It happened, late one afternoon, when David arose from his couch and was walking upon the roof of the king's house, that he saw from the roof a woman bathing; and the woman was very beautiful. ⁽³⁾And David sent and inquired about the woman. And one said, "Is not this Bathsheba, the daughter of Eliam, the wife of Uriah the Hittite?" ⁽⁴⁾So David sent messengers, and took her; and she came to him, and he lay with her. (Now she was purifying herself from her uncleanness.) Then she returned to her house. ⁽⁵⁾And the woman conceived; and she sent and told David, "I am with child."

⁽⁶⁾So David sent word to Joab, "Send me Uriah the Hittite." And Joab sent Uriah to David. ⁽⁷⁾When Uriah came to him, David asked how Joab was doing, and how the

people fared, and how the war prospered. (8)Then David said to Uriah, "Go down to your house, and wash your feet." And Uriah went out of the king's house, and there followed him a present from the king. (9)But Uriah slept at the door of the king's house with all the servants of his lord, and did not go down to his house. (10)When they told David, "Uriah did not go down to his house," David said to Uriah, "Have you not come from a journey? Why did you not go down to your house?" (11)Uriah said to David, "The ark and Israel and Judah dwell in booths; and my lord Joab and the servants of my lord are camping in the open field; shall I then go to my house, to eat and to drink, and to lie with my wife? As you live, and as your soul lives, I will not do this thing." (12)Then David said to Uriah, "Remain here today also, and tomorrow I will let you depart." So Uriah remained in Jerusalem that day, and the next. (13)And David invited him, and he ate in his presence and drank, so that he made him drunk; and in the evening he went out to lie on his couch with the servants of his lord, but he did not go down to his house.

(14)In the morning David wrote a letter to Joab, and sent it by the hand of Uriah. (15)In the letter he wrote, "Set Uriah in the forefront of the hardest fighting, and then draw back from him, that he may be struck down, and die." (16)And as Joab was besieging the city, he assigned Uriah to the place where he knew there were valiant men. (17)And the men of the city came out and fought with Joab; and some of the servants of David among the people fell. Uriah the Hittite was slain also. (18)Then Joab sent and told David all the news about the fighting; (19)and he instructed the messenger, "When you have finished telling all the news about the fighting to the king, (20)then, if the king's anger rises, and if he says to you, 'Why did you go so near the city to fight? Did you not know that they would shoot from the wall? (21)Who killed Abimelech the son of Jerubbesheth? Did not a woman cast an upper millstone upon him from the wall, so that he died at Thebez? Why did you go so near the wall?' then you shall say, 'Your servant Uriah the Hittite is dead also.' "

(22)So the messenger went, and came and told David all that Joab had sent him to tell. (23)The messenger said to David, "The men gained an advantage over us, and came out against us in the field; but we drove them back to the entrance of the gate. (24)Then the archers shot at your servants from the wall; some of the king's servants are dead; and your servant Uriah the Hittite is dead also." (25)David said to the messenger, "Thus shall you say to Joab, 'Do not let this matter trouble you, for the sword devours now one and now another; strengthen your attack upon the city, and overthrow it.' And encourage him."

(26)When the wife of Uriah heard that Uriah her husband was dead, she made lamentation for her husband. (27)And when the mourning was over, David sent and brought her to his house, and she became his wife, and bore him a son. But the thing that David had done displeased the LORD.

21 Nathan's Accusation, David's Repentance, Solomon's Birth

II Samuel 12:1–25

(1)And the LORD sent Nathan to David. He came to him, and said to him, "There were two men in a certain city, the one rich and the other poor. (2)The rich man had very many flocks and herds; (3)but the poor man had nothing but one little ewe lamb, which he had bought. And he brought it up, and it grew up with him and with his children; it used to eat of his morsel, and drink from his cup, and lie in his bosom, and it was like a daughter to him. (4)Now there came a traveler to the rich man, and he was unwilling to take one of his own flock or herd to prepare for the wayfarer who had come to him, but he took the poor man's lamb, and prepared it for the man who had come to him." (5)Then David's anger was greatly kindled against the man; and he said to Nathan, "As the LORD lives, the man who has done this deserves to die; (6)and he shall restore the lamb fourfold, because he did this thing, and because he had no pity."

(7)Nathan said to David, "You are the man. Thus says the LORD, the God of Israel, 'I anointed you king over Israel, and I delivered you out of the hand of Saul; (8)and I gave you your master's house, and your master's wives into your bosom, and gave you the house of Israel and of Judah; and if this were too little, I would add to you as much more. (9)Why have you despised the word of the LORD, to do what is evil in his sight? You have smitten Uriah the Hittite with the sword, and have taken his wife to be your wife, and have slain him with the sword of the Ammonites. (10)Now therefore the sword shall never depart from your house, because you have despised me, and have taken the wife of Uriah the Hittite to be your wife.' (11)Thus says the LORD, 'Behold, I will raise up evil against you out of your own house; and I will take your wives before your eyes, and give them to your neighbor, and he shall lie with your wives in the sight of this sun. (12)For you did it secretly; but I will do this thing before all Israel, and before the sun.' " (13)David said to Nathan, "I have sinned against the LORD." And Nathan said to David, "The LORD also has put away your sin; you shall not die. (14)Nevertheless, because by this deed you have utterly scorned the LORD, the child that is born to you shall die." (15)Then Nathan went to his house.

And the LORD struck the child that Uriah's wife bore to David, and it became sick. (16)David therefore besought God for the child; and David fasted, and went in and lay all night upon the ground. (17)And the elders of his house stood beside him, to raise him from the ground; but he would not, nor did he eat food with them. (18)On the seventh day the child died. And the servants of David feared to tell him that the child was dead; for they said, "Behold, while the child was yet alive, we spoke to him, and he did not listen to us; how then can we say to him the child is dead? He may do himself some harm." (19)But when David saw that his servants were whispering together, David perceived that the child was dead; and David said to his servants, "Is the child dead?" They said, "He is dead." (20)Then David arose from the earth, and washed, and anointed himself, and changed his clothes; and he went into the house of the LORD, and worshiped; he then went to his own house; and when he asked, they set food before him, and he ate. (21)Then his servants said to him, "What is this thing that you have done? You fasted and wept for the child while it was alive; but when the child died, you arose and ate food." (22)He said, "While the child was still alive, I fasted and wept; for I said, 'Who knows whether the LORD will be gracious to me, that the child may live?' (23)But now he is dead; why should I fast? Can I bring him back again? I shall go to him, but he will not return to me."

(24)Then David comforted his wife, Bathsheba, and went in to her, and lay with her; and she bore a son, and he called his name Solomon. And the LORD loved him, (25)and sent a message by Nathan the prophet; so he called his name Jedidiah, because of the LORD.

22 The Capture of Rabbah (Conclusion)

II Samuel 12:26–31

(26)Now Joab fought against Rabbah of the Ammonites, and took the royal city. (27)And Joab sent messengers to David, and said, "I have fought against Rabbah; moreover, I have taken the city of waters. (28)Now, then, gather the rest of the people together, and encamp against the city, and take it; lest I take the city, and it be called by my name." (29)So David gathered all the people together and went to Rabbah, and fought against it and took it. (30)And he took the crown of their king from his head; the weight of it was a talent of gold, and in it was a precious stone; and it was placed on David's head. And he brought forth the spoil of the city, a very great amount. /31/And he brought forth the people who were in it, and set them to labor with saws and iron picks and iron axes, and made them pass through the brickkilns; and thus he did to all the cities of the Ammonites. Then David and all the people returned to Jerusalem.

I Chronicles 20:1b–3

(1b)And Joab smote Rabbah, and overthrew it.

(2)And David took the crown of their king from his head; he found that it weighed a talent of gold, and in it was a precious stone; and it was placed on David's head. And he brought forth the spoil of the city, a very great amount. /3/And he brought forth the people who were in it, and sawed with saws and iron picks and axes;

and thus David did to all the cities of the Ammonites. Then David and all the people returned to Jerusalem.

23 The Rape of Tamar

II Samuel 13:1–22

(1)Now Absalom, David's son, had a beautiful sister, whose name was Tamar; and after a time Amnon, David's son, loved her. (2)And Amnon was so tormented that he made himself ill because of his sister Tamar; for she was a virgin, and it seemed impossible to Amnon to do anything to her. (3)But Amnon had a friend, whose name was Jonadab, the son of Shime-ah, David's brother; and Jonadab was a very crafty man. (4)And he said to him, "O son of the king, why are you so haggard morning after morning? Will you not tell me?" Amnon said to him, "I love Tamar, my brother Ab-

49

salom's sister." (5)Jonadab said to him, "Lie down on your bed, and pretend to be ill; and when your father comes to see you, say to him, 'Let my sister Tamar come and give me bread to eat, and prepare the food in my sight, that I may see it, and eat it from her hand.' " (6)So Amnon lay down, and pretended to be ill; and when the king came to see him, Amnon said to the king, "Pray let my sister Tamar come and make a couple of cakes in my sight, that I may eat from her hand."

(7)Then David sent home to Tamar, saying, "Go to your brother Amnon's house, and prepare food for him." (8)So Tamar went to her brother Amnon's house, where he was lying down. And she took dough, and kneaded it, and made cakes in his sight, and baked the cakes. (9)And she took the pan and emptied it out before him, but he refused to eat. And Amnon said, "Send out every one from me." So every one went out from him. (10)Then Amnon said to Tamar, "Bring the food into the chamber, that I may eat from your hand." And Tamar took the cakes she had made, and brought them into the chamber to Amnon her brother. (11)But when she brought them near him to eat, he took hold of her, and said to her, "Come, lie with me, my sister." (12)She answered him, "No, my brother, do not force me; for such a thing is not done in Israel; do not do this wanton folly. (13)As for me, where could I carry my shame? And as for you, you would be as one of the wanton fools in Israel. Now therefore, I pray you, speak to the king; for he will not withhold me from you." (14)But he would not listen to her; and being stronger than she, he forced her, and lay with her.

(15)Then Amnon hated her with very great hatred; so that the hatred with which he hated her was greater than the love with which he had loved her. And Amnon said to her, "Arise, be gone." (16)But she said to him, "No, my brother; for this wrong in sending me away is greater than the other which you did to me." But he would not listen to her. (17)He called the young man who served him and said, "Put this woman out of my presence, and bolt the door after her." (18)Now she was wearing a long robe with sleeves; for thus were the virgin daughters of the king clad of old. So his servant put her out, and bolted the door after her. (19)And Tamar put ashes on her head, and rent the long robe which she wore; and she laid her hand on her head, and went away, crying aloud as she went.

(20)And her brother Absalom said to her, "Has Amnon your brother been with you? Now hold your peace, my sister; he is your brother; do not take this to heart." So Tamar dwelt, a desolate woman, in her brother Absalom's house. (21)When King David heard of all these things, he was very angry. (22)But Absalom spoke to Amnon neither good nor bad; for Absalom hated Amnon, because he had forced his sister Tamar.

24 Absalom's Murder of Amnon

II Samuel 13:23–39

(23)After two full years Absalom had sheepshearers at Baal-hazor, which is near Ephraim, and Absalom invited all the king's sons. (24)And Absalom came to the king, and said, "Behold, your servant has sheepshearers; pray let the king and his servants go with your servant." (25)But the king said to Absalom, "No, my son, let us not all go, lest we be burdensome to you." He pressed him, but he would not go but gave him his blessing. (26)Then Absalom said, "If not, pray let my brother Amnon go with us." And the king said to him, "Why should he go with you?" (27)But Absalom pressed him until he let Amnon and all the king's sons go with him. (28)Then Absalom commanded his servants, "Mark when Amnon's heart is merry with wine, and when I say to you, 'Strike Amnon,' then kill him. Fear not; have I not commanded you? Be courageous and be valiant." (29)So the servants of Absalom did to Amnon as Absalom had commanded. Then all the king's sons arose, and each mounted his mule and fled.

(30)While they were on the way, tidings came to David, "Absalom has slain all the king's sons, and not one of them is left." (31)Then the king arose, and rent his garments, and lay on the earth; and all his servants who were standing by rent their garments. (32)But Jonadab the son of Shime-ah, David's brother, said, "Let not my lord suppose that they have killed all the young men the king's sons, for Amnon alone is dead, for by the command of Absalom this has been determined from the day he forced his sister Tamar. (33)Now therefore let not my lord the king so take it to heart as to suppose that all the king's sons are dead; for Amnon alone is dead."

(34)But Absalom fled. And the young man who kept the watch lifted up his eyes, and looked, and behold, many people were coming from the Horonaim road by the side of the mountain. (35)And Jonadab said to the king, "Behold, the king's sons have come; as your servant said, so it has come about." (36)And as soon as he had finished speaking, behold, the king's sons came, and lifted up their voice and wept; and the king also and all his servants wept very bitterly.

(37)But Absalom fled, and went to Talmai the son of Ammihud, king of Geshur. And David mourned for his son day after day. (38)So Absalom fled, and went to Geshur, and was there three years. (39)And the spirit of the king longed to go forth to Absalom; for he was comforted about Amnon, seeing he was dead.

25 Absalom's Return to Jerusalem

II Samuel 14:1–24

(1)Now Joab the son of Zeruiah perceived that the king's heart went out to Absalom. (2)And Joab sent to Tekoa, and fetched from there a wise woman, and said to her, "Pretend to be a mourner, and put on mourning garments; do not anoint yourself with oil, but behave like a woman who has been mourning many days for the dead; (3)and go to the king, and speak thus to him." So Joab put the words in her mouth.

(4)When the woman of Tekoa came to the king, she fell on her face to the ground, and did obeisance, and said, "Help, O king." (5)And the king said to her, "What is your trouble?" She answered, "Alas, I am a widow; my husband is dead. (6)And your handmaid had two sons, and they quarreled with one another in the field; there was no one to part them, and one struck the other and killed him. (7)And now the whole family has risen against your handmaid, and they say, 'Give up the man who struck his brother, that we may kill him for the life of his brother whom he slew'; and so they would destroy the heir also. Thus they would quench my coal which is left, and leave to my husband neither name nor remnant upon the face of the earth."

(8)Then the king said to the woman, "Go to your house, and I will give orders concerning you." (9)And the woman of Tekoa said to the king, "On me be the guilt, my lord the king, and on my father's house; let the king and his throne be guiltless." (10)The king said, "If any one says anything to you, bring him to me, and he shall never touch you again." (11)Then she said, "Pray let the king invoke the LORD your God, that the avenger of blood slay no more, and my son be not destroyed." He said, "As the LORD lives, not one hair of your son shall fall to the ground."

(12)Then the woman said, "Pray let your handmaid speak a word to my lord the king." He said, "Speak." (13)And the woman said, "Why then have you planned such a thing against the people of God? For in giving this decision the king convicts himself, inasmuch as the king does not bring his banished one home again. (14)We must all die, we are like water spilt on the ground, which cannot be gathered up again; but God will not take away the life of him who devises means not to keep his banished one an outcast. (15)Now I have come to say this to my lord the king because the people have made me afraid; and your handmaid thought, 'I will speak to the king; it may be that the king will perform the request of his servant. (16)For the king will hear, and deliver his servant from the hand of the man who would destroy me and my son together from the heritage of God.' (17)And your handmaid thought, 'The word of my lord the king will set me at rest'; for my lord the king is like the angel of God to discern good and evil. The LORD your God be with you!"

(18)Then the king answered the woman, "Do not hide from me anything I ask you." And the woman said, "Let my lord the king speak." (19)The king said, "Is the hand of Joab with you in all this?" The woman answered and said, "As surely as you live, my lord the king, one cannot turn to the right hand or to the left from anything that my lord the king has said. It was your servant Joab who bade me; it was he who put all these words in the mouth of your handmaid. (20)In order to change the course of affairs your servant Joab did this. But my lord has wisdom like the wisdom of the angel of God to know all things that are on the earth."

(21)Then the king said to Joab, "Behold now, I grant this; go, bring back the young man Absalom." (22)And Joab fell on his face to the ground, and did obeisance, and blessed the king; and Joab said, "Today your servant knows that I have found favor in your sight, my lord the king, in that the king has granted the request of his servant." (23)So Joab arose and went to Geshur, and brought Absalom to Jerusalem. (24)And the king said, "Let him dwell apart in his own house; he is not to come into my presence." So Absalom dwelt apart in his own house, and did not come into the king's presence.

26 David Is Reconciled with Absalom

II Samuel 14:25–33

(25)Now in all Israel there was no one so much to be praised for his beauty as Absalom; from the sole of his foot to the crown of his head there was no blemish in him. (26)And when he cut the hair of his head (for at the end of every year he used to cut it; when it was heavy on him, he cut it), he weighed the hair of his head, two hundred shekels by the king's weight. (27)There were born to Absalom three sons, and one daughter whose name was Tamar; she was a beautiful woman.

(28)So Absalom dwelt two full years in Jerusalem, without coming into the king's presence. (29)Then Absalom sent for Joab, to send him to the king; but Joab would not come to him. And he sent a second time, but Joab would not come. (30)Then he said to his servants, "See, Joab's field is next to mine, and he has barley there; go and set it on fire." So Absalom's servants set the field on fire. [31]Then Joab arose and went to Absalom at his house, and said to him, "Why have your servants set my field on fire?" [32]Absalom answered Joab, "Behold, I sent word to you, 'Come here, that I may send you to the king, to ask, "Why have I come from Geshur? It would be better for me to be there still." Now therefore let me go into the presence of the king; and if there is guilt in me, let him kill me.' " [33]Then Joab went to the king, and told him; and he summoned Absalom. So he came to the king, and bowed himself on his face to the ground before the king; and the king kissed Absalom.

27 Absalom Rebels, David Flees Jerusalem

II Samuel 15:1–37

[1]After this Absalom got himself a chariot and horses, and fifty men to run before him. [2]And Absalom used to rise early and stand beside the way of the gate; and when any man had a suit to come before the king for judgment, Absalom would call to him, and say, "From what city are you?" And when he said, "Your servant is of such and such a tribe in Israel," [3]Absalom would say to him, "See, your claims are good and right; but there is no man deputed by the king to hear you." [4]Absalom said moreover, "Oh that I were judge in the land! Then every man with a suit or cause might come to me, and I would give him justice." [5]And whenever a man came near to do obeisance to him, he would put out his hand, and take hold of him, and kiss him. [6]Thus Absalom did to all of Israel who came to the king for judgment; so Absalom stole the hearts of the men of Israel.

[7]And at the end of four years Absalom said to the king, "Pray let me go and pay my vow, which I have vowed to the LORD, in Hebron. [8]For your servant vowed a vow while I dwelt at Geshur in Aram, saying, 'If the LORD will indeed bring me back to Jerusalem, then I will offer worship to the LORD.' " [9]The king said to him, "Go in peace." So he arose, and went to Hebron. [10]But Absalom sent secret messengers throughout all the tribes of Israel, saying, "As soon as you hear the sound of the trumpet, then say, 'Absalom is king at Hebron!' " [11]With Absalom went two hundred men from Jerusalem who were invited guests, and they went in their simplicity, and knew nothing. [12]And while Absalom was offering the sacrifices, he sent for Ahithophel the Gilonite, David's counselor, from his city Giloh. And the conspiracy grew strong, and the people with Absalom kept increasing.

[13]And a messenger came to David, saying, "The hearts of the men of Israel have gone after Absalom." [14]Then David said to all his servants who were with him at Jerusalem, "Arise, and let us flee; or else there will be no escape for us from Absalom; go in haste, lest he overtake us quickly, and bring down evil upon us, and smite the city with the edge of the sword." [15]And the king's servants said to the king, "Behold, your servants are ready to do whatever my lord the king decides." [16]So the king went forth, and all his household after him. And the king left ten concubines to keep the house. [17]And the king went forth, and all the people after him; and they halted at the last house. [18]And all his servants passed by him; and all the Cherethites, and all the Pelethites, and all the six hundred Gittites who had followed him from Gath, passed on before the king.

(19)Then the king said to Ittai the Gittite, "Why do you also go with us? Go back, and stay with the king; for you are a foreigner, and also an exile from your home. (20)You came only yesterday, and shall I today make you wander about with us, seeing I go I know not where? Go back, and take your brethren with you; and may the LORD show steadfast love and faithfulness to you." (21)But Ittai answered the king, "As the LORD lives, and as my lord the king lives, wherever my lord the king shall be, whether for death or for life, there also will your servant be." (22)And David said to Ittai, "Go then, pass on." So Ittai the Gittite passed on, with all his men and all the little ones who were with him. (23)And all the country wept aloud as all the people passed by, and the king crossed the brook Kidron, and all the people passed on toward the wilderness.

(24)And Abiathar came up, and lo, Zadok came also, with all the Levites, bearing the ark of the covenant of God; and they set down the ark of God, until the people had all passed out of the city. (25)Then the king said to Zadok, "Carry the ark of God back into the city. If I find favor in the eyes of the LORD, he will bring me back and let me see both it and his habitation; (26)but if he says, 'I have no pleasure in you,' behold, here I am, let him do to me what seems good to him." (27)The king also said to Zadok the priest, "Look, go back to the city in peace, you and Abiathar, with your two sons, Ahima-az your son, and Jonathan the son of Abiathar. (28)See, I will wait at the fords of the wilderness, until word comes from you to inform me." (29)So Zadok and Abiathar carried the ark of God back to Jerusalem; and they remained there.

(30)But David went up the ascent of the Mount of Olives, weeping as he went, barefoot and with his head covered; and all the people who were with him covered their heads, and they went up, weeping as they went. (31)And it was told David, "Ahithophel is among the conspirators with Absalom." And David said, "O LORD, I pray thee, turn the counsel of Ahithophel into foolishness."

(32)When David came to the summit, where God was worshiped, behold, Hushai the Archite came to meet him with his coat rent and earth upon his head. (33)David said to him, "If you go on with me, you will be a burden to me. (34)But if you return to the city, and say to Absalom, 'I will be your servant, O king; as I have been your father's servant in time past, so now I will be your servant,' then you will defeat for me the counsel of Ahithophel. (35)Are not Zadok and Abiathar the priests with you there? So whatever you hear from the king's house, tell it to Zadok and Abiathar the priests. (36)Behold, their two sons are with them there, Ahima-az, Zadok's son, and Jonathan, Abiathar's son; and by them you shall send to me everything you hear." (37)So Hushai, David's friend, came into the city, just as Absalom was entering Jerusalem.

28 David Makes His Way to the Jordan

II Samuel 16:1–14

(1)When David had passed a little beyond the summit, Ziba the servant of Mephibosheth met him, with a couple of asses saddled, bearing two hundred loaves of bread, a hundred bunches of raisins, a hundred of summer fruits, and a skin of wine. (2)And the king said to Ziba, "Why have you brought these?" Ziba answered, "The asses are for the king's household to ride on, the bread and summer fruit for the young men to eat, and the wine for those who faint in the wilderness to drink." (3)And the king said,

"And where is your master's son?" Ziba said to the king, "Behold, he remains in Jerusalem; for he said, 'Today the house of Israel will give me back the kingdom of my father.' " (4)Then the king said to Ziba, "Behold, all that belonged to Mephibosheth is now yours." And Ziba said, "I do obeisance; let me ever find favor in your sight, my lord the king."

(5)When King David came to Bahurim, there came out a man of the family of the house of Saul, whose name was Shime-i, the son of Gera; and as he came he cursed continually. (6)And he threw stones at David, and at all the servants of King David; and all the people and all the mighty men were on his right hand and on his left. (7)And Shime-i said as he cursed, "Begone, begone, you man of blood, you worthless fellow! (8)The LORD has avenged upon you all the blood of the house of Saul, in whose place you have reigned; and the LORD has given the kingdom into the hand of your son Absalom. See, your ruin is on you; for you are a man of blood."

(9)Then Abishai the son of Zeruiah said to the king, "Why should this dead dog curse my lord the king? Let me go over and take off his head." (10)But the king said, "What have I to do with you, you sons of Zeruiah? If he is cursing because the LORD has said to him, 'Curse David,' who then shall say, 'Why have you done so?' " (11)And David said to Abishai and to all his servants, "Behold, my own son seeks my life; how much more now may this Benjaminite! Let him alone, and let him curse; for the LORD has bidden him. (12)It may be that the LORD will look upon my affliction, and that the LORD will repay me with good for this cursing of me today." (13)So David and his men went on the road, while Shime-i went along on the hillside opposite him and cursed as he went, and threw stones at him and flung dust. (14)And the king, and all the people who were with him, arrived weary at the Jordan; and there he refreshed himself.

29 Absalom Violates David's Concubines

II Samuel 16:15–23

(15)Now Absalom and all the people, the men of Israel, came to Jerusalem, and Ahithophel with him. (16)And when Hushai the Archite, David's friend, came to Absalom, Hushai said to Absalom, "Long live the king! Long live the king!" (17)And Absalom said to Hushai, "Is this your loyalty to your friend? Why did you not go with your friend?" (18)And Hushai said to Absalom, "No; for whom the LORD and this people and all the men of Israel have chosen, his I will be, and with him I will remain. (19)And again, whom should I serve? Should it not be his son? As I have served your father, so I will serve you."

(20)Then Absalom said to Ahithophel, "Give your counsel; what shall we do?" (21)Ahithophel said to Absalom, "Go in to your father's concubines, whom he has left to keep the house; and all Israel will hear that you have made yourself odious to your father, and the hands of all who are with you will be strengthened." (22)So they pitched a tent for Absalom upon the roof; and Absalom went in to his father's concubines in the sight of all Israel. (23)Now in those days the counsel which Ahithophel gave was as if one consulted the oracle of God; so was all the counsel of Ahithophel esteemed, both by David and by Absalom.

30 Ahithophel's Counsel Overruled

II Samuel 17:1–23

[1]Moreover Ahithophel said to Absalom, "Let me choose twelve thousand men, and I will set out and pursue David tonight. [2]I will come upon him while he is weary and discouraged, and throw him into a panic; and all the people who are with him will flee. I will strike down the king only, [3]and I will bring all the people back to you as a bride comes home to her husband. You seek the life of only one man, and all the people will be at peace." [4]And the advice pleased Absalom and all the elders of Israel.

[5]Then Absalom said, "Call Hushai the Archite also, and let us hear what he has to say." [6]And when Hushai came to Absalom, Absalom said to him, "Thus has Ahithophel spoken; shall we do as he advises? If not, you speak." [7]Then Hushai said to Absalom, "This time the counsel which Ahithophel has given is not good." [8]Hushai said moreover, "You know that your father and his men are mighty men, and that they are enraged, like a bear robbed of her cubs in the field. Besides, your father is expert in war; he will not spend the night with the people. [9]Behold, even now he has hidden himself in one of the pits, or in some other place. And when some of the people fall at the first attack, whoever hears it will say, 'There has been a slaughter among the people who follow Absalom.' [10]Then even the valiant man, whose heart is like the heart of a lion, will utterly melt with fear; for all Israel knows that your father is a mighty man, and that those who are with him are valiant men. [11]But my counsel is that all Israel be gathered to you, from Dan to Beer-sheba, as the sand by the sea for multitude, and that you go to battle in person. [12]So we shall come upon him in some place where he is to be found, and we shall light upon him as the dew falls on the ground; and of him and all the men with him not one will be left. [13]If he withdraws into a city, then all Israel will bring ropes to that city, and we shall drag it into the valley, until not even a pebble is to be found there." [14]And Absalom and all the men of Israel said, "The counsel of Hushai the Archite is better than the counsel of Ahithophel." For the LORD had ordained to defeat the good counsel of Ahithophel, so that the LORD might bring evil upon Absalom.

[15]Then Hushai said to Zadok and Abiathar the priests, "Thus and so did Ahithophel counsel Absalom and the elders of Israel; and thus and so have I counseled. [16]Now therefore send quickly and tell David, 'Do not lodge tonight at the fords of the wilderness, but by all means pass over; lest the king and all the people who are with him be swallowed up.' " [17]Now Jonathan and Ahima-az were waiting at En-rogel; a maidservant used to go and tell them, and they would go and tell King David; for they must not be seen entering the city. [18]But a lad saw them, and told Absalom; so both of them went away quickly, and came to the house of a man at Bahurim, who had a well in his courtyard; and they went down into it. [19]And the woman took and spread a covering over the well's mouth, and scattered grain upon it; and nothing was known of it. [20]When Absalom's servants came to the woman at the house, they said, "Where are Ahima-az and Jonathan?" And the woman said to them, "They have gone over the brook of water." And when they had sought and could not find them, they returned to Jerusalem.

[21]After they had gone, the men came up out of the well, and went and told King David. They said to David, "Arise, and go quickly over the water; for thus and so has Ahithophel counseled against you." [22]Then David arose, and all the people who were

with him, and they crossed the Jordan; by daybreak not one was left who had not crossed the Jordan.

(23)When Ahithophel saw that his counsel was not followed, he saddled his ass, and went off home to his own city. And he set his house in order, and hanged himself; and he died, and was buried in the tomb of his father.

31 David Reaches Mahanaim

II Samuel 17:24–29

(24)Then David came to Mahanaim. And Absalom crossed the Jordan with all the men of Israel. (25)Now Absalom had set Amasa over the army instead of Joab. Amasa was the son of a man named Ithra the Ishmaelite, who had married Abigal the daughter of Nahash, sister of Zeruiah, Joab's mother. (26)And Israel and Absalom encamped in the land of Gilead.

(27)When David came to Mahanaim, Shobi the son of Nahash from Rabbah of the Ammonites, and Machir the son of Ammi-el from Lo-debar, and Barzillai the Gileadite from Rogelim, (28)brought beds, basins, and earthen vessels, wheat, barley, meal, parched grain, beans and lentils, (29)honey and curds and sheep and cheese from the herd, for David and the people with him to eat; for they said, "The people are hungry and weary and thirsty in the wilderness."

32 The Defeat and Death of Absalom

II Samuel 18:1–33

(1)Then David mustered the men who were with him, and set over them commanders of thousands and commanders of hundreds. (2)And David sent forth the army, one third under the command of Joab, one third under the command of Abishai the son of Zeruiah, Joab's brother, and one third under the command of Ittai the Gittite. And the king said to the men, "I myself will also go out with you." (3)But the men said, "You shall not go out. For if we flee, they will not care about us. If half of us die, they will not care about us. But you are worth ten thousand of us; therefore it is better that you send us help from the city." (4)The king said to them, "Whatever seems best to you I will do." So the king stood at the side of the gate, while all the army marched out by hundreds and by thousands. (5)And the king ordered Joab and Abishai and Ittai, "Deal gently for my sake with the young man Absalom." And all the people heard when the king gave orders to all the commanders about Absalom.

(6)So the army went out into the field against Israel; and the battle was fought in the forest of Ephraim. (7)And the men of Israel were defeated there by the servants of David, and the slaughter there was great on that day, twenty thousand men. (8)The battle spread over the face of all the country; and the forest devoured more people that day than the sword.

(9)And Absalom chanced to meet the servants of David. Absalom was riding upon his mule, and the mule went under the thick branches of a great oak, and his head caught fast in the oak, and he was left hanging between heaven and earth, while the mule that was under him went on. (10)And a certain man saw it, and told Joab, "Behold, I saw Absalom hanging in an oak." (11)Joab said to the man who told him, "What, you saw him! Why then did you not strike him there to the ground? I would have been glad to give you ten pieces of silver and a girdle." (12)But the man said to Joab, "Even if I felt in my hand the weight of a thousand pieces of silver, I would not put forth my hand against the king's son; for in our hearing the king commanded you and Abishai and Ittai, 'For my sake protect the young man Absalom.' (13)On the other hand, if I had dealt treacherously against his life (and there is nothing hidden from the king), then you yourself would have stood aloof." (14)Joab said, "I will not waste time like this with you." And he took three darts in his hand, and thrust them into the heart of Absalom, while he was still alive in the oak. (15)And ten young men, Joab's armor-bearers, surrounded Absalom and struck him, and killed him.

(16)Then Joab blew the trumpet, and the troops came back from pursuing Israel; for Joab restrained them. (17)And they took Absalom, and threw him into a great pit in the forest, and raised over him a very great heap of stones; and all Israel fled every one to his own home. (18)Now Absalom in his lifetime had taken and set up for himself the pillar which is in the King's Valley, for he said, "I have no son to keep my name in remembrance"; he called the pillar after his own name, and it is called Absalom's monument to this day.

(19)Then said Ahima-az the son of Zadok, "Let me run, and carry tidings to the king that the LORD has delivered him from the power of his enemies." (20)And Joab said to him, "You are not to carry tidings today; you may carry tidings another day, but today you shall carry no tidings, because the king's son is dead." (21)Then Joab said to the Cushite, "Go, tell the king what you have seen." The Cushite bowed before Joab, and ran. (22)Then Ahima-az the son of Zadok said again to Joab, "Come what may, let me also run after the Cushite." And Joab said, "Why will you run, my son, seeing that you will have no reward for the tidings?" (23)"Come what may," he said, "I will run." So he said to him, "Run." Then Ahima-az ran by the way of the plain, and outran the Cushite.

(24)Now David was sitting between the two gates; and the watchman went up to the roof of the gate by the wall, and when he lifted up his eyes and looked, he saw a man running alone. (25)And the watchman called out and told the king. And the king said, "If he is alone, there are tidings in his mouth." And he came apace, and drew near. (26)And the watchman saw another man running; and the watchman called to the gate and said, "See, another man running alone!" The king said, "He also brings tidings." (27)And the watchman said, "I think the running of the foremost is like the running of Ahima-az the son of Zadok." And the king said, "He is a good man, and comes with good tidings."

(28)Then Ahima-az cried out to the king, "All is well." And he bowed before the king with his face to the earth, and said, "Blessed be the LORD your God, who has delivered up the men who raised their hand against my lord the king." (29) And the king said, "Is it well with the young man Absalom?" Ahima-az answered, "When Joab sent your servant, I saw a great tumult, but I do not know what it was." (30)And the king said, "Turn aside, and stand here." So he turned aside, and stood still.

(31)And behold, the Cushite came; and the Cushite said, "Good tidings for my lord the king! For the LORD has delivered you this day from the power of all who rose up against you." (32)The king said to the Cushite, "Is it well with the young man Absalom?"

And the Cushite answered, "May the enemies of my lord the king, and all who rise up against you for evil, be like that young man." (33)And the king was deeply moved, and went up to the chamber over the gate, and wept; and as he went, he said, "O my son Absalom, my son, my son Absalom! Would I had died instead of you, O Absalom, my son, my son!"

33 David's Restoration

II Samuel 19:1–43

(1)It was told Joab, "Behold, the king is weeping and mourning for Absalom." (2)So the victory that day was turned into mourning for all the people; for the people heard that day, "The king is grieving for his son." (3)And the people stole into the city that day as people steal in who are ashamed when they flee in battle. (4)The king covered his face, and the king cried with a loud voice, "O my son Absalom, O Absalom, my son, my son!" (5)Then Joab came into the house to the king, and said, "You have today covered with shame the faces of all your servants, who have this day saved your life, and the lives of your sons and your daughters, and the lives of your wives and your concubines, (6)because you love those who hate you and hate those who love you. For you have made it clear today that commanders and servants are nothing to you; for today I perceive that if Absalom were alive and all of us were dead today, then you would be pleased. (7)Now therefore arise, go out and speak kindly to your servants; for I swear by the LORD, if you do not go, not a man will stay with you this night; and this will be worse for you than all the evil that has come upon you from your youth until now." (8)Then the king arose, and took his seat in the gate. And the people were all told, "Behold, the king is sitting in the gate"; and all the people came before the king.

Now Israel had fled every man to his own home. (9)And all the people were at strife throughout all the tribes of Israel, saying, "The king delivered us from the hand of our enemies, and saved us from the hand of the Philistines; and now he has fled out of the land from Absalom. (10)But Absalom, whom we anointed over us, is dead in battle. Now therefore why do you say nothing about bringing the king back?"

(11)And King David sent this message to Zadok and Abiathar the priests, "Say to the elders of Judah, 'Why should you be the last to bring the king back to his house, when the word of all Israel has come to the king? (12)You are my kinsmen, you are my bone and my flesh; why then should you be the last to bring back the king?' (13)And say to Amasa, 'Are you not my bone and my flesh? God do so to me, and more also, if you are not commander of my army henceforth in place of Joab.' " (14)And he swayed the heart of all the men of Judah as one man; so that they sent word to the king, "Return, both you and all your servants." (15)So the king came back to the Jordan; and Judah came to Gilgal to meet the king and to bring the king over the Jordan.

(16)And Shime-i the son of Gera, the Benjaminite, from Bahurim, made haste to come down with the men of Judah to meet King David; (17)and with him were a thousand men from Benjamin. And Ziba the servant of the house of Saul, with his fifteen sons and his twenty servants, rushed down to the Jordan before the king, (18)and they crossed the ford to bring over the king's household, and to do his pleasure. And Shime-i the son of Gera fell down before the king, as he was about to cross the Jordan, (19)and said to the king, "Let not my lord hold me guilty or remember how your servant did wrong

59

on the day my lord the king left Jerusalem; let not the king bear it in mind. (20)For your servant knows that I have sinned; therefore, behold, I have come this day, the first of all the house of Joseph to come down to meet my lord the king." (21)Abishai the son of Zeruiah answered, "Shall not Shime-i be put to death for this, because he cursed the LORD's anointed?" (22)But David said, "What have I to do with you, you sons of Zeruiah, that you should this day be as an adversary to me? Shall any one be put to death in Israel this day? For do I not know that I am this day king over Israel?" (23)And the king said to Shime-i, "You shall not die." And the king gave him his oath.

(24)And Mephibosheth the son of Saul came down to meet the king; he had neither dressed his feet, nor trimmed his beard, nor washed his clothes, from the day the king departed until the day he came back in safety. (25)And when he came from Jerusalem to meet the king, the king said to him, "Why did you not go with me, Mephibosheth?" (26)He answered, "My lord, O king, my servant deceived me; for your servant said to him, 'Saddle an ass for me, that I may ride upon it and go with the king.' For your servant is lame. (27)He has slandered your servant to my lord the king. But my lord the king is like the angel of God; do therefore what seems good to you. (28)For all my father's house were but men doomed to death before my lord the king; but you set your servant among those who eat at your table. What further right have I, then, to cry to the king?" (29)And the king said to him, "Why speak any more of your affairs? I have decided: you and Ziba shall divide the land." (30)And Mephibosheth said to the king, "Oh, let him take it all, since my lord the king has come safely home."

(31)Now Barzillai the Gileadite had come down from Rogelim; and he went on with the king to the Jordan, to escort him over the Jordan. (32)Barzillai was a very aged man, eighty years old; and he had provided the king with food while he stayed at Mahanaim; for he was a very wealthy man. (33)And the king said to Barzillai, "Come over with me, and I will provide for you with me in Jerusalem." (34)But Barzillai said to the king, "How many years have I still to live, that I should go up with the king to Jerusalem? (35)I am this day eighty years old; can I discern what is pleasant and what is not? Can your servant taste what he eats or what he drinks? Can I still listen to the voice of singing men and singing women? Why then should your servant be an added burden to my lord the king? (36)Your servant will go a little way over the Jordan with the king. Why should the king recompense me with such a reward? (37)Pray let your servant return, that I may die in my own city, near the grave of my father and my mother. But here is your servant Chimham; let him go over with my lord the king; and do for him whatever seems good to you." (38)And the king answered, "Chimham shall go over with me, and I will do for him whatever seems good to you; and all that you desire of me I will do for you." (39)Then all the people went over the Jordan, and the king went over; and the king kissed Barzillai and blessed him, and he returned to his own home. (40)The king went on to Gilgal, and Chimham went on with him; all the people of Judah, and also half the people of Israel, brought the king on his way.

(41)Then all the men of Israel came to the king, and said to the king, "Why have our brethren the men of Judah stolen you away, and brought the king and his household over the Jordan, and all David's men with him?" (42)All the men of Judah answered the men of Israel, "Because the king is near of kin to us. Why then are you angry over this matter? Have we eaten at all at the king's expense? Or has he given us any gift?" (43)And the men of Israel answered the men of Judah, "We have ten shares in the king, and in David also we have more than you. Why then did you despise us? Were we not the first to speak of bringing back our king?'' But the words of the men of Judah were fiercer than the words of the men of Israel.

34 Sheba's Rebellion Put Down

II Samuel 20:1–26

(1)Now there happened to be there a worthless fellow, whose name was Sheba, the son of Bichri, a Benjaminite; and he blew the trumpet, and said,

"We have no portion in David,
and we have no inheritance in the son of Jesse;
every man to his tents, O Israel!"

(2)So all the men of Israel withdrew from David, and followed Sheba the son of Bichri; but the men of Judah followed their king steadfastly from the Jordan to Jerusalem.

(3)And David came to his house at Jerusalem; and the king took the ten concubines whom he had left to care for the house, and put them in a house under guard, and provided for them, but did not go in to them. So they were shut up until the day of their death, living as if in widowhood.

(4)Then the king said to Amasa, "Call the men of Judah together to me within three days, and be here yourself." (5)So Amasa went to summon Judah; but he delayed beyond the set time which had been appointed him. (6)And David said to Abishai, "Now Sheba the son of Bichri will do us more harm than Absalom; take your lord's servants and pursue him, lest he get himself fortified cities, and cause us trouble." (7)And there went out after Abishai, Joab and the Cherethites and the Pelethites, and all the mighty men; they went out from Jerusalem to pursue Sheba the son of Bichri. (8)When they were at the great stone which is in Gibeon, Amasa came to meet them. Now Joab was wearing a soldier's garment, and over it was a girdle with a sword in its sheath fastened upon his loins, and as he went forward it fell out. (9)And Joab said to Amasa, "Is it well with you, my brother?" And Joab took Amasa by the beard with his right hand to kiss him. (10)But Amasa did not observe the sword which was in Joab's hand; so Joab struck him with it in the body, and shed his bowels to the ground, without striking a second blow; and he died.

Then Joab and Abishai his brother pursued Sheba the son of Bichri. (11)And one of Joab's men took his stand by Amasa, and said, "Whoever favors Joab, and whoever is for David, let him follow Joab." (12)And Amasa lay wallowing in his blood in the highway. And any one who came by, seeing him, stopped; and when the man saw that all the people stopped, he carried Amasa out of the highway into the field, and threw a garment over him. (13)When he was taken out of the highway, all the people went on after Joab to pursue Sheba the son of Bichri.

(14)And Sheba passed through all the tribes of Israel to Abel of Beth-maacah; and all the Bichrites assembled, and followed him in. (15)And all the men who were with Joab came and besieged him in Abel of Beth-maacah; they cast up a mound against the city, and it stood againt the rampart; and they were battering the wall, to throw it down. (16)Then a wise woman called from the city, "Hear! Hear! Tell Joab, 'Come here, that

I may speak to you.' " (17)And he came near her; and the woman said, "Are you Joab?" He answered, "I am." Then she said to him, "Listen to the words of your maidservant." And he answered, "I am listening." (18)Then she said, "They were wont to say in old time, 'Let them but ask counsel at Abel'; and so they settled a matter. (19)I am one of those who are peaceable and faithful in Israel; you seek to destroy a city which is a mother in Israel; why will you swallow up the heritage of the LORD?" (20)Joab answered, "Far be it from me, far be it, that I should swallow up or destroy! (21)That is not true. But a man of the hill country of Ephraim, called Sheba the son of Bichri, has lifted up his hand against King David; give up him alone, and I will withdraw from the city." And the woman said to Joab, "Behold, his head shall be thrown to you over the wall." (22)Then the woman went to all the people in her wisdom. And they cut off the head of Sheba the son of Bichri, and threw it out to Joab. So he blew the trumpet, and they dispersed from the city, every man to his home. And Joab returned to Jerusalem to the king.

(23)Now Joab was in command of all the army of Israel; and Benaiah the son of Jehoiada was in command of the Cherethites and the Pelethites; (24)and Adoram was in charge of the forced labor; and Jehoshaphat the son of Ahilud was the recorder; (25)and Sheva was secretary; and Zadok and Abiathar were priests; (26)and Ira the Jairite was also David's priest.

35 The Execution of the Saulites

II Samuel 21:1–14

(1)Now there was a famine in the days of David for three years, year after year; and David sought the face of the LORD. And the LORD said, "There is bloodguilt on Saul and on his house, because he put the Gibeonites to death." (2)So the king called the Gibeonites. Now the Gibeonites were not of the people of Israel, but of the remnant of the Amorites; although the people of Israel had sworn to spare them, Saul had sought to slay them in his zeal for the people of Israel and Judah. (3)And David said to the Gibeonites, "What shall I do for you? And how shall I make expiation, that you may bless the heritage of the LORD?" (4)The Gibeonites said to him, "It is not a matter of silver or gold between us and Saul or his house; neither is it for us to put any man to death in Israel." And he said, "What do you say that I shall do for you?" (5)They said to the king, "The man who consumed us and planned to destroy us, so that we should have no place in all the territory of Israel, (6)let seven of his sons be given to us, so that we may hang them up before the LORD at Gibeon on the mountain of the LORD." And the king said, "I will give them."

(7)But the king spared Mephibosheth, the son of Saul's son Jonathan, because of the oath of the LORD which was between them, between David and Jonathan the son of Saul. (8)The king took the two sons of Rizpah the daughter of Aiah, whom she bore to Saul, Armoni and Mephibosheth; and the five sons of Merab the daughter of Saul, whom she bore to Adri-el the son of Barzillai the Meholathite; (9)and he gave them into the hands of the Gibeonites, and they hanged them on the mountain before the LORD, and the seven of them perished together. They were put to death in the first days of harvest, at the beginning of barley harvest.

(10)Then Rizpah the daughter of Aiah took sackcloth, and spread it for herself on the rock, from the beginning of harvest until rain fell upon them from the heavens; and she did not allow the birds of the air to come upon them by day, or the beasts of the field by night. (11)When David was told what Rizpah the daughter of Aiah, the concubine of Saul, had done, (12)David went and took the bones of Saul and the bones of his son Jonathan from the men of Jabesh-gilead, who had stolen them from the public square of Beth-shan, where the Philistines had hanged them, on the day the Philistines killed Saul on Gilboa; (13)and he brought up from there the bones of Saul and the bones of his son Jonathan; and they gathered the bones of those who were hanged. (14)And they buried the bones of Saul and his son Jonathan in the land of Benjamin in Zela, in the tomb of Kish his father; and they did all that the king commanded. And after that God heeded supplications for the land.

36 Further Battles with the Philistines

II Samuel 21:15–22	*I Chronicles 20:4–8*
(15)The Philistines had war again with Israel, and David went down together with his servants, and they fought against the Philistines; and David grew weary. (16)And Ishbi-benob, one of the descendants of the giants, whose spear weighed three hundred shekels of bronze, and who was girded with a new sword, thought to kill David. (17)But Abishai the son of Zeruiah came to his aid, and attacked the Philistine and killed him. Then David's men adjured him, "You shall no more go out with us to battle, lest you quench the lamp of Israel."	
/18/And after this there <u>was again</u> war with the Philistines at Gob; then Sibbecai the Hushathite slew <u>Saph,</u> who was one of the descendants of the giants.	(4)And after this there <u>arose</u> war with the Philistines at Gezer; then Sibbecai the Hushathite slew <u>Sippai,</u> who was one of the descendants of the giants; <u>and the Philistines were subdued.</u>
(19)And there was again war with the Philistines <u>at Gob;</u> and Elhanan the son of Jaare-<u>oregim,</u> <u>the Bethlehemite,</u> slew Goliath the Gittite, the shaft of whose spear was like a weaver's beam. (20)And	(5)And there was again war with the Philistines; and Elhanan the son of Jair slew <u>Lahmi the brother of</u> Goliath the Gittite, the shaft of whose spear was like a weaver's beam. (6)And

63

there was again war at Gath, where
there was a man of great stature,
who had six fingers on each hand,
and six toes on each foot, twenty-
four in number; and he also was
descended from the giants. (21)And
when he taunted Israel, Jonathan the
son of Shime-i, David's brother, slew
him. (22)These four were descended
from the giants in Gath; and they fell
by the hand of David and by the hand
of his servants.

there was again war at Gath, where
there was a man of great stature,
who had six fingers on each hand,
and six toes on each foot, twenty-
four in number; and he also was
descended from the giants. (7)And
when he taunted Israel, Jonathan the
son of Shime-a, David's brother, slew
him. (8)These were descended
from the giants in Gath; and they fell
by the hand of David and by the hand
of his servants.

37 David's Psalm of Deliverance

II Samuel 22:1–51

(1)And David
spoke
to the LORD the words of this song
on the day when the LORD delivered
him from the hand of all his enemies,
and from the hand of Saul.
/2/He said,

The LORD is my rock, and my
fortress, and my deliverer,
(3)God, my rock, in whom I take
refuge,
my shield and the horn of my
salvation,
my stronghold and my refuge,
my savior; thou savest me
from violence.
(4)I call upon the LORD, who is
worthy to be praised,
and I am saved from my enemies.

/5/For the waves of death
encompassed me,
the torrents of perdition
assailed me;
(6)the cords of Sheol entangled me,
the snares of death
confronted me.

Psalm 18:1–50

To the choirmaster. A Psalm of David
the servant of the LORD, who addressed
the words of this song to the LORD
on the day when the LORD delivered
him from the hand of all his enemies,
and from the hand of Saul.
He said:

(1)I love thee, O LORD, my strength.
/2/The LORD is my rock, and my
fortress, and my deliverer,
my God, my rock, in whom I take
refuge,
my shield and the horn of my
salvation, my stronghold.

(3)I call upon the LORD, who is
worthy to be praised,
and I am saved from my enemies.

(4)The cords of death
encompassed me,
the torrents of perdition
assailed me;
(5)the cords of Sheol entangled me,
the snares of death
confronted me.

/7/In my distress I called upon
    the LORD;
    to my God I called.
    From his temple he heard my voice,
    and my cry came to his ears.

/8/Then the earth reeled and rocked;
    the foundations of the
     heavens trembled
    and quaked, because he was angry.
(9)Smoke went up from his nostrils,
    and devouring fire from
    his mouth;
    glowing coals flamed forth
    from him.
(10)He bowed the heavens, and
    came down;
    thick darkness was under
    his feet.
(11)He rode on a cherub, and flew;
    he was seen upon the
    wings of the wind.
(12)He made darkness
    around him
    his canopy, thick clouds,
    a gathering of water.
(13)Out of the brightness before him

    coals of fire flamed forth.
(14)The LORD thundered
    from heaven,
    and the Most High uttered
    his voice.

(15)And he sent out arrows,
    and scattered them;
    lightning,
    and routed them.
(16)Then the channels of the sea
    were seen,
    the foundations of the
    world were laid bare,
    at the rebuke of the LORD,
    at the blast of the breath
    of his nostrils.

(6)In my distress I called upon
    the LORD;
    to my God I cried for help.
    From his temple he heard my voice,
    and my cry to him reached
    his ears.

(7)Then the earth reeled and rocked;
    the foundations also of the
    mountains trembled
    and quaked, because he was angry.
(8)Smoke went up from his nostrils,
    and devouring fire from
    his mouth;
    glowing coals flamed forth
    from him.
(9)He bowed the heavens, and
    came down;
    thick darkness was under
    his feet.
(10)He rode on a cherub, and flew;
    he came swiftly upon the
    wings of the wind.
(11)He made darkness his covering
    around him,
    his canopy thick clouds
    dark with water.
(12)Out of the brightness before him
    there broke through his clouds
    hailstones and coals of fire.
(13)The LORD also thundered
    in the heavens,
    and the Most High uttered
    his voice,
    hailstones and coals of fire.
(14)And he sent out his arrows,
    and scattered them;
    he flashed forth lightnings,
    and routed them.
(15)Then the channels of the sea
    were seen,
    and the foundations of the
    world were laid bare,
    at thy rebuke, O LORD,
    at the blast of the breath
    of thy nostrils.

/17/ He reached from on high, he
    took me,
    he drew me out of many waters.
(18) He delivered me from my
    strong enemy,
    from those who hated me;
    for they were too mighty for me.
(19) They came upon me in the day of
    my calamity;
    but the LORD was my stay.
(20) He brought me forth into a
    broad place;
    he delivered me, because he
    delighted in me.

/21/ The LORD rewarded me according
    to my righteousness;
    according to the cleanness of
    my hands he recompensed me.
(22) For I have kept the ways of
    the LORD,
    and have not wickedly departed
    from my God.
(23) For all his ordinances were
    before me,
    and from his statutes I did
    not turn aside.
(24) I was blameless before him,
    and I kept myself from guilt.
(25) Therefore the LORD has recompensed
    me according to
    my righteousness,
    according to my cleanness
    in his sight.

/26/ With the loyal thou dost show
    thyself loyal;
    with the blameless man thou dost
    show thyself blameless;
(27) with the pure thou dost show
    thyself pure,
    and with the crooked thou dost
    show thyself perverse.
(28) Thou dost deliver a humble
    people,
    but thy eyes are upon the
    haughty to bring them down.

(16) He reached from on high, he
    took me,
    he drew me out of many waters.
(17) He delivered me from my
    strong enemy,
    and from those who hated me;
    for they were too mighty for me.
(18) They came upon me in the day of
    my calamity;
    but the LORD was my stay.
(19) He brought me forth into a
    broad place;
    he delivered me, because he
    delighted in me.

(20) The LORD rewarded me according
    to my righteousness;
    according to the cleanness of
    my hands he recompensed me.
(21) For I have kept the ways of
    the LORD,
    and have not wickedly departed
    from my God.
(22) For all his ordinances were
    before me,
    and his statutes I did
    not put away from me.
(23) I was blameless before him,
    and I kept myself from guilt.
(24) Therefore the LORD has recompensed
    me according to
    my righteousness,
    according to the cleanness
    of my hands in his sight.

(25) With the loyal thou dost show
    thyself loyal;
    with the blameless man thou dost
    show thyself blameless;
/26/ with the pure thou dost show
    thyself pure,
    and with the crooked thou dost
    show thyself perverse.
/27/ For thou dost deliver a humble
    people,
    but the haughty eyes
    thou dost bring down.

(29)Yea, thou art my lamp, O LORD,
  and my God lightens my
    darkness.
(30)Yea, by thee I can crush a troop,
  and by my God I can leap over
    a wall.
(31)This God—his way is perfect;
  the promise of the LORD
    proves true;
  he is a shield for all those
    who take refuge in him.

/32/ For who is God, but the LORD?
  And who is a rock, except
    our God?
(33) This God is my strong refuge,

  and has set free his way.
(34) He made his feet like
    hinds' feet,
  and set me secure on the
    heights.
(35)He trains my hands for war,
  so that my arms can bend a bow
    of bronze.
(36)Thou hast given me the shield of
    thy salvation,

  and thy help made me
    great.
(37)Thou didst give a wide place for
    my steps under me,
  and my feet did not slip.
(38)I pursued my enemies and
    destroyed them,
  and did not turn back until
    they were consumed.
(39)I consumed them; I thrust them
    through, so that they did
    not rise;
  they fell under my feet.
(40)For thou didst gird me with
    strength for the battle;
  thou didst make my assailants
    sink under me.

(28)Yea, thou dost light my lamp;
  the LORD my God lightens my
    darkness.
(29)Yea, by thee I can crush a troop;
  and by my God I can leap over
    a wall.
(30)This God—his way is perfect;
  the promise of the LORD
    proves true;
  he is a shield for all those
    who take refuge in him.

(31)For who is God, but the LORD?
  And who is a rock, except
    our God?—
(32)the God who girded me with
      strength,
  and made my way safe.
(33)He made my feet like
    hinds' feet,
  and set me secure on the
    heights.
(34)He trains my hands for war,
  so that my arms can bend a bow
    of bronze.
(35)Thou hast given me the shield of
    thy salvation,
  and thy right hand supported
    me,
  and thy gentleness made me
    great.
(36)Thou didst give a wide place for
    my steps under me,
  and my feet did not slip.
/37/ I pursued my enemies and
    overtook them;
  and did not turn back until
    they were consumed.
(38)I thrust them
    through, so that they were
    not able to rise;
  they fell under my feet.
(39)For thou didst gird me with
    strength for the battle;
  thou didst make my assailants
    sink under me.

(41)Thou didst make my enemies turn
    their backs to me,
  those who hated me, _and_ I
    destroyed _them_.
(42)They _looked_, but there
    was none to save;
  they cried to the LORD, but he
    did not answer them.
(43)I beat them fine as _the_ dust
    of the earth,
  I _crushed_ them _and stamped them_
    down like the mire of
    the streets.

(44)Thou didst deliver me from strife
    with my people;
  thou didst _keep_ me as the head
    of the nations;
  people whom I had not known
    served me.
(45)Foreigners came cringing to me;
  as soon as they heard of me,
    they obeyed me.

(46)Foreigners lost heart,
  and _girded themselves_ out of
    their fastnesses.

/47/The LORD lives; and blessed be
    my rock,
  and exalted be _my_ God,
    the rock of my salvation,
(48)the God who gave me vengeance
  and _brought down_ peoples under
    me,
(49)who _brought_ me _out_ from my
    enemies;
  thou didst exalt me above
    my adversaries,
  thou didst deliver me from men
    of violence.

/50/For this I will extol thee,
    O LORD, among the nations,
  and sing praises to thy name.
/51/Great triumphs he gives to his
    king,

(40)Thou didst make my enemies turn
    their backs to me,
  those who hated me I
    destroyed.
/41/They _cried for help_, but there
    was none to save;
  they cried to the LORD, but he
    did not answer them.
(42)I beat them fine as dust
    before the wind;
  I cast them _out_
    like the mire of
    the streets.

(43)Thou didst deliver me from strife
    with the people;
  thou didst _make_ me the head
    of the nations;
  people whom I had not known
    served me.

/44/As soon as they heard of me,
    they obeyed me;
  foreigners came cringing to me.
(45)Foreigners lost heart,
  and _came trembling_ out of
    their fastnesses.

(46)The LORD lives; and blessed be
    my rock,
  and exalted be _the_ God
    of my salvation,
(47)the God who gave me vengeance
  and subdued peoples under
    me;
(48)who delivered me from my
    enemies;
  yea, thou didst exalt me above
    my adversaries;
  thou didst deliver me from men
    of violence.

(49)For this I will extol thee,
    O LORD, among the nations,
  and sing praises to thy name.
(50)Great triumphs he gives to his
    king,

and shows steadfast love to
  his anointed,
to David, and his descendants
  for ever.

and shows steadfast love to
  his anointed,
to David, and his descendants
  for ever.

38 David's "Last Words"

II Samuel 23:1–7

(1)Now these are the last words of David:
  The oracle of David, the son of Jesse,
    the oracle of the man who was raised on high,
  the anointed of the God of Jacob,
    the sweet psalmist of Israel:
(2)"The Spirit of the LORD speaks by me,
    his word is upon my tongue.
(3)The God of Israel has spoken,
    the Rock of Israel has said to me:
  When one rules justly over men,
    ruling in the fear of God,
(4)he dawns on them like the morning light,
    like the sun shining forth upon a cloudless morning,
    like rain that makes grass to sprout from the earth.
(5)Yea, does not my house stand so with God?
    For he has made with me an everlasting covenant,
    ordered in all things and secure.
  For will he not cause to prosper
    all my help and my desire?
(6)But godless men are all like thorns that are thrown away;
    for they cannot be taken with the hand;
(7)but the man who touches them
    arms himself with iron and the shaft of a spear,
    and they are utterly consumed with fire."

39 The Roll of David's Mightiest Warriors

II Samuel 23:8–39   *I Chronicles 11:10–47*

(10)Now these are the chiefs of
David's mighty men, who gave him
strong support in his kingdom,
together with all Israel, to make him
king, according to the word of the
LORD concerning Israel.

69

[8]These are the names of the
mighty men whom David had:
Josheb-basshebeth a Tah-chemonite;
he was chief of the three;
he . . .⁽*⁾against
eight hundred
whom he slew at one time.
⁽9⁾And next to him among the
three mighty men was Eleazar
the son of Dodo, son of Ahohi.
He was with David
when they defied the Philistines who
were gathered there for battle, and
the men of Israel withdrew. ⁽10⁾He
rose and struck down the Philistines
until his hand was weary, and his hand
cleaved to the sword; and the LORD
wrought a great victory that day; and
the men returned after him only to
strip the slain.
⁽11⁾And next to him was Shammah,
the son of Agee the Hararite.
The Philistines
gathered together at Lehi,
where there was a plot of ground
full of lentils; and the men fled
from the Philistines. ⁽12⁾But he
took his stand in the midst of the
plot, and defended it, and slew the
Philistines; and the LORD wrought
a great victory.
⁽13⁾And three of the thirty chief
men went down,
and came about harvest time to David
at the cave of Adullam,
when a band of Philistines was
encamped in the valley of Rephaim.
⁽14⁾David was then in the stronghold;
and the garrison of the Philistines
was then at Bethlehem. ⁽15⁾And David
said longingly, "O that some one
would give me water to drink from the
well of Bethlehem which is by the
gate!" ⁽16⁾Then the three mighty men
broke through the camp of the
Philistines, and drew water out of

⁽11⁾This is an account of
David's mighty men:
Jashobe-am, a Hachmonite,
was chief of the thirty;
he wielded his spear against
three hundred
whom he slew at one time.
⁽12⁾And next to him among the
three mighty men was Eleazar
the son of Dodo, the Ahohite.
⁽13⁾He was with David

at Pasdammim when the Philistines were
gathered there for battle.
There was a plot of ground
full of barley, and the men fled
from the Philistines. ⁽14⁾But they
took their stand in the midst of the
plot, and defended it, and slew the
Philistines; and the LORD saved
them by a great victory.
⁽15⁾Three of the thirty chief
men went down
to the rock to David
at the cave of Adullam,
when the army of Philistines was
encamped in the valley of Rephaim.
⁽16⁾David was then in the stronghold;
and the garrison of the Philistines
was then at Bethlehem. ⁽17⁾And David
said longingly, "O that some one
would give me water to drink from the
well of Bethlehem which is by the
gate!" ⁽18⁾Then the three mighty men
broke through the camp of the
Philistines, and drew water out of

*Hebrew is obscure.

the well of Bethlehem which was by
the gate, and took and brought it to
David. But he would not drink
of it; he poured it out to the LORD,
(17)and said, "Far be it from me,
O LORD, that
I should do this. Shall I drink
the blood of the men who went
at the risk of their lives?"

Therefore he would not drink it.
These things did the three
mighty men.
   (18)Now Abishai, the brother
of Joab, the son of Zeruiah,
was chief of the three. And he
wielded his spear against three
hundred men and slew them, and won a
name beside the three. (19)Was he
the most renowned of the three? And
he became their commander; but he
did not attain to the three.
   (20)And Benaiah the son of
Jehoiada was a valiant man of
Kabzeel, a doer of great deeds;
he smote two ariels of Moab.
He also went down and slew a lion in
a pit on a day when snow had fallen.
(21)And he slew an Egyptian,
a handsome man.

The Egyptian had a spear in his hand;

but Benaiah went down to him with a
staff, and snatched the spear out of
the Egyptian's hand, and slew him
with his own spear. (22)These
things did Benaiah the son of
Jehoiada, and won a name beside the
three mighty men. (23)He was renowned
among the thirty, but he did not
attain to the three. And David set
him over his bodyguard.

   (24)Asahel the brother of Joab

the well of Bethlehem which was by
the gate, and took and brought it to
David. But David would not drink
of it; he poured it out to the LORD,
(19)and said, "Far be it from me
before my God that
I should do this. Shall I drink
the lifeblood of these men?
For at the risk of their lives
they brought it."
Therefore he would not drink it.
These things did the three
mighty men.
   (20)Now Abishai, the brother
of Joab,
was chief of the three. And he
wielded his spear against three
hundred men and slew them, and won a
name beside the three. (21)He was
the most renowned of the three, and
he became their commander; but he
did not attain to the three.
   (22)And Benaiah the son of
Jehoiada was a valiant man of
Kabzeel, a doer of great deeds;
he smote two ariels of Moab.
He also went down and slew a lion in
a pit on a day when snow had fallen.
(23)And he slew an Egyptian,
a man of great stature,
five cubits tall.
The Egyptian had in his hand a spear
like a weaver's beam;*
but Benaiah went down to him with a
staff, and snatched the spear out of
the Egyptian's hand, and slew him
with his own spear. (24)These
things did Benaiah the son of
Jehoiada, and won a name beside the
three mighty men. (25)He was renowned
among the thirty, but he did not
attain to the three. And David set
him over his bodyguard.
   (26)The mighty men
of the armies were
Asahel the brother of Joab,

*Cf. I Sam. 17:7.

was one of the thirty;
Elhanan the son of Dodo of Bethlehem,
(25)Shammah of Harod,
Elika of Harod,
(26)Helez the Paltite,
Ira the son of Ikkesh of Tekoa,
(27)Abi-ezer of Anathoth,
Mebunnai the Hushathite,
(28)Zalmon the Ahohite,
Maharai of Netophah,
(29)Heleb the son of Baanah of
Netophah, Ittai the son of Ribai
of Gibe-ah of the Benjaminites,
(30)Benaiah of Pirathon,
Hiddai of the brooks of Gaash,
(31)Abi-albon the Arbathite,
Azmaveth of Bahurim,
(32)Eliahba of Sha-albon,
the sons of Jashen,
Jonathan,
(33)Shammah the Hararite,
Ahiam the son of Sharar the
Hararite,
(34)Eliphelet the son of Ahasbai
of Maacah,
Eliam the son of Ahithophel of Gilo,

(35)Hezro of Carmel,
Paarai the Arbite,
(36)Igal the son of Nathan of Zobah,
Bani the Gadite,

(37)Zelek the Ammonite,
Naharai of Be-eroth, the armor-bearer
of Joab the son of Zeruiah,
(38)Ira the Ithrite,
Gareb the Ithrite,
(39)Uriah the Hittite:
thirty-seven in all.

Elhanan the son of Dodo of Bethlehem,
(27)Shammoth the Harorite,

Helez the Pelonite,
(28)Ira the son of Ikkesh of Tekoa,
Abi-ezer of Anathoth,
(29)Sibbecai the Hushathite,
Ilai the Ahohite,
(30)Maharai of Netophah,
Heled the son of Baanah of
Netophah, (31)Ithai the son of Ribai
of Gibe-ah of the Benjaminites,
Benaiah of Pirathon,
(32)Hurai of the brooks of Gaash,
Abiel the Arbathite,
(33)Azmaveth of Baharum,
Eliahba of Sha-albon,
(34)the sons of Hashem the Gizonite,
Jonathan
the son of Shagee the Hararite,
(35)Ahiam the son of Sachar the
Hararite,
Eliphal the son of Ur,

(36)Hepher the Mecherathite,
Ahijah the Pelonite,
(37)Hezro of Carmel,
Naarai the son of Ezbai,
(38)Joel the brother of Nathan,

Mibhar the son of Hagri,
(39)Zelek the Ammonite,
Naharai of Be-eroth, the armor-bearer
of Joab the son of Zeruiah,
(40)Ira the Ithrite,
Gareb the Ithrite,
(41)Uriah the Hittite,

Zabad the son of Ahlai, (42)Adina
the son of Shiza the Reubenite, a
leader of the Reubenites, and thirty
with him, (43)Hanan the son of
Maacah, and Joshaphat the Mithnite,
(44)Uzzia the Ashterathite, Shama
and Je-iel the sons of Hotham the

Aroerite, (45)Jedia-el the son of
Shimri, and Joha his brother,
the Tizite, (46)Eliel the Mahavite,
and Jeribai, and Joshaviah, the sons
of Elnaam, and Ithmah the Moabite,
(47)Eliel, and Obed, and Ja-asiel
the Mezoba-ite.

40 Additional Rolls of David's Fighters

I Chronicles 12:1–40

(1)Now these are the men who came to David at Ziklag, while he could not move about freely because of Saul the son of Kish; and they were among the mighty men who helped him in war. (2)They were bowmen, and could shoot arrows and sling stones with either the right or the left hand; they were Benjaminites, Saul's kinsmen. (3)The chief was Ahi-ezer, then Joash, both sons of Shemaah of Gibe-ah; also Jezi-el and Pelet the sons of Azmaveth; Beracah, Jehu of Anathoth, (4)Ishmaiah of Gibeon, a mighty man among the thirty and a leader over the thirty; Jeremiah, Jahaziel, Johanan, Jozabad of Gederah, (5)Eluzai, Jerimoth, Bealiah, Shemariah, Shephatiah the Haruphite; (6)Elkanah, Isshiah, Azarel, Jo-ezer, and Jashobe-am, the Korahites; (7)and Jo-elah and Zebadiah, the sons of Jeroham of Gedor.

(8)From the Gadites there went over to David at the stronghold in the wilderness mighty and experienced warriors, expert with shield and spear, whose faces were like the faces of lions, and who were swift as gazelles upon the mountains: (9)Ezer the chief, Obadiah second, Eliab third, (10)Mishmannah fourth, Jeremiah fifth, (11)Attai sixth, Eliel seventh, (12)Johanan eighth, Elzabad ninth, (13)Jeremiah tenth, Machbannai eleventh. (14)These Gadites were officers of the army, the lesser over a hundred and the greater over a thousand. (15)These are the men who crossed the Jordan in the first month, when it was overflowing all its banks, and put to flight all those in the valleys, to the east and to the west.

(16)And some of the men of Benjamin and Judah came to the stronghold to David. (17)David went out to meet them and said to them, "If you have come to me in friendship to help me, my heart will be knit to you; but if to betray me to my adversaries, although there is no wrong in my hands, then may the God of our fathers see and rebuke you." (18)Then the Spirit came upon Amasai, chief of the thirty, and he said,

> "We are yours, O David;
> and with you, O son of Jesse!
> Peace, peace to you,
> and peace to your helpers!
> For your God helps you."

Then David received them, and made them officers of his troops.
(19)Some of the men of Manasseh deserted to David when he came with the Philistines for the battle against Saul. (Yet he did not help them, for the rulers of the Philistines

73

took counsel and sent him away, saying, "At peril to our heads he will desert to his master Saul.") (20)As he went to Ziklag these men of Manasseh deserted to him: Adnah, Jozabad, Jedia-el, Michael, Jozabad, Elihu, and Zillethai, chiefs of thousands in Manasseh. (21)They helped David against the band of raiders; for they were all mighty men of valor, and were commanders in the army. (22)For from day to day men kept coming to David to help him, until there was a great army, like an army of God.

(23)These are the numbers of the divisions of the armed troops, who came to David in Hebron, to turn the kingdom of Saul over to him, according to the word of the LORD. (24)The men of Judah bearing shield and spear were six thousand eight hundred armed troops. (25)Of the Simeonites, mighty men of valor for war, seven thousand one hundred. (26)Of the Levites four thousand six hundred. (27)The prince Jehoiada, of the house of Aaron, and with him three thousand seven hundred. (28)Zadok, a young man mighty in valor, and twenty-two commanders from his own father's house. (29)Of the Benjaminites, the kinsmen of Saul, three thousand, of whom the majority had hitherto kept their allegiance to the house of Saul. (30)Of the Ephraimites twenty thousand eight hundred, mighty men of valor, famous men in their fathers' houses. (31)Of the half-tribe of Manasseh eighteen thousand, who were expressly named to come and make David king. (32)Of Issachar men who had understanding of the times, to know what Israel ought to do, two hundred chiefs, and all their kinsmen under their command. (33)Of Zebulun fifty thousand seasoned troops, equipped for battle with all the weapons of war, to help David with singleness of purpose. (34)Of Naphtali a thousand commanders with whom were thirty-seven thousand men armed with shield and spear. (35)Of the Danites twenty-eight thousand six hundred men equipped for battle. (36)Of Asher forty thousand seasoned troops ready for battle. (37)Of the Reubenites and Gadites and the half-tribe of Manasseh from beyond the Jordan, one hundred and twenty thousand men armed with all the weapons of war.

(38)All these, men of war, arrayed in battle order, came to Hebron with full intent to make David king over all Israel; likewise all the rest of Israel were of a single mind to make David king. (39)And they were there with David for three days, eating and drinking, for their brethren had made preparation for them. (40)And also their neighbors, from as far as Issachar and Zebulun and Naphtali, came bringing food on asses and on camels and on mules and on oxen, abundant provisions of meal, cakes of figs, clusters of raisins, and wine and oil, oxen and sheep, for there was joy in Israel.

41 David's Census of Israel

II Samuel 24:1–25	*I Chronicles 21:1–22:1*
(1)Again the anger of the LORD was kindled against Israel, and he	(1)Satan stood up against Israel, and
incited David against them, saying, "Go, number Israel and Judah."	incited David to number Israel.
(2)So the king said to Joab the commander of the army	(2)So David said to Joab and the commanders of the army,

who was with him,
"Go through all the tribes of Israel,
from Dan to Beer-sheba,
and number the people,
that I may know the number
of the people."
(3)But Joab said to the king,
"May the LORD your God add to the
people a hundred times as many
as they are,
while the eyes of

my lord the king
still see it;

but why does my lord the king
delight in this thing?"

/4/But the king's word
prevailed against Joab
and the commanders of the army.
So Joab
and the commanders of the army
departed
from the presence of the king
to number the people of Israel.
(5)They crossed the Jordan, and
began from Aroer, and from the city
that is in the middle of the valley,
toward Gad and on to Jazer. (6)Then
they came to Gilead, and to Kadesh
in the land of the Hittites; and they
came to Dan, and from Dan they went
around to Sidon, (7)and came to the
fortress of Tyre and to all the cities
of the Hivites and Canaanites;
and they went out to the Negeb of
Judah at Beer-sheba.
(8)So when they had
gone through all the land,
they came to Jerusalem
at the end of nine months
and twenty days.
(9)And Joab gave the sum of the
numbering of the people to the king:
in Israel there were

"Go, number Israel,
from Beer-sheba to Dan,
and bring me a report,
that I may know their number."

(3)But Joab said,
"May the LORD add to his
people a hundred times as many
as they are!

Are they not,
my lord the king,

all of them my lord's servants?
Why then should my lord
require this?
Why should he bring guilt
upon Israel?"
(4)But the king's word
prevailed against Joab.

So Joab

departed and

went throughout all Israel,
and came back to Jerusalem.

(5)And Joab gave the sum of the
numbering of the people to David.
In all Israel there were

eight hundred thousand
valiant men who drew the sword,
and the men of Judah were
five hundred thousand.

(10)But David's heart smote him
after he had numbered the people.
And David said to the LORD,
"I have sinned greatly
in what I have done.
But now, O LORD, I pray thee,
take away the iniquity of thy servant;
for I have done very foolishly."
(11)And when David arose
in the morning,
the word of the LORD came
to the prophet Gad, David's seer,
saying, (12)"Go and say to David,
'Thus says the LORD,
Three things I hold over you;
choose one of them, that I may do
it to you.' " (13)So Gad came to
David and
told him, and
said to him,

"Shall seven years of famine
come to you in your land?
Or will you flee three months
before your foes
while they pursue you?

Or shall there be three days'

pestilence in your land?

Now consider, and
decide what answer I shall

---

one million one hundred thousand
men who drew the sword,
and in Judah
four hundred and seventy thousand
who drew the sword.
(6)But he did not include Levi and
Benjamin in the numbering, for the
king's command was abhorrent to Joab.
(7)But God was displeased
with this thing, and
he smote Israel.

(8)And David said to God,
"I have sinned greatly
in that I have done this thing.
But now, I pray thee,
take away the iniquity of thy servant;
for I have done very foolishly."

(9)And the LORD spoke
to Gad, David's seer,
saying, (10)"Go and say to David,
'Thus says the LORD,
Three things I offer you;
choose one of them, that I may do
it to you.' " (11)So Gad came to
David and

said to him,
"Thus says the LORD,
'Take which you will:
(12)either three years of famine;

or three months of devastation
by your foes,

while the sword of your enemies
overtakes you;
or else three days
of the sword of the LORD,
pestilence upon the land,
and the angel of the LORD
destroying throughout all
the territory of Israel.'
Now
decide what answer I shall

return to him who sent me."
(14)Then David said to Gad,
"I am in great distress;
let us fall into the hand of
the LORD, for his mercy is great;
but let me not fall into the
hand of man."
(15)So the LORD sent a
pestilence upon Israel
from the morning until
the appointed time;
and there died
of the people from Dan to Beer-sheba
seventy thousand men.

(16)And when the angel
stretched forth his hand
toward Jerusalem to destroy it,

the LORD
repented of the evil,
and said to the angel
who was working destruction
among the people,
"It is enough; now stay your hand."
And the angel of the LORD was

by the threshing floor of
Araunah the Jebusite.

(17)Then David spoke to the LORD
when he saw the angel who was
smiting the people, and said,

"Lo, I have sinned, and
I have done wickedly;
but these sheep, what have they done?
Let thy hand, I pray thee,

be against me and
against my father's house."

return to him who sent me."
(13)Then David said to Gad,
"I am in great distress;
let me fall into the hand of
the LORD, for his mercy is very great;
but let me not fall into the
hand of man."
(14)So the LORD sent a
pestilence upon Israel;

and there fell

seventy thousand men of Israel.
(15)And God sent
the angel

to Jerusalem to destroy it;
but when he was about to destroy it,
the LORD saw, and
he repented of the evil;
and he said to the destroying angel,

"It is enough; now stay your hand."
And the angel of the LORD was
standing
by the threshing floor of
Ornan the Jebusite.
(16)And David lifted his eyes and
saw the angel of the LORD standing
between earth and heaven, and
in his hand a drawn sword stretched
out over Jerusalem. Then David and
the elders, clothed in sackcloth,
fell upon their faces.
/17/Then David said to God,

"Was it not I who gave command
to number the people?
It is I who have sinned and
done very wickedly.
But these sheep, what have they done?
Let thy hand, I pray thee,
O LORD my God,
be against me and
against my father's house;

	but let not the plague
	be upon thy people."
	(18)Then the angel of the LORD
	commanded Gad
(18)And Gad	
came that day to David,	
and said to him,	
"Go up, rear an altar	to say to David that
to the LORD on the threshing floor	David should go up and rear an altar
of Araunah the Jebusite."	to the LORD on the threshing floor
(19)So David went up at Gad's word,	of Ornan the Jebusite.
as	(19)So David went up at Gad's word,
the LORD commanded.	which he had spoken
	in the name of the LORD.
	(20)Now Ornan was threshing wheat;
	he turned and saw the angel,
	and his four sons who were with him
	hid themselves.
	(21)As David came to Ornan,
(20)And when Araunah looked down,	Ornan looked
he saw the king	and saw David
and his servants coming on toward him;	
and Araunah went forth,	and went forth
	from the threshing floor,
and did obeisance to the king	and did obeisance to David
with his face to the ground.	with his face to the ground.
(21)And Araunah said, "Why has my	
lord the king come to his servant?"	
David said,	(22)And David said to Ornan,
"To buy the	"Give me the site of the
threshing floor of you, in order to	threshing floor that I may
build an altar to the LORD,	build on it an altar to the LORD—
	give it to me at its full price—
that the plague may be averted	that the plague may be averted
from the people."	from the people."
(22)Then Araunah said to David,	(23)Then Ornan said to David,
	"Take it; and
"Let my lord the king	let my lord the king
take and offer up	do
what seems good to him;	what seems good to him;
here are the oxen for	see, I give the oxen for
the burnt offering, and	burnt offerings, and
the threshing sledges and	the threshing sledges
the yokes of the oxen	
for the wood.	for the wood,
	and the wheat for a cereal offering.
(23)All this, O king, Araunah	I give it all."
gives to the king."	
And Araunah said to the king,	

78

"The LORD your God accept you."
(24)But the king said to Araunah,
"No, but I will buy it of you
for a price;

I will not offer burnt offerings
to the LORD my God
which cost me nothing."
So David bought
the threshing floor and the oxen
for fifty shekels of silver.

(25)And David built there an altar
to the LORD, and offered
burnt offerings and peace offerings.

So the LORD heeded supplications
for the land,

and the plague was averted
from Israel.

(24)But King David said to Ornan,
"No, but I will buy it
for the full price;
I will not take for the LORD
what is yours,
nor offer burnt offerings

which cost me nothing."
(25)So David paid Ornan

six hundred shekels of gold
by weight for the site.
/26/ And David built there an altar
to the LORD, and offered
burnt offerings and peace offerings,
and called upon the LORD,

and he answered him with fire
from heaven upon the altar of
burnt offering.

(27)Then the LORD commanded the
angel; and he put his sword back into
its sheath.
(28)At that time, when David saw
that the LORD had answered him at the
threshing floor of Ornan the Jebusite,
he made his sacrifices there.
(29)For the tabernacle of the LORD,
which Moses had made in the
wilderness, and the altar of burnt
offering were at that time in the
high place at Gibeon; (30)but David
could not go before it to inquire of
God, for he was afraid of the sword
of the angel of the LORD.
(22:1)Then David said, "Here shall
be the house of the LORD God and here
the altar of burnt offering for
Israel."

42 Adonijah's Abortive Rebellion

I Kings 1:1–53

[1]Now King David was old and advanced in years; and although they covered him with clothes, he could not get warm. [2]Therefore his servants said to him, "Let a young maiden be sought for my lord the king, and let her wait upon the king, and be his nurse; let her lie in your bosom, that my lord the king may be warm." [3]So they sought for a beautiful maiden throughout all the territory of Israel, and found Abishag the Shunammite, and brought her to the king. [4]The maiden was very beautiful; and she became the king's nurse and ministered to him; but the king knew her not.

[5]Now Adonijah the son of Haggith exalted himself, saying, "I will be king"; and he prepared for himself chariots and horsemen, and fifty men to run before him. [6]His father had never at any time displeased him by asking, "Why have you done thus and so?" He was also a very handsome man; and he was born next after Absalom. [7]He conferred with Joab the son of Zeruiah and with Abiathar the priest; and they followed Adonijah and helped him. [8]But Zadok the priest, and Benaiah the son of Jehoiada, and Nathan the prophet, and Shime-i, and Rei, and David's mighty men were not with Adonijah.

[9]Adonijah sacrificed sheep, oxen, and fatlings by the Serpent's Stone, which is beside En-rogel, and he invited all his brothers, the king's sons, and all the royal officials of Judah, [10]but he did not invite Nathan the prophet or Benaiah or the mighty men or Solomon his brother.

[11]Then Nathan said to Bathsheba the mother of Solomon, "Have you not heard that Adonijah the son of Haggith has become king and David our lord does not know it? [12]Now therefore come, let me give you counsel, that you may save your own life and the life of your son Solomon. [13]Go in at once to King David, and say to him, 'Did you not, my lord the king, swear to your maidservant, saying, "Solomon your son shall reign after me, and he shall sit upon my throne"? Why then is Adonijah king?' [14]Then while you are still speaking with the king, I also will come in after you and confirm your words."

[15]So Bathsheba went to the king into his chamber (now the king was very old, and Abishag the Shunammite was ministering to the king). [16]Bathsheba bowed and did obeisance to the king, and the king said, "What do you desire?" [17]She said to him, "My lord, you swore to your maidservant by the LORD your God, saying, 'Solomon your son shall reign after me, and he shall sit upon my throne.' [18]And now, behold, Adonijah is king, although you, my lord the king, do not know it. [19]He has sacrificed oxen, fatlings, and sheep in abundance, and has invited all the sons of the king, Abiathar the priest, and Joab the commander of the army; but Solomon your servant he has not invited. [20]And now, my lord the king, the eyes of all Israel are upon you, to tell them who shall sit on the throne of my lord the king after him. [21]Otherwise it will come to pass, when my lord the king sleeps with his fathers, that I and my son Solomon will be counted offenders."

[22]While she was still speaking with the king, Nathan the prophet came in. [23]And they told the king, "Here is Nathan the prophet." And when he came in before the king, he bowed before the king, with his face to the ground. [24]And Nathan said, "My lord the king, have you said, 'Adonijah shall reign after me, and he shall sit upon my

throne'? (25)For he has gone down this day, and has sacrificed oxen, fatlings, and sheep in abundance, and has invited all the king's sons, Joab the commander of the army, and Abiathar the priest; and behold, they are eating and drinking before him, and saying, 'Long live King Adonijah!' (26)But me, your servant, and Zadok the priest, and Benaiah the son of Jehoiada, and your servant Solomon, he has not invited. (27)Has this thing been brought about by my lord the king and you have not told your servants who should sit on the throne of my lord the king after him?"

(28)Then King David answered, "Call Bathsheba to me." So she came into the king's presence, and stood before the king. (29)And the king swore, saying, "As the LORD lives, who has redeemed my soul out of every adversity, (30)as I swore to you by the LORD, the God of Israel, saying, 'Solomon your son shall reign after me, and he shall sit upon my throne in my stead'; even so will I do this day." (31)Then Bathsheba bowed with her face to the ground, and did obeisance to the king, and said, "May my lord King David live for ever!"

(32)King David said, "Call to me Zadok the priest, Nathan the prophet, and Benaiah the son of Jehoiada." So they came before the king. (33)And the king said to them, "Take with you the servants of your lord, and cause Solomon my son to ride on my own mule, and bring him down to Gihon; (34)and let Zadok the priest and Nathan the prophet there anoint him king over Israel; then blow the trumpet, and say, 'Long live King Solomon!' (35)You shall then come up after him, and he shall come and sit upon my throne; for he shall be king in my stead; and I have appointed him to be ruler over Israel and over Judah." (36)And Benaiah the son of Jehoiada answered the king, "Amen! May the LORD, the God of my lord the king, say so. (37)As the LORD has been with my lord the king, even so may he be with Solomon, and make his throne greater than the throne of my lord King David."

(38)So Zadok the priest, Nathan the prophet, and Benaiah the son of Jehoiada, and the Cherethites and the Pelethites, went down and caused Solomon to ride on King David's mule, and brought him to Gihon. (39)There Zadok the priest took the horn of oil from the tent, and anointed Solomon. Then they blew the trumpet; and all the people said, "Long live King Solomon!" (40)And all the people went up after him, playing on pipes, and rejoicing with great joy, so that the earth was split by their noise.

(41)Adonijah and all the guests who were with him heard it as they finished feasting. And when Joab heard the sound of the trumpet, he said, "What does this uproar in the city mean?" (42)While he was still speaking, behold, Jonathan the son of Abiathar the priest came; and Adonijah said, "Come in, for you are a worthy man and bring good news." (43)Jonathan answered Adonijah, "No, for our lord King David has made Solomon king; (44)and the king has sent with him Zadok the priest, Nathan the prophet, and Benaiah the son of Jehoiada, and the Cherethites and the Pelethites; and they have caused him to ride on the king's mule; (45)and Zadok the priest and Nathan the prophet have anointed him king at Gihon; and they have gone up from there rejoicing, so that the city is in an uproar. This is the noise that you have heard. (46)Solomon sits upon the royal throne. (47)Moreover the king's servants came to congratulate our lord King David, saying, 'Your God make the name of Solomon more famous than yours, and make his throne greater than your throne.' And the king bowed himself upon the bed. (48)And the king also said, 'Blessed be the LORD, the God of Israel, who has granted one of my offspring to sit on my throne this day, my own eyes seeing it.' "

(49)Then all the guests of Adonijah trembled, and rose, and each went his own way.

$^{(50)}$And Adonijah feared Solomon; and he arose, and went, and caught hold of the horns of the altar. $^{(51)}$And it was told Solomon, "Behold, Adonijah fears King Solomon; for, lo, he has laid hold of the horns of the altar, saying, 'Let King Solomon swear to me first that he will not slay his servant with the sword.' " $^{(52)}$And Solomon said, "If he prove to be a worthy man, not one of his hairs shall fall to the earth; but if wickedness is found in him, he shall die." $^{(53)}$So King Solomon sent, and they brought him down from the altar. And he came and did obeisance to King Solomon; and Solomon said to him, "Go to your house."

43 David's Charge to Solomon, I

I Kings 2:1–9

$^{(1)}$When David's time to die drew near, he charged Solomon his son, saying, $^{(2)}$"I am about to go the way of all the earth. Be strong, and show yourself a man, $^{(3)}$and keep the charge of the LORD your God, walking in his ways and keeping his statutes, his commandments, his ordinances, and his testimonies, as it is written in the law of Moses, that you may prosper in all that you do and wherever you turn; $^{(4)}$that the LORD may establish his word which he spoke concerning me, saying, 'If your sons take heed to their way, to walk before me in faithfulness with all their heart and with all their soul, there shall not fail you a man on the throne of Israel.'

$^{(5)}$"Moreover you know also what Joab the son of Zeruiah did to me, how he dealt with the two commanders of the armies of Israel, Abner the son of Ner, and Amasa the son of Jether, whom he murdered, avenging in time of peace blood which had been shed in war, and putting innocent blood upon the girdle about my loins, and upon the sandals on my feet. $^{(6)}$Act therefore according to your wisdom, but do not let his gray head go down to Sheol in peace. $^{(7)}$But deal loyally with the sons of Barzillai the Gileadite, and let them be among those who eat at your table; for with such loyalty they met me when I fled from Absalom your brother. $^{(8)}$And there is also with you Shime-i the son of Gera, the Benjaminite from Bahurim, who cursed me with a grievous curse on the day when I went to Mahanaim; but when he came down to meet me at the Jordan, I swore to him by the LORD, saying, 'I will not put you to death with the sword.' $^{(9)}$Now therefore hold him not guiltless, for you are a wise man; you will know what you ought to do to him, and you shall bring his gray head down with blood to Sheol."

44 David's Charge to Solomon, II

I Chronicles 22:2–19

$^{(2)}$David commanded to gather together the aliens who were in the land of Israel, and he set stonecutters to prepare dressed stones for building the house of God. $^{(3)}$David also provided great stores of iron for nails for the doors of the gates and for clamps, as well as bronze in quantities beyond weighing, $^{(4)}$and cedar timbers without number; for the Sidonians and Tyrians brought great quantities of cedar to David. $^{(5)}$For David said, "Solomon my son is young and inexperienced, and the house that is to be built for the LORD must be exceedingly magnificent, of fame and glory throughout all lands; I will therefore make preparation for it." So David provided materials in great quantity before his death.

(6)Then he called for Solomon his son, and charged him to build a house for the LORD, the God of Israel. (7)David said to Solomon, "My son, I had it in my heart to build a house to the name of the LORD my God. (8)But the word of the LORD came to me, saying, 'You have shed much blood and have waged great wars: you shall not build a house to my name, because you have shed so much blood before me upon the earth. (9)Behold, a son shall be born to you; he shall be a man of peace. I will give him peace from all his enemies round about; for his name shall be Solomon, and I will give peace and quiet to Israel in his days. (10)He shall build a house for my name. He shall be my son, and I will be his father, and I will establish his royal throne in Israel for ever.' (11)Now, my son, the LORD be with you, so that you may succeed in building the house of the LORD your God, as he has spoken concerning you. (12)Only, may the LORD grant you discretion and understanding, that when he gives you charge over Israel you may keep the law of the LORD your God. (13)Then you will prosper if you are careful to observe the statutes and the ordinances which the LORD commanded Moses for Israel. Be strong, and of good courage. Fear not; be not dismayed. (14)With great pains I have provided for the house of the LORD a hundred thousand talents of gold, a million talents of silver, and bronze and iron beyond weighing, for there is so much of it; timber and stone too I have provided. To these you must add. (15)You have an abundance of workmen: stonecutters, masons, carpenters, and all kinds of craftsmen without number, skilled in working (16)gold, silver, bronze, and iron. Arise and be doing! The LORD be with you!"

(17)David also commanded all the leaders of Israel to help Solomon his son, saying, (18)"Is not the LORD your God with you? And has he not given you peace on every side? For he has delivered the inhabitants of the land into my hand; and the land is subdued before the LORD and his people. (19)Now set your mind and heart to seek the LORD your God. Arise and build the sanctuary of the LORD God, so that the ark of the covenant of the LORD and the holy vessels of God may be brought into a house built for the name of the LORD."

45 The Divisions of the Levites

I Chronicles 23:1–32

(1)When David was old and full of days, he made Solomon his son king over Israel.

(2)David assembled all the leaders of Israel and the priests and the Levites. (3)The Levites, thirty years old and upward, were numbered, and the total was thirty-eight thousand men. (4)"Twenty-four thousand of these," David said, "shall have charge of the work in the house of the LORD, six thousand shall be officers and judges, (5)four thousand gatekeepers, and four thousand shall offer praises to the LORD with the instruments which I have made for praise." (6)And David organized them in divisions corresponding to the sons of Levi: Gershom, Kohath, and Merari.

(7)The sons of Gershom were Ladan and Shime-i. (8)The sons of Ladan: Jehiel the chief, and Zetham, and Joel, three. (9)The sons of Shime-i: Shelomoth, Hazi-el, and Haran, three. These were the heads of the fathers' houses of Ladan. (10)And the sons of Shime-i: Jahath, Zina, and Jeush, and Beriah. These four were the sons of Shime-i. (11)Jahath was the chief, and Zizah the second; but Jeush and Beriah had not many sons, therefore they became a father's house in one reckoning.

(12)The sons of Kohath: Amram, Izhar, Hebron, and Uzziel, four. (13)The sons of Amram: Aaron and Moses. Aaron was set apart to consecrate the most holy things, that he and his sons for ever should burn incense before the LORD, and minister to him and pronounce blessings in his name for ever. (14)But the sons of Moses the man of God were named among the tribe of Levi. (15)The sons of Moses: Gershom and Eliezer. (16)The sons of Gershom: Shebuel the chief. (17)The sons of Eliezer: Rehabiah the chief; Eliezer had no other sons, but the sons of Rehabiah were very many. (18)The sons of Izhar: Shelomith the chief. (19)The sons of Hebron: Jeriah the chief, Amariah the second, Jahaziel the third, and Jekameam the fourth. (20)The sons of Uzziel: Micah the chief and Isshiah the second.

(21)The sons of Merari: Mahli and Mushi. The sons of Mahli: Eleazar and Kish. (22)Eleazar died having no sons, but only daughters; their kinsmen, the sons of Kish, married them. (23)The sons of Mushi: Mahli, Eder, and Jeremoth, three.

(24)These were the sons of Levi by their fathers' houses, the heads of fathers' houses as they were registered according to the number of the names of the individuals from twenty years old and upward who were to do the work for the service of the house of the LORD. (25)For David said, "The LORD, the God of Israel, has given peace to his people; and he dwells in Jerusalem for ever. (26)And so the Levites no longer need to carry the tabernacle or any of the things for its service"—(27)for by the last words of David these were the number of the Levites from twenty years old and upward—(28)"but their duty shall be to assist the sons of Aaron for the service of the house of the LORD, having the care of the courts and the chambers, the cleansing of all that is holy, and any work for the service of the house of God; (29)to assist also with the showbread, the flour for the cereal offering, the wafers of unleavened bread, the baked offering, the offering mixed with oil, and all measures of quantity or size. (30)And they shall stand every morning, thanking and praising the LORD, and likewise at evening, (31)and whenever burnt offerings are offered to the LORD on sabbaths, new moons, and feast days, according to the number required of them, continually before the LORD. (32)Thus they shall keep charge of the tent of meeting and the sanctuary, and shall attend the sons of Aaron, their brethren, for the service of the house of the LORD."

46 The Divisions of the Sons of Aaron

I Chronicles 24:1–19

(1)The divisions of the sons of Aaron were these. The sons of Aaron: Nadab, Abihu, Eleazar, and Ithamar. (2)But Nadab and Abihu died before their father, and had no children, so Eleazar and Ithamar became the priests. (3)With the help of Zadok of the sons of Eleazar, and Ahimelech of the sons of Ithamar, David organized them according to the appointed duties in their service. (4)Since more chief men were found among the sons of Eleazar than among the sons of Ithamar, they organized them under sixteen heads of fathers' houses of the sons of Eleazar, and eight of the sons of Ithamar. (5)They organized them by lot, all alike, for there were officers of the sanctuary and officers of

God among both the sons of Eleazar and the sons of Ithamar. (6)And the scribe Shemaiah the son of Nethanel, a Levite, recorded them in the presence of the king, and the princes, and Zadok the priest, and Ahimelech the son of Abiathar, and the heads of the fathers' houses of the priests and of the Levites; one father's house being chosen for Eleazar and one chosen for Ithamar.

(7)The first lot fell to Jehoiarib, the second to Jedaiah, (8)the third to Harim, the fourth to Se-orim, (9)the fifth to Malchijah, the sixth to Mijamin, (10)the seventh to Hakkoz, the eighth to Abijah, (11)the ninth to Jeshua, the tenth to Shecaniah, (12)the eleventh to Eliashib, the twelfth to Jakim, (13)the thirteenth to Huppah, the fourteenth to Jeshebe-ab, (14)the fifteenth to Bilgah, the sixteenth to Immer, (15)the seventeenth to Hezir, the eighteenth to Happizzez, (16)the nineteenth to Pethahiah, the twentieth to Jehezkel, (17)the twenty-first to Jachin, the twenty-second to Gamul, (18)the twenty-third to Delaiah, the twenty-fourth to Ma-aziah. (19)These had as their appointed duty in their service to come into the house of the LORD according to the procedure established for them by Aaron their father, as the LORD God of Israel had commanded him.

47 Additional Lists of Levites

I Chronicles 24:20–31

(20)And of the rest of the sons of Levi: of the sons of Amram, Shuba-el; of the sons of Shuba-el, Jehdeiah. (21)Of Rehabiah: of the sons of Rehabiah, Isshiah the chief. (22)Of the Izharites, Shelomoth; of the sons of Shelomoth, Jahath. (23)The sons of Hebron: Jeriah the chief, Amariah the second, Jahaziel the third, Jekameam the fourth. (24)The sons of Uzziel, Micah; of the sons of Micah, Shamir. (25)The brother of Micah, Isshiah; of the sons of Isshiah, Zechariah. (26)The sons of Merari: Mahli and Mushi. The sons of Ja-aziah: Beno. (27)The sons of Merari: of Ja-aziah, Beno, Shoham, Zaccur, and Ibri. (28)Of Mahli: Eleazar, who had no sons. (29)Of Kish, the sons of Kish: Jerahmeel. (30)The sons of Mushi: Mahli, Eder, and Jerimoth. These were the sons of the Levites according to their fathers' houses. (31)These also, the head of each father's house and his younger brother alike, cast lots, just as their brethren the sons of Aaron, in the presence of King David, Zadok, Ahimelech, and the heads of fathers' houses of the priests and of the Levites.

48 The Divisions of the Leaders of Music

I Chronicles 25:1–31

(1)David and the chiefs of the service also set apart for the service certain of the sons of Asaph, and of Heman, and of Jeduthun, who should prophesy with lyres, with harps, and with cymbals. The list of those who did the work and of their duties was: (2)Of the sons of Asaph: Zaccur, Joseph, Nethaniah, and Asharelah, sons of Asaph, under the direction of Asaph, who prophesied under the direction of the king. (3)Of Jeduthun, the sons of Jeduthun: Gedaliah, Zeri, Jeshaiah, Shime-i, Hashabiah, and Mattithiah, six, under the direction of their father Jeduthun, who prophesied with the lyre in thanksgiving and praise to the LORD. (4)Of Heman, the sons of Heman: Bukkiah, Mattaniah,

Uzziel, Shebuel, and Jerimoth, Hananiah, Hanani, Eliathah, Giddalti, and Romamti-ezer, Joshbekashah, Mallothi, Hothir, Mahazi-oth. (5)All these were the sons of Heman the king's seer, according to the promise of God to exalt him; for God had given Heman fourteen sons and three daughters. (6)They were all under the direction of their father in the music in the house of the LORD with cymbals, harps, and lyres for the service of the house of God. Asaph, Jeduthun, and Heman were under the order of the king. (7)The number of them along with their brethren, who were trained in singing to the LORD, all who were skilful, was two hundred and eighty-eight. (8)And they cast lots for their duties, small and great, teacher and pupil alike.

(9)The first lot fell for Asaph to Joseph; the second to Gedaliah, to him and his brethren and his sons, twelve; (10)the third to Zaccur, his sons and his brethren, twelve; (11)the fourth to Izri, his sons and his brethren, twelve; (12)the fifth to Nethaniah, his sons and his brethren, twelve; (13)the sixth to Bukkiah, his sons and his brethren, twelve; (14)the seventh to Jesharelah, his sons and his brethren, twelve; (15)the eighth to Jeshaiah, his sons and his brethren, twelve; (16)the ninth to Mattaniah, his sons and his brethren, twelve; (17)the tenth to Shime-i, his sons and his brethren, twelve; (18)the eleventh to Azarel, his sons and his brethren, twelve; (19)the twelfth to Hashabiah, his sons and his brethren, twelve; (20)to the thirteenth, Shuba-el, his sons and his brethren, twelve; (21)to the fourteenth, Mattithiah, his sons and his brethren, twelve; (22)to the fifteenth, to Jeremoth, his sons and his brethren, twelve; (23)to the sixteenth, to Hananiah, his sons and his brethren, twelve; (24)to the seventeenth, to Joshbekashah, his sons and his brethren, twelve; (25)to the eighteenth, to Hanani, his sons and his brethren, twelve; (26)to the nineteenth, to Mallothi, his sons and his brethren, twelve; (27)to the twentieth, to Eliathah, his sons and his brethren, twelve; (28)to the twenty-first, to Hothir, his sons and his brethren, twelve; (29)to the twenty-second, to Giddalti, his sons and his brethren, twelve; (30)to the twenty-third, to Mahazi-oth, his sons and his brethren, twelve; (31)to the twenty-fourth, to Romamti-ezer, his sons and his brethren, twelve.

49 The Divisions of the Gatekeepers

I Chronicles 26:1–19

(1)As for the divisions of the gatekeepers: of the Korahites, Meshelemiah the son of Kore, of the sons of Asaph. (2)And Meshelemiah had sons: Zechariah the first-born, Jedia-el the second, Zebadiah the third, Jathni-el the fourth, (3)Elam the fifth, Jeho-hanan the sixth, Elie-ho-enai the seventh. (4)And Obed-edom had sons: Shemaiah the first-born, Jehozabad the second, Joah the third, Sachar the fourth, Nethanel the fifth, (5)Ammi-el the sixth, Issachar the seventh, Pe-ullethai the eighth; for God blessed him. (6)Also to his son Shemaiah were sons born who were rulers in their fathers' houses, for they were men of great ability. (7)The sons of Shemaiah: Othni, Repha-el, Obed, and Elzabad, whose brethren were able men, Elihu and Semachiah. (8)All these were of the sons of Obed-edom with their sons and brethren, able men qualified for the service; sixty-two of Obed-edom. (9)And Meshelemiah had sons and brethren, able men, eighteen. (10)And Hosah, of the sons of Merari, had sons: Shimri the chief (for though he was not the first-born, his father made him chief), (11)Hilkiah the second, Tebaliah the third, Zechariah the fourth: all the sons and brethren of Hosah were thirteen.

(12)These divisions of the gatekeepers, corresponding to their chief men, had duties, just as their brethren did, ministering in the house of the LORD; (13)and they cast lots by fathers' houses, small and great alike, for their gates. (14)The lot for the east fell to Shelemiah. They cast lots also for his son Zechariah, a shrewd counselor, and his lot came out for the north. (15)Obed-edom's came out for the south, and to his sons was allotted the storehouse. (16)For Shuppim and Hosah it came out for the west, at the gate of Shallecheth on the road that goes up. Watch corresponded to watch. (17)On the east there were six each day, on the north four each day, on the south four each day, as well as two and two at the storehouse; (18)and for the parbar on the west there were four at the road and two at the parbar. (19)These were the divisions of the gatekeepers among the Korahites and the sons of Merari.

50 Additional Lists of Levites and Other Officials

I Chronicles 26:20–27:34

(20)And of the Levites, Ahijah had charge of the treasuries of the house of God and the treasuries of the dedicated gifts. (21)The sons of Ladan, the sons of the Gershonites belonging to Ladan, the heads of the fathers' houses belonging to Ladan the Gershonite: Jehieli.
(22)The sons of Jehieli, Zetham and Joel his brother, were in charge of the treasuries of the house of the LORD. (23)Of the Amramites, the Izharites, the Hebronites, and the Uzzielites—(24)and Shebuel the son of Gershom, son of Moses, was chief officer in charge of the treasuries. (25)His brethren: from Eliezer were his son Rehabiah, and his son Jeshaiah, and his son Joram, and his son Zichri, and his son Shelomoth. (26)This Shelomoth and his brethren were in charge of all the treasuries of the dedicated gifts which David the king, and the heads of the fathers' houses, and the officers of the thousands and the hundreds, and the commanders of the army, had dedicated. (27)From spoil won in battles they dedicated gifts for the maintenance of the house of the LORD. (28)Also all that Samuel the seer, and Saul the son of Kish, and Abner the son of Ner, and Joab the son of Zeruiah had dedicated—all dedicated gifts were in the care of Shelomoth and his brethren.
(29)Of the Izharites, Chenaniah and his sons were appointed to outside duties for Israel, as officers and judges. (30)Of the Hebronites, Hashabiah and his brethren, one thousand seven hundred men of ability, had the oversight of Israel westward of the Jordan for all the work of the LORD and for the service of the king. (31)Of the Hebronites, Jerijah was chief of the Hebronites of whatever genealogy or fathers' houses. (In the fortieth year of David's reign search was made and men of great ability among them were found at Jazer in Gilead.) (32)King David appointed him and his brethren, two thousand seven hundred men of ability, heads of fathers' houses, to have the oversight of the Reubenites, the Gadites, and the half-tribe of the Manassites for everything pertaining to God and for the affairs of the king.
(27:1)This is the list of the people of Israel, the heads of fathers' houses, the commanders of thousands and hundreds, and their officers who served the king in all matters concerning the divisions that came and went, month after month throughout the year, each division numbering twenty-four thousand:

(2)Jashobeam the son of Zabdi-el was in charge of the first division in the first month; in his division were twenty-four thousand. (3)He was a descendant of Perez, and was chief of all the commanders of the army for the first month. (4)Dodai the Ahohite was in charge of the division of the second month; in his division were twenty-four thousand. (5)The third commander, for the third month, was Benaiah, the son of Jehoiada the priest, as chief; in his division were twenty-four thousand. (6)This is the Benaiah who was a mighty man of the thirty and in command of the thirty; Ammizabad his son was in charge of his division. (7)Asahel the brother of Joab was fourth, for the fourth month, and his son Zebadiah after him; in his division were twenty-four thousand. (8)The fifth commander, for the fifth month, was Shamhuth, the Izrahite; in his division were twenty-four thousand. (9)Sixth, for the sixth month, was Ira, the son of Ikkesh the Tekoite; in his division were twenty-four thousand. (10)Seventh, for the seventh month, was Helez the Pelonite, of the sons of Ephraim; in his division were twenty-four thousand. (11)Eighth, for the eighth month, was Sibbecai the Hushathite, of the Zerahites; in his division were twenty-four thousand. (12)Ninth, for the ninth month, was Abi-ezer of Anathoth, a Benjaminite; in his division were twenty-four thousand. (13)Tenth, for the tenth month, was Maharai of Netophah, of the Zerahites; in his division were twenty-four thousand. (14)Eleventh, for the eleventh month, was Benaiah of Pirathon, of the sons of Ephraim; in his division were twenty-four thousand. (15)Twelfth, for the twelfth month, was Heldai the Netophathite, of Othni-el; in his division were twenty-four thousand.

(16)Over the tribes of Israel, for the Reubenites Eliezer the son of Zichri was chief officer; for the Simeonites, Shephatiah the son of Maacah; (17)for Levi, Hashabiah the son of Kemuel; for Aaron, Zadok; (18)for Judah, Elihu, one of David's brothers; for Issachar, Omri the son of Michael; (19)for Zebulun, Ishmaiah the son of Obadiah; for Naphtali, Jeremoth the son of Azriel; (20)for the Ephraimites, Hoshea the son of Azaziah; for the half-tribe of Manasseh, Joel the son of Pedaiah; (21)for the half-tribe of Manasseh in Gilead, Iddo the son of Zechariah; for Benjamin, Ja-asiel the son of Abner; (22)for Dan, Azarel the son of Jeroham. These were the leaders of the tribes of Israel. (23)David did not number those below twenty years of age, for the LORD had promised to make Israel as many as the stars of heaven. (24)Joab the son of Zeruiah began to number, but did not finish; yet wrath came upon Israel for this, and the number was not entered in the chronicles of King David.

(25)Over the king's treasuries was Azmaveth the son of Adi-el; and over the treasuries in the country, in the cities, in the villages, and in the towers, was Jonathan the son of Uzziah; (26)and over those who did the work of the field for tilling the soil was Ezri the son of Chelub; (27)and over the vineyards was Shime-i the Ramathite; and over the produce of the vineyards for the wine cellars was Zabdi the Shiphmite. (28)Over the olive and sycamore trees in the Shephelah was Baal-hanan the Gederite; and over the stores of oil was Joash. (29)Over the herds that pastured in Sharon was Shitrai the Sharonite; over the herds in the valleys was Shaphat the son of Adlai. (30)Over the camels was Obil the Ishmaelite; and over the she-asses was Jehdeiah the Meronothite. Over the flocks was Jaziz the Hagrite. (31)All these were stewards of King David's property.

(32)Jonathan, David's uncle, was a counselor, being a man of understanding and a scribe; he and Jehiel the son of Hachmoni attended the king's sons. (33)Ahithophel was the king's counselor, and Hushai the Archite was the king's friend. (34)Ahithophel was succeeded by Jehoiada the son of Benaiah, and Abiathar. Joab was commander of the king's army.

51 David's Charge to Israel and to Solomon

I Chronicles 28:1–29:9

(1)David assembled at Jerusalem all the officials of Israel, the officials of the tribes, the officers of the divisions that served the king, the commanders of thousands, the commanders of hundreds, the stewards of all the property and cattle of the king and his sons, together with the palace officials, the mighty men, and all the seasoned warriors. (2)Then King David rose to his feet and said: "Hear me, my brethren and my people. I had it in my heart to build a house of rest for the ark of the covenant of the LORD, and for the footstool of our God; and I made preparations for building. (3)But God said to me, 'You may not build a house for my name, for you are a warrior and have shed blood.' (4)Yet the LORD God of Israel chose me from all my father's house to be king over Israel for ever; for he chose Judah as leader, and in the house of Judah my father's house, and among my father's sons he took pleasure in me to make me king over all Israel. (5)And of all my sons (for the LORD has given me many sons) he has chosen Solomon my son to sit upon the throne of the kingdom of the LORD over Israel. (6)He said to me, 'It is Solomon your son who shall build my house and my courts, for I have chosen him to be my son, and I will be his father. (7)I will establish his kingdom for ever if he continues resolute in keeping my commandments and my ordinances, as he is today.' (8)Now therefore in the sight of all Israel, the assembly of the LORD, and in the hearing of our God, observe and seek out all the commandments of the LORD your God; that you may possess this good land, and leave it for an inheritance to your children after you for ever.

(9)"And you, Solomon, my son, know the God of your father, and serve him with a whole heart and with a willing mind; for the LORD searches all hearts, and understands every plan and thought. If you seek him, he will be found by you; but if you forsake him, he will cast you off for ever. (10)Take heed now, for the LORD has chosen you to build a house for the sanctuary; be strong, and do it."

(11)Then David gave Solomon his son the plan of the vestibule of the temple, and of its houses, its treasuries, its upper rooms, and its inner chambers, and of the room for the mercy seat; (12)and the plan of all that he had in mind for the courts of the house of the LORD, all the surrounding chambers, the treasuries of the house of God, and the treasuries for dedicated gifts; (13)for the divisions of the priests and of the Levites, and all the work of the service in the house of the LORD; for all the vessels for the service in the house of the LORD, (14)the weight of gold for all golden vessels for each service, the weight of silver vessels for each service, (15)the weight of the golden lampstands and their lamps, the weight of gold for each lampstand and its lamps, the weight of silver for a lampstand and its lamps, according to the use of each lampstand in the service, (16)the weight of gold for each table for the showbread, the silver for the silver tables, (17)and pure gold for the forks, the basins, and the cups; for the golden bowls and the weight of each; for the silver bowls and the weight of each; (18)for the altar of incense made of refined gold, and its weight; also his plan for the golden chariot of the cherubim that spread their wings and covered the ark of the covenant of the LORD. (19)All this he made clear by the writing from the hand of the LORD concerning it, all the work to be done according to the plan.

(20)Then David said to Solomon his son, "Be strong and of good courage, and do it. Fear not, be not dismayed; for the LORD God, even my God, is with you. He will not fail you or forsake you, until all the work for the service of the house of the LORD is finished. (21)And behold the divisions of the priests and the Levites for all the service of the house of God; and with you in all the work will be every willing man who has skill for any kind of service; also the officers and all the people will be wholly at your command."

(29:1)And David the king said to all the assembly, "Solomon my son, whom alone God has chosen, is young and inexperienced, and the work is great; for the palace will not be for man but for the LORD God. (2)So I have provided for the house of my God, so far as I was able, the gold for the things of gold, the silver for the things of silver, and the bronze for the things of bronze, the iron for the things of iron, and wood for the things of wood, besides great quantities of onyx and stones for setting, antimony, colored stones, all sorts of precious stones, and marble. (3)Moreover, in addition to all that I have provided for the holy house, I have a treasure of my own of gold and silver, and because of my devotion to the house of my God I give it to the house of my God: (4)three thousand talents of gold, of the gold of Ophir, and seven thousand talents of refined silver, for overlaying the walls of the house, (5)and for all the work to be done by craftsmen, gold for the things of gold and silver for the things of silver. Who then will offer willingly, consecrating himself today to the LORD?"

(6)Then the heads of fathers' houses made their freewill offerings, as did also the leaders of the tribes, the commanders of thousands and of hundreds, and the officers over the king's work. (7)They gave for the service of the house of God five thousand talents and ten thousand darics of gold, ten thousand talents of silver, eighteen thousand talents of bronze, and a hundred thousand talents of iron. (8)And whoever had precious stones gave them to the treasury of the house of the LORD, in the care of Jehiel the Gershonite. (9)Then the people rejoiced because these had given willingly, for with a whole heart they had offered freely to the LORD; David the king also rejoiced greatly.

52 David's Prayer

I Chronicles 29:10–22a

(10)Therefore David blessed the LORD in the presence of all the assembly; and David said: "Blessed art thou, O LORD, the God of Israel our father, for ever and ever. (11)Thine, O LORD, is the greatness, and the power, and the glory, and the victory, and the majesty; for all that is in the heavens and in the earth is thine; thine is the kingdom, O LORD, and thou art exalted as head above all. (12)Both riches and honor come from thee, and thou rulest over all. In thy hand are power and might; and in thy hand it is to make great and to give strength to all. (13)And now we thank thee, our God, and praise thy glorious name.

(14)"But who am I, and what is my people, that we should be able thus to offer willingly? For all things come from thee, and of thy own have we given thee. (15)For we are strangers before thee, and sojourners, as all our fathers were; our days on the earth are like a shadow, and there is no abiding. (16)O LORD our God, all this abundance that we have provided for building thee a house for thy holy name comes from thy hand and is all thy own. (17)I know, my God, that thou triest the heart, and hast pleasure in uprightness; in the uprightness of my heart I have freely offered all these things, and now I have seen thy people, who are present here, offering freely and joyously to thee. (18)O LORD, the God of Abraham, Isaac, and Israel, our fathers, keep for ever such purposes and thoughts in the hearts of thy people, and direct their hearts toward thee. (19)Grant to Solomon my son that with a whole heart he may keep thy commandments, thy testimonies, and thy statutes, performing all, and that he may build the palace for which I have made provision."

(20)Then David said to all the assembly, "Bless the LORD your God." And all the assembly blessed the LORD, the God of their fathers, and bowed their heads, and worshiped the LORD, and did obeisance to the king. (21)And they performed sacrifices to the LORD, and on the next day offered burnt offerings to the LORD, a thousand bulls, a thousand rams, and a thousand lambs, with their drink offerings, and sacrifices in abundance for all Israel; (22)and they ate and drank before the LORD on that day with great gladness.

53 The Death of David

I Kings 2:10–12

I Chronicles 29:22b–30

(22b)And they made Solomon the son of David king the second time, and they anointed him as prince for the LORD, and Zadok as priest. (23)Then Solomon sat on the throne of the LORD as king instead of David his father; and he prospered, and all Israel obeyed him.* (24)All the leaders and the mighty men, and also all the sons of King David, pledged their allegiance to King Solomon. (25)And the LORD gave Solomon great repute in the sight of all Israel, and bestowed upon him such royal majesty as had not been on any king before him in Israel.

(10)Then David slept with his fathers, and was buried in the city of David.

(11)And the time that David reigned over Israel was forty years; he reigned seven years in Hebron, and thirty-three years in Jerusalem.

(26)Thus David the son of Jesse reigned over all Israel. (27)The time that he reigned over Israel was forty years; he reigned seven years in Hebron, and thirty-three years in Jerusalem. (28)Then he died in a good old age, full of days, riches, and honor; and

*Cf. I Kings 1:46; 2:12.

(12)So Solomon sat upon the throne of David his father;*

Solomon his son reigned in his stead.

and his kingdom was firmly established.

(29)Now the acts of King David, from first to last, are written in the Chronicles of Samuel the seer, and in the Chronicles of Nathan the prophet, and in the Chronicles of Gad the seer, (30)with accounts of all his rule and his might and of the circumstances that came upon him and upon Israel, and upon all the kingdoms of the countries.

54 Solomon Settles Old Scores

I Kings 2:13–46a

(13)Then Adonijah the son of Haggith came to Bathsheba the mother of Solomon. And she said, "Do you come peaceably?" He said, "Peaceably." (14)Then he said, "I have something to say to you." She said, "Say on." (15)He said, "You know that the kingdom was mine, and that all Israel fully expected me to reign; however, the kingdom has turned about and become my brother's, for it was his from the LORD. (16)And now I have one request to make of you; do not refuse me." She said to him, "Say on." (17)And he said, "Pray ask King Solomon—he will not refuse you—to give me Abishag the Shunammite as my wife." (18)Bathsheba said, "Very well; I will speak for you to the king."

(19)So Bathsheba went to King Solomon, to speak to him on behalf of Adonijah. And the king rose to meet her, and bowed down to her; then he sat on his throne, and had a seat brought for the king's mother; and she sat on his right. (20)Then she said, "I have one small request to make of you; do not refuse me." And the king said to her, "Make your request, my mother; for I will not refuse you." (21)She said, "Let Abishag the Shunammite be given to Adonijah your brother as his wife." (22)King Solomon answered his mother, "And why do you ask Abishag the Shunammite for Adonijah? Ask for him the kingdom also; for he is my elder brother, and on his side are Abiathar the priest and Joab the son of Zeruiah." (23)Then King Solomon swore by the LORD, saying, "God do so to me and more also if this word does not cost Adonijah his life! (24)Now therefore as the LORD lives, who has established me, and placed me on the throne of David my father, and who has made me a house, as he promised, Adonijah shall be put to death

*Cf. I Chron. 29:23.

this day." (25)So King Solomon sent Benaiah the son of Jehoiada; and he struck him down, and he died.

(26)And to Abiathar the priest the king said, "Go to Anathoth, to your estate; for you deserve death. But I will not at this time put you to death, because you bore the ark of the LORD God before David my father, and because you shared in all the affliction of my father." (27)So Solomon expelled Abiathar from being priest to the LORD, thus fulfilling the word of the LORD which he had spoken concerning the house of Eli in Shiloh.

(28)When the news came to Joab—for Joab had supported Adonijah although he had not supported Absalom—Joab fled to the tent of the LORD and caught hold of the horns of the altar. (29)And when it was told King Solomon, "Joab has fled to the tent of the LORD, and behold, he is beside the altar," Solomon sent Benaiah the son of Jehoiada, saying, "Go, strike him down." (30)So Benaiah came to the tent of the LORD, and said to him, "The king commands, 'Come forth.' " But he said, "No, I will die here." Then Benaiah brought the king word again, saying, "Thus said Joab, and thus he answered me." (31)The king replied to him, "Do as he has said, strike him down and bury him; and thus take away from me and from my father's house the guilt for the blood which Joab shed without cause. (32)The LORD will bring back his bloody deeds upon his own head, because, without the knowledge of my father David, he attacked and slew with the sword two men more righteous and better than himself, Abner the son of Ner, commander of the army of Israel, and Amasa the son of Jether, commander of the army of Judah. (33)So shall their blood come back upon the head of Joab and upon the head of his descendants for ever; but to David, and to his descendants, and to his house, and to his throne, there shall be peace from the LORD for evermore." (34)Then Benaiah the son of Jehoiada went up, and struck him down and killed him; and he was buried in his own house in the wilderness. (35)The king put Benaiah the son of Jehoiada over the army in place of Joab, and the king put Zadok the priest in the place of Abiathar.

(36)Then the king sent and summoned Shime-i, and said to him, "Build yourself a house in Jerusalem, and dwell there, and do not go forth from there to any place whatever. (37)For on the day you go forth, and cross the brook Kidron, know for certain that you shall die; your blood shall be upon your own head." (38)And Shime-i said to the king, "What you say is good; as my lord the king has said, so will your servant do." So Shime-i dwelt in Jerusalem many days.

(39)But it happened at the end of three years that two of Shime-i's slaves ran away to Achish, son of Maacah, king of Gath. And when it was told Shime-i, "Behold, your slaves are in Gath," (40)Shime-i arose and saddled an ass, and went to Gath to Achish, to seek his slaves; Shime-i went and brought his slaves from Gath. (41)And when Solomon was told that Shime-i had gone from Jerusalem to Gath and returned, (42)the king sent and summoned Shime-i, and said to him, "Did I not make you swear by the LORD, and solemnly admonish you, saying, 'Know for certain that on the day you go forth and go to any place whatever, you shall die'? And you said to me, 'What you say is good; I obey.' (43)Why then have you not kept your oath to the LORD and the commandment with which I charged you?" (44)The king also said to Shime-i, "You know in your own heart all the evil that you did to David my father; so the LORD will bring back your evil upon your own head. (45)But King Solomon shall be blessed, and the throne of David shall be established before the LORD for ever." (46)Then the king commanded Benaiah the son of Jehoiada; and he went out and struck him down, and he died.

55 Solomon's Prayer for Wisdom

I Kings 2:46b–3:15	*II Chronicles 1:1–13*

(46b)So the kingdom was established in the hand of Solomon.

(1)Solomon the son of David established himself in his kingdom, and the LORD his God was with him and made him exceedingly great.

(3:1)Solomon made a marriage alliance with Pharaoh king of Egypt; he took Pharaoh's daughter, and brought her into the city of David, until he had finished building his own house and the house of the LORD and the wall around Jerusalem. (2)The people were sacrificing at the high places, however, because no house had yet been built for the name of the LORD. (3)Solomon loved the LORD, walking in the statutes of David his father; only, he sacrificed and burnt incense at the high places.

(2)Solomon spoke to all Israel, to the commanders of thousands and of hundreds, to the judges, and to all the leaders in all Israel, the heads of fathers' houses. (3)And Solomon, and all the assembly with him, went to the high place that was at Gibeon;

(4)And the king

went to Gibeon to sacrifice there, for that was the great high place;

for the tent of meeting of God, which Moses the servant of the LORD had made in the wilderness, was there. (4)(But David had brought up the ark of God from Kiriath-jearim to the place that David had prepared for it, for he had pitched a tent for it in Jerusalem.) (5)Moreover the bronze altar that Bezalel the son of Uri, son of Hur, had made, was there before the tabernacle of the LORD. And Solomon and the assembly sought the LORD. (6)And Solomon went up there to the bronze altar before the LORD, which was at the tent of meeting,

Solomon used
to offer a thousand burnt
offerings upon that altar.
(5)At Gibeon
the LORD appeared
to Solomon in a dream by night;
and God said,
"Ask what I shall give you."
(6)And Solomon said,
"Thou hast shown great and steadfast
love to thy servant David my father,
because he walked before thee in
faithfulness, in righteousness,
and in uprightness of heart toward
thee; and thou hast kept for him
this great and steadfast love, and
hast given him a son to sit on his
throne this day.|(7)And now,
O LORD my God,
thou hast made thy servant king
in place of David my father,
although I am but a little child;
I do not know how to go out or
come in.*|(8)And thy servant is in
the midst of thy people whom thou
hast chosen, a great

people,
that cannot be numbered or counted
for multitude. |

(9)Give thy servant therefore
an understanding mind

to govern thy people,

that I may discern between
good and evil;
for who is able to govern
this thy great people?" |

(10)It pleased the LORD
that Solomon had asked this.|

*Cf. II Chron. 1:10.

and offered a thousand burnt
offerings upon it.

(7)In that night God appeared
to Solomon,
and said to him,
"Ask what I shall give you."
(8)And Solomon said to God,
"Thou has shown great and steadfast
love to David my father, and

hast made me king
in his stead.

(9)O LORD God, let thy promise to
David my father be now fulfilled,
for thou hast made me king over a†
people

as many as the dust of the earth.
(10)Give me now
wisdom and knowledge
to go out and come in
before this people,‡

for who can rule
this thy people, that is so great?"

†Cf. I Kings 3:7.
‡Cf. I Kings 3:7.

/11/And God said to him,
"Because
you have asked this,

and you have not asked for yourself
long life or riches

or the life of your enemies,

but have asked for yourself
understanding to discern
what is right, |

(12)behold, I now do according
to your word.
Behold, I give you a wise
and discerning mind,
so that none like you has been
before you and none like you
shall arise after you.*
(13)I give you also
what you have not asked,
both riches and honor,
so that no other king shall
compare with you, all your days. |

(14)And if you will walk in my
ways, keeping my statutes and my
commandments, as your father David
walked, then I will lengthen your
days." |
    (15)And Solomon awoke,
and behold, it was a dream.
Then he came

to Jerusalem,
and stood before the ark of
the covenant of the LORD, and
offered up burnt offerings and
peace offerings, and made a
feast for all his servants. |

(11)God answered Solomon,
"Because

this was in your heart,
and you have not asked

possessions, wealth, honor,
or the life of those who hate you,
and have not even asked long life,
but have asked
wisdom and knowledge for yourself

that you may rule my people over
whom I have made you king,

(12)wisdom and knowledge
are granted to you.

I will also give you

riches, possessions, and honor.

such as none of the kings had
who were before you, and none
after you shall have the like."†

(13)So Solomon came from the
high place at Gibeon, from before
the tent of meeting,
to Jerusalem.

And he reigned over Israel.

*Cf. II Chron. 1:13.   †Cf. I Kings 3:12.

56 Solomon's Judgment of the Harlots

I Kings 3:16–28

(16)Then two harlots came to the king, and stood before him. (17)The one woman said, "Oh, my lord, this woman and I dwell in the same house; and I gave birth to a child while she was in the house. (18)Then on the third day after I was delivered, this woman also gave birth; and we were alone; there was no one else with us in the house, only we two were in the house. (19)And this woman's son died in the night, because she lay on it. (20)And she arose at midnight, and took my son from beside me, while your maidservant slept, and laid it in her bosom, and laid her dead son in my bosom. (21)When I rose in the morning to nurse my child, behold, it was dead; but when I looked at it closely in the morning, behold, it was not the child that I had borne." (22)But the other woman said, "No, the living child is mine, and the dead child is yours." The first said, "No, the dead child is yours, and the living child is mine." Thus they spoke before the king.

(23)Then the king said, "The one says, 'This is my son that is alive, and your son is dead'; and the other says, 'No; but your son is dead, and my son is the living one.' " (24)And the king said, "Bring me a sword." So a sword was brought before the king. (25)And the king said, "Divide the living child in two, and give half to the one, and half to the other." (26)Then the woman whose son was alive said to the king, because her heart yearned for her son, "Oh, my lord, give her the living child, and by no means slay it." But the other said, "It shall be neither mine not yours; divide it." (27)Then the king answered and said, "Give the living child to the first woman, and by no means slay it; she is its mother." (28)And all Israel heard of the judgment which the king had rendered; and they stood in awe of the king, because they perceived that the wisdom of God was in him, to render justice.

57 Solomon's Officials

I Kings 4:1–19

(1)King Solomon was king over all Israel, (2)and these were his high officials: Azariah the son of Zadok was the priest; (3)Elihoreph and Ahijah the sons of Shisha were secretaries; Jehoshaphat the son of Ahilud was recorder; (4)Benaiah the son of Jehoiada was in command of the army; Zadok and Abiathar were priests; (5)Azariah the son of Nathan was over the officers; Zabud the son of Nathan was priest and king's friend; (6)Ahishar was in charge of the palace; and Adoniram the son of Abda was in charge of the forced labor.

(7)Solomon had twelve officers over all Israel, who provided food for the king and his household; each man had to make provision for one month in the year. (8)These were their names: Ben-hur, in the hill country of Ephraim; (9)Ben-deker, in Makaz, Shaalbim, Beth-shemesh, and Elonbeth-hanan; (10)Ben-hesed, in Arubboth (to him belonged Socoh and all the land of Hepher); (11)Ben-abinadab, in all Naphath-dor (he had Taphath the daughter of Solomon as his wife); (12)Baana the son of Ahilud, in Taanach, Megiddo, and all Beth-shean which is beside Zarethan below Jezreel, and from Beth-shean to Abel-meholah, as far as the other side of Jokmeam; (13)Ben-geber, in Ramoth-gilead (he had the villages of Jair the son of Manasseh, which are in Gilead, and he had the region of Argob, which is in Bashan, sixty great cities with walls and bronze bars); (14)Ahinadab the son of Iddo, in Mahanaim; (15)Ahima-az, in Naphtali (he had taken Basemath the daughter of Solomon as his wife); (16)Baana the son of Hushai, in Asher and Bealoth; (17)Jehoshaphat the son of Paruah, in Issachar; (18)Shime-i the son of Ela, in Benjamin; (19)Geber the son of Uri, in the land of Gilead, the country of Sihon king of the Amorites and of Og king of Bashan. And there was one officer in the land of Judah.

58 The Extent of Solomon's Kingdom

I Kings 4:20–21   II Chronicles 9:26

(20)Judah and Israel were
as many as the sand by the sea;
they ate and drank and were happy.
(21)Solomon ruled over all the
kingdoms from the Euphrates to
the land of the Philistines
and to the border of Egypt;
they brought tribute and served
Solomon all the days of his life.

/26/And he ruled over all the
kings from the Euphrates to
the land of the Philistines
and to the border of Egypt.

59 Solomon's Wealth and Power

I Kings 4:22–28

(22)Solomon's provision for one day was thirty cors of fine flour, and sixty cors of meal, (23)ten fat oxen, and twenty pasture-fed cattle, a hundred sheep, besides harts, gazelles, roebucks, and fatted fowl. (24)For he had dominion over all the region west of the Euphrates from Tiphsah to Gaza, over all the kings west of the Euphrates; and he had peace on all sides round about him. (25)And Judah and Israel dwelt in safety, from Dan even to Beer-sheba, every man under his vine and under his fig tree, all the days of Solomon. (26)Solomon also had forty thousand stalls of horses for his chariots, and twelve thousand horsemen. (27)And those officers supplied provisions for King Solomon, and for all who came to King Solomon's table, each one in his month; they let nothing be lacking. (28)Barley also and straw for the horses and swift steeds they brought to the place where it was required, each according to his charge.

60 Solomon's Wisdom

I Kings 4:29–34

(29)And God gave Solomon wisdom and understanding beyond measure, and largeness of mind like the sand on the seashore, (30)so that Solomon's wisdom surpassed the wisdom of all the people of the east, and all the wisdom of Egypt. (31)For he was wiser than all other men, wiser than Ethan the Ezrahite, and Heman, Calcol, and Darda, the sons of Mahol; and his fame was in all the nations round about. (32)He also uttered three thousand proverbs; and his songs were a thousand and five. (33)He spoke of trees, from the cedar that is in Lebanon to the hyssop that grows out of the wall; he spoke also of beasts, and of birds, and of reptiles, and of fish. (34)And men came from all peoples to hear the wisdom of Solomon, and from all the kings of the earth, who had heard of his wisdom.

61 Solomon's Preparations for the Temple Construction

I Kings 5:1–18; 7:13–14   *II Chronicles 2:1–18*

I Kings 5:1–8

(1)Now Hiram king of Tyre sent his servants to Solomon, when he heard that they had anointed him king in place of his father; for Hiram always loved David.

                                  (1)Now Solomon purposed to build a temple for the name of the LORD, and a royal palace for himself.*
(2)And Solomon assigned seventy thousand men to bear burdens and eighty thousand to quarry in the hill country, and three thousand six hundred to oversee them.†

(2)And Solomon sent word to Hiram,
    (3)And Solomon sent word to Huram the king of Tyre:

(3)"You know that David my father could not build a house for the name of the LORD his God because of the warfare with which his enemies surrounded him, until the LORD put them under the soles of his feet. (4)But now the LORD my God has given me rest on every side; there is neither adversary nor misfortune.

    "As you dealt with David my father and sent him cedar to build himself a house to dwell in, so deal with me.
(4)Behold,
I am about to build a house for the name of the LORD my God

(5)And so
I purpose to build a house for the name of the LORD my God, as the LORD said to David my father,

*Cf. I Kings 5:5.
†Cf. I Kings 5:15.

'Your son, whom I will set upon your throne in your place, shall build the house for my name.'

and dedicate it to him for the burning of incense of sweet spices before him, and for the continual offering of the showbread, and for burnt offerings morning and evening, on the sabbaths and the new moons and the appointed feasts of the LORD our God, as ordained for ever for Israel. (5)The house which I am to build will be great, for our God is greater than all gods. (6)But who is able to build him a house, since heaven, even highest heaven, cannot contain him?* Who am I to build a house for him, except as a place to burn incense before him? (7)So now send me a man skilled to work in gold, silver, bronze, and iron, and in purple, crimson, and blue fabrics, trained also in engraving, to be with the skilled workers who are with me in Judah and Jerusalem, whom David my father provided.

(6)Now therefore command that cedars

(8)Send me also
cedar,
cypress, and algum timber

of Lebanon
be cut for me;
and my servants will join

from Lebanon,

for I know that
your servants

your servants,
and I will pay you for your servants such wages as you set;
for you know that there is no one among us who knows how to cut timber like the Sidonians."

know how to cut timber

in Lebanon.
And my servants will be with your servants, (9)to prepare timber for me in abundance, for the house I am

*Cf. I Kings 8:27

to build will be great and wonderful.
(10)I will give for your servants,
the hewers who cut timber, twenty
thousand cors of crushed wheat,
twenty thousand cors of barley,
twenty thousand baths of wine, and
twenty thousand baths of oil."*

(7)When Hiram heard the words
of Solomon, he rejoiced greatly,
and said,

(11)Then Huram the king of
Tyre answered in a letter which he
sent to Solomon,
"Because the LORD loves his people
he has made you king over them."
(12)Huram also said,

"Blessed be the LORD

this day,
who has given to David a wise son
to be over this great people."

"Blessed be the LORD God of Israel,
who made heaven and earth,

who has given King David a wise son,

endued with discretion and
understanding, who will build a
temple for the LORD, and
a royal palace for himself.

(8)And Hiram sent to Solomon,
saying, "I have heard the message
which you have sent to me; I am
ready to do all you desire in the
matter of cedar and cypress timber.

I Kings 7:13–14

(13)And King Solomon sent
and brought

(13)"Now I have sent

a skilled man,
endued with understanding,
Huramabi,

Hiram from Tyre.
(14)He was
the son of a widow of the
tribe of Naphtali,
and his father was a man of Tyre,

(14)the son of a woman of the
daughters of Dan,
and his father was a man of Tyre.
He is trained
to work in
gold, silver,

a worker in

bronze;

bronze,

*Cf. I Kings 5:11.

iron, stone, and wood, and in
purple, blue, and crimson fabrics
and fine linen, and to do
all sorts of engraving and execute
any design that may be assigned him,
with your craftsmen, the craftsmen of
my lord, David your father.

and he was full of wisdom,
understanding, and skill, for making
any work in bronze. He came to King
Solomon, and did all his work.

(15)Now therefore the wheat
and barley, oil and wine, of which
my lord has spoken, let him send to
his servants;

I Kings 5:9–18
(9)My servants shall bring it
down to the sea

(16)and we will cut whatever
timber you need
from Lebanon,

from Lebanon;
and I will make it into rafts
to go by sea to the place you direct,
and I will have them broken up there,
and you shall receive it;

and bring it to you in rafts
by sea to Joppa,

so that you may take it
up to Jerusalem."

and you shall meet my wishes by
providing food for my household."
(10)So Hiram supplied Solomon with
all the timber of cedar and cypress
that he desired, (11)while Solomon
gave Hiram twenty thousand cors of
wheat as food for his household, and
twenty thousand cors of beaten oil.*
Solomon gave this to Hiram year by
year. (12)And the LORD gave Solomon
wisdom, as he promised him; and there
was peace between Hiram and Solomon;
and the two of them made a treaty.
(13)King Solomon
raised a levy of forced labor
out of all

(17)Then Solomon

took a census of all the aliens
who were in the land of

*Cf. II Chron. 2:10.

Israel;

and the levy numbered
thirty thousand men.

(14)And he sent them to Lebanon,
ten thousand a month in relays; they
would be a month in Lebanon and two
months at home; Adoniram was in
charge of the levy.
/15/Solomon also had
seventy thousand

burden-bearers and
eighty thousand to quarry
in the hill country,
(16)besides Solomon's
three thousand three hundred
chief officers
who were over the work,
who had charge of

the people who carried on the work.
(17)At the king's command, they
quarried out great, costly stones in
order to lay the foundation of the
house with dressed stones. (18)So
Solomon's builders and Hiram's
builders and the men of Gebal did
the hewing and prepared the timber
and the stone to build the house.

Israel,
after the census of them which
David his father had taken;
and there were found
a hundred and fifty-three thousand
six hundred.

(18)Seventy thousand
of them he assigned to
bear burdens,
eighty thousand to quarry
in the hill country, and

three thousand six hundred as

overseers

to make
the people work.

62 The Construction of the Temple

I Kings 6:1 –38; II Chronicles 3:1 –14

I Kings 6:1–3

(1)In the four hundred and
eightieth year after the people of
Israel came out of the land of Egypt,
in the fourth year of Solomon's reign
over Israel, in the month of Ziv,
which is the second month,
he began to build

II Chronicles 3:1 –4a

(1)Then Solomon began to build

the house of the LORD.

the house of the LORD
in Jerusalem on Mount Moriah,
where the LORD had appeared to
David his father, at the place that
David had appointed, on the threshing
floor of Ornan the Jebusite. ⁽²⁾He
began to build in the second month of
the fourth year of his reign.
⁽³⁾Thesè are Solomon's measurements
for building the house
of God:
the length,
in cubits of the old standard,
was sixty cubits,
and the breadth twenty cubits.

⁽²⁾The house which King Solomon built
for the LORD was

sixty cubits long,
twenty cubits wide,
and thirty cubits high.
⁽³⁾The vestibule in front
of the nave of the house was
twenty cubits long,
equal to the width of the house,
and ten cubits deep in front
of the house.

^[4]The vestibule in front
of the nave of the house was
twenty cubits long,
. . .*

and its height was a hundred
and twenty cubits.†

I Kings 6:4–20a

⁽⁴⁾And he made for the house windows with recessed frames. ⁽⁵⁾He also built a structure against the wall of the house, running round the walls of the house, both the nave and the inner sanctuary; and he made side chambers all around. ⁽⁶⁾The lowest story was five cubits broad, the middle one was six cubits broad, and the third was seven cubits broad; for around the outside of the house he made offsets on the wall in order that the supporting beams should not be inserted into the walls of the house.

⁽⁷⁾When the house was built, it was with stone prepared at the quarry; so that neither hammer nor axe nor any tool of iron was heard in the temple, while it was being built.

⁽⁸⁾The entrance for the lowest story was on the south side of the house; and one went up by stairs to the middle story, and from the middle story to the third. ⁽⁹⁾So he built the house, and finished it; and he made the ceiling of the house of beams and planks of cedar. ⁽¹⁰⁾He built the structure against the whole house, each story five cubits high, and it was joined to the house with timbers of cedar.

⁽¹¹⁾Now the word of the LORD came to Solomon, ⁽¹²⁾"Concerning this house which you are building, if you will walk in my statutes and obey my ordinances and keep all my commandments and walk in them, then I will establish my word with you, which I spoke to David your father. ⁽¹³⁾And I will dwell among the children of Israel, and will not forsake my people Israel."

*Hebrew is uncertain.
†Cf. I Kings 6:20.

(14)So Solomon built the house, and finished it. (15)He lined the walls of the house on the inside with boards of cedar; from the floor of the house to the rafters of the ceiling, he covered them on the inside with wood; and he covered the floor of the house with boards of cypress. (16)He built twenty cubits of the rear of the house with boards of cedar from the floor to the rafters, and he built this within as an inner sanctuary, as the most holy place. (17)The house, that is, the nave in front of the inner sanctuary, was forty cubits long. (18)The cedar within the house was carved in the form of gourds and open flowers; all was cedar, no stone was seen. (19)The inner sanctuary he prepared in the innermost part of the house, to set there the ark of the covenant of the LORD. (20)The inner sanctuary was twenty cubits long, twenty cubits wide, and twenty cubits high; and

I Kings 6:20b–38	*II Chronicles 3:4b–14*
he overlaid it with pure gold. He also made an altar of cedar.	He overlaid it on the inside with pure gold.
	(5)The nave he lined with cypress,
(21)And Solomon overlaid the inside of the house with pure gold, and he drew chains of gold across, in front of the inner sanctuary, and overlaid it with gold.	and covered it with fine gold, and made palms and chains on it.
	(6)He adorned the house with settings of precious stones. The gold was gold of Parvaim. (7)So he lined the house with gold—
(22)And he overlaid the whole house with gold,	its beams, its thresholds, its walls, and its doors; and he carved cherubim on the walls.
until all the house was finished. Also the whole altar that belonged to the inner sanctuary he overlaid with gold.	
	(8)And he made the most holy place; its length, corresponding to the breadth of the house, was twenty cubits, and its breadth was twenty cubits; he overlaid it with six hundred talents of fine gold. (9)The weight of the nails was one shekel to fifty shekels of gold. And he overlaid the upper chambers with gold.

105

⁽²³⁾In the <u>inner sanctuary</u>
he made two cherubim
<u>of olivewood,</u>
<u>each ten cubits high.</u>

^[10]In the <u>most holy place</u>
he made two cherubim
. . .⊛

and they overlaid them with gold.
⁽¹¹⁾The wings of the cherubim
together extended twenty cubits:
one wing of the one,
of five cubits,
touched the wall of the house,
and its other wing,
of five cubits,
touched the wing of the other cherub;

⁽²⁴⁾Five cubits <u>was the length</u>
of one wing of <u>the cherub,</u>†

and five cubits <u>the length</u>
<u>of the other wing of the cherub;</u>

it was ten cubits from the tip of
one wing to the tip of the other.
⁽²⁵⁾The other cherub also measured
ten cubits; both cherubim had the
same measure and the same form.
⁽²⁶⁾The height of one cherub was
ten cubits, and so was that of the other
cherub. ⁽²⁷⁾He put the cherubim
in the innermost part of the house;
and the wings of the cherubim
were spread out so that
<u>a wing of one</u>

⁽¹²⁾and of this cherub, one wing,
of five cubits,
touched the wall of the house,
and the other wing,
also of five cubits,
was joined to the wing
of the first cherub.

touched the one wall,
and a wing of the other cherub

touched the other wall;
their other wings touched each other
in the middle of the house.

^{⟨13⟩}The wings of these cherubim
extended twenty cubits; they
stood on their feet, facing the
nave.

⁽²⁸⁾And he overlaid
the cherubim with gold.
  ⁽²⁹⁾He carved all the walls of
the house round about with carved
figures of cherubim and palm trees
and open flowers, in the inner and
outer rooms. ⁽³⁰⁾The floor of the

†Cf. I Kings 6:27

*Hebrew uncertain.

106

house he overlaid with gold in the
inner and outer rooms.

(31)For the entrance to the
inner sanctuary he made doors of
olivewood; the lintel and the
doorposts formed a pentagon. (32)He
covered the two doors of olivewood
with carvings of cherubim, palm trees,
and open flowers; he overlaid them
with gold, and spread gold upon the
cherubim and upon the palm trees.

(14)And he made the veil of blue and
purple and crimson fabrics and fine
linen, and worked cherubim on it.

(33)So also he made for the
entrance to the nave doorposts of
olivewood, in the form of a square,
(34)and two doors of cypress wood;
the two leaves of the one door were
folding, and the two leaves of the
other door were folding. (35)On
them he carved cherubim and palm
trees and open flowers; and he
overlaid them with gold evenly
applied upon the carved work.
(36)He built the inner court
with three courses of hewn stone
and one course of cedar beams.

(37)In the fourth year the
foundation of the house of the
LORD was laid, in the month of
Ziv. (38)And in the eleventh
year, in the month of Bul, which
is the eighth month, the house was
finished in all its parts, and
according to all its specifications.
He was seven years in building it.

63 The Construction of the Royal Palace

I Kings 7:1–12

(1)Solomon was building his own house thirteen years, and he finished his entire
house.

(2)He built the House of the Forest of Lebanon; its length was a hundred cubits, and
its breadth fifty cubits, and its height thirty cubits, and it was built upon three rows of

cedar pillars, with cedar beams upon the pillars. [3]And it was covered with cedar above the chambers that were upon the forty-five pillars, fifteen in each row. [4]There were window frames in three rows, and window opposite window in three tiers. [5]All the doorways and windows had square frames, and window was opposite window in three tiers.

[6]And he made the Hall of Pillars; its length was fifty cubits, and its breadth thirty cubits; there was a porch in front with pillars, and a canopy before them.

[7]And he made the Hall of the Throne where he was to pronounce judgment, even the Hall of Judgment; it was finished with cedar from floor to rafters.

[8]His own house where he was to dwell, in the other court back of the hall, was of like workmanship. Solomon also made a house like this hall for Pharaoh's daughter whom he had taken in marriage.

[9]All these were made of costly stones, hewn according to measure, sawed with saws, back and front, even from the foundation to the coping, and from the court of the house of the LORD to the great court. [10]The foundation was of costly stones, huge stones, stones of eight and ten cubits. [11]And above were costly stones, hewn according to measurement, and cedar. [12]The great court had three courses of hewn stone round about, and a course of cedar beams; so had the inner court of the house of the LORD, and the vestibule of the house.

64 The Accessories for the Temple

I Kings 7:13–51	*II Chronicles 2:13–14; 3:15–5:1*
	II Chronicles 2:13–14
[13]And King Solomon sent and brought	[13]"Now I have sent
	a skilled man, endued with understanding,
Hiram from Tyre. [14]He was the son of a widow of the tribe of Naphtali, and his father was a man of Tyre,	Huramabi, [14]the son of a woman of the daughters of Dan, and his father was a man of Tyre. He is trained
a worker in	to work in gold, silver,
bronze;	bronze, iron, stone, and wood, and in purple, blue, and crimson fabrics and fine linen, and to do all sorts of engraving and execute any design that may be assigned him, with your craftsmen, the craftsmen of my lord, David your father."

and he was full of wisdom,
understanding, and skill, for making
any work in bronze. He came to King
Solomon, and did all his work.

II Chronicles 3:15–5:1

(15)In front of the house
he made two pillars

(15)He cast two pillars
of bronze.
Eighteen cubits was the height
of one pillar,

thirty-five cubits high,

with a capital of five cubits on
the top of each.

and a line of twelve cubits measured
its circumference; it was hollow,
and its thickness was four fingers;
the second pillar was the same.
(16)He also made two capitals of molten
bronze, to set upon the tops of the
pillars; the height of the one capital
was five cubits, and the height of
the other capital was five cubits.
[17]. . .*

⟨16⟩He made

nets of checker work with wreaths of
chain work

chains
in the inner sanctuary

for the capitals

and put them
on the tops of the pillars;

upon the tops of the pillars;
seven for the one capital,
and seven for the other capital.
[18]Likewise he made
pillars;
in two rows round about upon
the one network, to cover the capital
that was upon the top of the
pomegranates;†

and he made a hundred

pomegranates,
and put them on the chains.

and he did the same with the other
capital. (19)Now the capitals that
were upon the tops of the pillars in
the vestibule were of lily-work, four
cubits. (20)The capitals were upon
the two pillars and also above the
rounded projection which was beside

*Hebrew lacks "He made two."
†The Hebrew words for "pillars" and "pomegranates" appear to have been transposed through
scribal error.

the network; there were two hundred
pomegranates, in two rows round about;
and so with the other capital.
(21)He set up the pillars
at the vestibule of the temple;
he set up the pillar
on the south
and called its name Jachin;
and he set up the pillar
on the north
and called its name Boaz.

(17)He set up the pillars
in front of the temple,
one
on the south,

and the other
on the north;

that on the south he called Jachin,
and that on the north Boaz.

(22)And upon the tops of the pillars
was lily-work. Thus the work of the
pillars was finished.

(4:1)He made an altar of bronze,
twenty cubits long, and twenty cubits
wide, and ten cubits high.

(23)Then he made the molten sea;
it was round, ten cubits from brim to
brim, and five cubits high, and a
line of thirty cubits measured its
circumference.
(24)Under its brim were gourds,
for ten cubits, compassing the sea
round about; the gourds were in two
rows, cast with it when it was cast.
(25)It stood upon twelve oxen,
three facing north,
three facing west,
three facing south, and
three facing east;
the sea was set upon them, and all
their hinder parts were inward.
(26)Its thickness was a
handbreadth; and its brim was made
like the brim of a cup,
like the flower of a lily;
it held two thousand baths.
(27)He also made the ten stands
of bronze; each stand was four cubits
long, four cubits wide, and three
cubits high. (28)This was the
construction of the stands: they had
panels, and the panels were set in
the frames (29)and on the panels

(2)Then he made the molten sea;
it was round, ten cubits from brim to
brim, and five cubits high, and a
line of thirty cubits measured its
circumference.
(3)Under it were figures of oxen,
for ten cubits, compassing the sea
round about; the oxen were in two
rows, cast with it when it was cast.
(4)It stood upon twelve oxen,
three facing north,
three facing west,
three facing south, and
three facing east;
the sea was set upon them, and all
their hinder parts were inward.
(5)Its thickness was a
handbreadth; and its brim was made
like the brim of a cup,
like the flower of a lily;
it held over three thousand baths.

that were set in the frames were
lions, oxen, and cherubim. Upon the
frames, both above and below the
lions and oxen, there were wreaths
of beveled work. (30)Moreover each
stand had four bronze wheels and axles
of bronze; and at the four corners
were supports for a laver. The
supports were cast, with wreaths at
the side of each. (31)Its opening
was within a crown which projected
upward one cubit; its opening was
round, as a pedestal is made, a cubit
and a half deep. At its opening there
were carvings; and its panels were
square, not round. (32)And the four
wheels were underneath the panels;
the axles of the wheels were of one
piece with the stands; and the height
of a wheel was a cubit and a half.
(33)The wheels were made like a
chariot wheel; their axles, their
rims, their spokes, and their hubs,
were all cast. (34)There were four
supports at the four corners of each
stand; the supports were of one piece
with the stands. (35)And on the
top of the stand there was a round
band half a cubit high; and on the
top of the stand its stays and its
panels were of one piece with it.
(36)And on the surfaces of its stays
and on its panels, he carved cherubim,
lions, and palm trees, according to
the space of each, with wreaths
round about. (37)After this manner
he made the ten stands; all of them
were cast alike, of the same measure
and the same form.

(38)And he made ten lavers
of bronze;

(6)He also made ten lavers

in which to wash,

each laver held forty baths,
each laver measured four cubits,
and there was a laver for each
of the ten stands.
(39)And he set the stands,

and set

111

five on the south side
of the house, and
five on the north side
of the house;

five on the south side,
and
five on the north side.

In these they were to rinse off
what was used for the burnt offering,
and the sea was for the priests to
wash in.
(7)And he made ten golden
lampstands as prescribed, and set
them in the temple, five on the
south side and five on the north.
(8)He also made ten tables, and
placed them in the temple, five on
the south side and five on the north.
And he made a hundred basins of gold.
(9)He made the court of the
priests, and the great court, and
doors for the court, and overlaid
their doors with bronze;

and he set the sea at the
southeast corner of the house.
(40)Hiram also made the pots,
the shovels, and the basins. So
Hiram finished all the work that he
did for King Solomon on the house of
the LORD: (41)the two pillars,
the two bowls of the capitals
that were on the tops of the pillars,
and the two networks to cover the
two bowls of the capitals that were
on the tops of the pillars; (42)and
the four hundred pomegranates for the
two networks, two rows of pomegranates
for each network, to cover the two
bowls of the capitals that were upon
the pillars;

(10)and he set the sea at the
southeast corner of the house.
(11)Huram also made the pots,
the shovels, and the basins. So
Huram finished the work that he
did for King Solomon on the house of
God: (12)the two pillars,
the bowls, and the two capitals
on the top of the pillars;
and the two networks to cover the
two bowls of the capitals that were
on the top of the pillars; (13)and
the four hundred pomegranates for the
two networks, two rows of pomegranates
for each network, to cover the two
bowls of the capitals that were upon
the pillars.
(14)He made
the stands also, and
the lavers upon the stands,
(15)and the one sea, and the twelve
oxen underneath it.
(16)The pots, the shovels,

(43)the ten stands, and
the ten lavers upon the stands;
(44)and the one sea, and the twelve
oxen underneath the sea.
(45)Now the pots, the shovels,
and the basins,

all these vessels in
the house of the LORD, which

the forks,

Hiram made
for King Solomon,
were of burnished bronze.

(46)In the plain of the Jordan
the king cast them, in the clay
ground between Succoth and Zarethan.
(47)And Solomon left all the vessels
unweighed, because there were so many
of them;

the weight of the bronze was not
found out.
(48)So Solomon made all the
vessels that were in the house of
the LORD: the golden altar,
the golden table for
the bread of the Presence,
(49)the lampstands
of pure gold,
five on the south side and
five on the north,

before the inner sanctuary;

the flowers, the lamps, and
the tongs, of gold;
(50)the cups,
snuffers, basins, dishes for incense,
and firepans, of pure gold;
and the sockets of gold,

for the doors of the innermost part
of the house,
the most holy place,
and for the doors of the nave
of the temple.
(51)Thus all the work that
King Solomon did on the house of
the LORD was finished. And Solomon
brought in the things which David
his father had dedicated,

the silver, the gold, and

and all the equipment for these
Huramabi made

of burnished bronze
for King Solomon
for the house of the LORD
(17)In the plain of the Jordan
the king cast them, in the clay
ground between Succoth and Zeredah.
/18/Solomon

made all these things
in great quantities, so that
the weight of the bronze was not
found out.
(19)So Solomon made all the
things that were in the house of
God: the golden altar,
the tables for
the bread of the Presence,
(20)the lampstands and their lamps
of pure gold

to burn
before the inner sanctuary,
as prescribed;
(21)the flowers, the lamps, and
the tongs, of purest gold;
(22)the
snuffers, basins, dishes for incense,
and firepans, of pure gold;

and the door of the house
for the inner doors to

the most holy place,
and for the doors of the nave
of the temple were of gold.
(5:1)Thus all the work that
Solomon did for the house of
the LORD was finished. And Solomon
brought in the things which David
his father had dedicated,
and stored
the silver, the gold, and

the vessels,
and stored them
in the treasuries of the house of
the LORD.

all the vessels

in the treasuries of the house of
God.

65 The Dedication of the Temple

I Kings 8:1–66; Psalm 136:1; Psalm   *II Chronicles 5:2–7:10*
132:8–10, 1

I Kings 8:1–10a

(1)Then Solomon assembled the
elders of Israel and all the heads of
the tribes, the leaders of the
fathers' houses of the people of
Israel, before King Solomon
in Jerusalem, to bring up the ark
of the covenant of the LORD out of
the city of David, which is Zion.
/2/And all the men of Israel
assembled before King Solomon
at the feast in the month Ethanim,
which is the seventh month.
(3)And all the elders of Israel
came, and the priests took up the
ark. (4)And they brought up the ark
of the LORD,
the tent of meeting, and all the holy
vessels that were in the tent;
the priests and the Levites
brought them up. (5)And King Solomon
and all the congregation of Israel,
who had assembled before him, were
with him before the ark,
sacrificing so many sheep and oxen
that they could not be counted or
numbered. (6)Then the priests
brought the ark of the covenant
of the LORD to its place, in the
inner sanctuary of the house, in the
most holy place, underneath the wings
of the cherubim. (7)For the cherubim
spread out their wings over the place
of the ark, so that the cherubim made
a covering above the ark and its

(2)Then Solomon assembled the
elders of Israel and all the heads of
the tribes, the leaders of the
fathers' houses of the people of
Israel,
in Jerusalem, to bring up the ark
of the covenant of the LORD out of
the city of David, which is Zion.
(3)And all the men of Israel
assembled before the king
at the feast
which is in the seventh month.
(4)And all the elders of Israel
came, and the Levites took up the
ark. (5)And they brought up the ark,

the tent of meeting, and all the holy
vessels that were in the tent;
the priests and the Levites
brought them up. (6)And King Solomon
and all the congregation of Israel,
who had assembled before him, were
before the ark,
sacrificing so many sheep and oxen
that they could not be counted or
numbered. /7/Then the priests
brought the ark of the covenant
of the LORD to its place, in the
inner sanctuary of the house, in the
most holy place, underneath the wings
of the cherubim. (8)For the cherubim
spread out their wings over the place
of the ark, so that the cherubim made
a covering above the ark and its

poles. (8)And the poles were so long
that the ends of the poles were seen
from the holy place before the inner
sanctuary; but they could not be seen
from outside; and they are there to
this day. (9)There was nothing in
the ark except the two tables
of stone
which Moses put there at Horeb,
where the LORD made a covenant with
the people of Israel, when they came
out of the land of Egypt.
(10)And when the priests came out
of the holy place,

poles. (9)And the poles were so long
that the ends of the poles were seen
from the holy place before the inner
sanctuary; but they could not be seen
from outside; and they are there to
this day. (10)There was nothing in
the ark except the two tables
which Moses put there at Horeb,
where the LORD made a covenant with
the people of Israel, when they came
out of Egypt.
/11/And when the priests came out
of the holy place,
(for all the priests who were present
had sanctified themselves, without
regard to their divisions; (12)and
all the Levitical singers, Asaph,
Heman, and Jeduthun, their sons and
kinsmen, arrayed in fine linen, with
cymbals, harps, and lyres, stood east
of the altar with a hundred and twenty
priests who were trumpeters; (13)and
it was the duty of the trumpeters and
singers to make themselves heard in
unison in praise and thanksgiving to
the LORD),
and when the song was raised, with
trumpets and cymbals and other
musical instruments,

Psalm 136:1

O give thanks to the LORD,
   for he is good,
  for his steadfast love endures
    for ever.

in praise to the LORD,
   "For he is good,
  for his steadfast love endures
    for ever,"

I Kings 8:10b–53

a cloud filled
the house of the LORD,

the house, the house of the LORD,
was filled with a cloud,
(14)so that the priests could not
stand to minister because of the
cloud; for the glory of the LORD
filled the house of God.
  (6:1)Then Solomon said,

(11)so that the priests could not
stand to minister because of the
cloud; for the glory of the LORD
filled the house of the LORD.
  (12)Then Solomon said,

115

"The LORD has said that he would
  dwell in thick darkness.
(13)I have built thee an exalted
  house,
  a place for thee to dwell in
    for ever."

(14)Then the king faced about, and
blessed all the assembly of Israel,
while all the assembly of Israel
stood. (15)And he said, "Blessed
be the LORD, the God of Israel, who
with his hand has fulfilled what he
promised with his mouth to David my
father, saying, (16)'Since the day
that I brought my people Israel out of
Egypt, I chose no city in
all the tribes of Israel in which to
build a house, that my name might be
there;

but I chose David to be
over my people Israel.'
(17)Now it was in the heart of David
my father to build a house for the
name of the LORD, the God of Israel.
(18)But the LORD said to David my
father, 'Whereas it was in your heart
to build a house for my name, you did
well that it was in your heart;
(19)nevertheless you shall not build
the house, but your son who shall be
born to you shall build the house for
my name.' (20)Now the LORD has
fulfilled his promise which he made;
for I have risen in the place of David
my father, and sit on the throne of
Israel, as the LORD promised, and I
have built the house for the name
of the LORD, the God of Israel.
/21/And there I have
provided a place for
the ark, in which is the covenant of
the LORD, which he made with

"The LORD has said that he would
  dwell in thick darkness.
(2)I have built thee an exalted
  house,
  a place for thee to dwell in
    for ever."

(3)Then the king faced about, and
blessed all the assembly of Israel,
while all the assembly of Israel
stood. (4)And he said, "Blessed
be the LORD, the God of Israel, who
with his hand has fulfilled what he
promised with his mouth to David my
father, saying, (5)'Since the day
that I brought my people out of
the land of Egypt, I chose no city in
all the tribes of Israel in which to
build a house, that my name might be
there,
and I chose no man as prince
over my people Israel;
(6)but I have chosen Jerusalem
that my name may be there
and I have chosen David to be
over my people Israel.'
(7)Now it was in the heart of David
my father to build a house for the
name of the LORD, the God of Israel.
(8)But the LORD said to David my
father, 'Whereas it was in your heart
to build a house for my name, you did
well that it was in your heart;
(9)nevertheless you shall not build
the house, but your son who shall be
born to you shall build the house for
my name.' (10)Now the LORD has
fulfilled his promise which he made;
for I have risen in the place of David
my father, and sit on the throne of
Israel, as the LORD promised, and I
have built the house for the name
of the LORD, the God of Israel.
(11)And there I have
set
the ark, in which is the covenant of
the LORD, which he made with

our fathers, when he brought them out
of the land of Egypt."

(22)Then Solomon stood before the
altar of the LORD in the presence of
all the assembly of Israel, and
spread forth his hands

the people of Israel."
(12)Then Solomon stood before the
altar of the LORD in the presence of
all the assembly of Israel, and
spread forth his hands.
(13)Solomon had made a bronze
platform five cubits long, five
cubits wide, and three cubits high,
and had set it in the court; and
he stood upon it. Then he knelt upon
his knees in the presence of
all the assembly of Israel, and
spread forth his hands

toward heaven;
(23)and said, "O LORD, God of Israel,
there is no God like thee, in heaven
above or on earth beneath, keeping
covenant and showing steadfast love
to thy servants who walk before thee
with all their heart; (24)who hast
kept with thy servant David my father
what thou didst declare to him; yea,
thou didst speak with thy mouth, and
with thy hand hast fulfilled it this
day. (25)Now therefore, O LORD,
God of Israel, keep with thy servant
David my father what thou hast
promised him, saying, 'There shall
never fail you a man before me to sit
upon the throne of Israel, if only
your sons take heed to their way, to
walk before me
as you have walked before me.'
(26)Now therefore, O
God of Israel,
let thy word be confirmed, which thou
hast spoken to thy servant David
my father.
(27)"But will God indeed dwell

on the earth? Behold, heaven and the
highest heaven cannot contain thee;
how much less this house which I have
built! (28)Yet have regard to the
prayer of thy servant and to his

toward heaven;
(14)and said, "O LORD, God of Israel,
there is no God like thee, in heaven
or on earth, keeping
covenant and showing steadfast love
to thy servants who walk before thee
with all their heart; (15)who hast
kept with thy servant David my father
what thou didst declare to him; yea,
thou didst speak with thy mouth, and
with thy hand hast fulfilled it this
day. (16)Now therefore, O LORD,
God of Israel, keep with thy servant
David my father what thou hast
promised him, saying, 'There shall
never fail you a man before me to sit
upon the throne of Israel, if only
your sons take heed to their way, to
walk in my law
as you have walked before me.'
(17)Now therefore, O LORD,
God of Israel,
let thy word be confirmed, which thou
hast spoken to thy servant David.

(18)"But will God indeed dwell
with man
on the earth? Behold, heaven and the
highest heaven cannot contain thee;
how much less this house which I have
built! (19)Yet have regard to the
prayer of thy servant and to his

supplication, O LORD my God,
hearkening to the cry and to the
prayer which thy servant prays before
thee this day;
⁽²⁹⁾that thy eyes may be open night
and day toward this house, the place
of which thou hast said,
'My name shall be there,'
that thou mayest hearken to the
prayer which thy servant offers
toward this place. ⁽³⁰⁾And hearken
thou to the supplication of thy
servant and of thy people Israel,
when they pray toward this place;
yea, hear thou in heaven thy
dwelling place; and when thou
hearest, forgive.

⁽³¹⁾"If a man sins against his
neighbor and is made to take an oath,
and comes and swears his oath before
thine altar in this house, ⁽³²⁾then
hear thou in heaven, and act, and
judge thy servants, condemning the
guilty by bringing his conduct upon
his own head, and vindicating the
righteous by rewarding him
according to his righteousness.

⁽³³⁾"When thy people Israel are
defeated before the enemy because
they have sinned against thee, if
they turn again to thee, and
acknowledge thy name, and pray and
make supplication to thee in this
house; ⁽³⁴⁾then hear thou in
heaven, and forgive the sin of thy
people Israel, and bring them again
to the land which thou gavest

to their fathers.

⁽³⁵⁾"When heaven is shut up and
there is no rain because they have
sinned against thee, if they pray
toward this place, and acknowledge
thy name, and turn from their sin,
when thou dost afflict them,
⁽³⁶⁾then hear thou in heaven, and
forgive the sin of thy servants,

supplication, O LORD my God,
hearkening to the cry and to the
prayer which thy servant prays before
thee;
⁽²⁰⁾that thy eyes may be open day
and night toward this house, the place
where thou hast promised
to set thy name,
that thou mayest hearken to the
prayer which thy servant offers
toward this place. ⁽²¹⁾And hearken
thou to the supplications of thy
servant and of thy people Israel,
when they pray toward this place;
yea, hear thou from heaven thy
dwelling place; and when thou
hearest, forgive.

^{/22/}"If a man sins against his
neighbor and is made to take an oath,
and comes and swears his oath before
thine altar in this house, ⁽²³⁾then
hear thou from heaven, and act, and
judge thy servants, requiting the
guilty by bringing his conduct upon
his own head, and vindicating the
righteous by rewarding him
according to his righteousness.

^{/24/}"If thy people Israel are
defeated before the enemy because
they have sinned against thee, when
they turn again and
acknowledge thy name, and pray and
make supplication to thee in this
house; ⁽²⁵⁾then hear thou from
heaven, and forgive the sin of thy
people Israel, and bring them again
to the land which thou gavest
to them and
to their fathers.

⁽²⁶⁾"When heaven is shut up and
there is no rain because they have
sinned against thee, if they pray
toward this place, and acknowledge
thy name, and turn from their sin,
when thou dost afflict them,
⁽²⁷⁾then hear thou in heaven, and
forgive the sin of thy servants,

thy people Israel, when thou dost
teach them the good way in
which they should walk; and grant
rain upon thy land, which thou hast
given to thy people as an inheritance.
(37)"If there is famine in the
land, if there is pestilence or blight
or mildew or locust or caterpillar;
if their enemy besieges them in any
of their cities; whatever plague,
whatever sickness there is;
(38)whatever prayer, whatever
supplication is made by any man or by
all thy people Israel, each knowing
the affliction of his own heart and

stretching out his hands toward this
house; (39)then hear thou in heaven
thy dwelling place, and forgive, and
act, and
render to each whose heart thou
knowest, according to all his ways
(for thou, thou only, knowest the
hearts of all the children of men);
(40)that they may fear thee

all the days that they live in the
land which thou gavest to our fathers.
(41)"Likewise when a foreigner,
who is not of thy people Israel,
comes from a far country for
thy name's
sake
(42)(for they shall hear of
thy great name,
and thy mighty hand, and of
thy outstretched arm), when he comes
and prays toward this house, (43)hear
thou in heaven thy dwelling place,
and do according to all for which the
foreigner calls to thee; in order
that all the peoples of the earth may
know thy name and fear thee, as do thy
people Israel, and that they may know
that this house which I have built is
called by thy name.
(44)"If thy people go out to

thy people Israel, when thou dost
teach them toward the good way in
which they should walk; and grant
rain upon thy land, which thou hast
given to thy people as an inheritance.
(28)"If there is famine in the
land, if there is pestilence or blight
or mildew or locust or caterpillar;
if their enemies besiege them in any
of their cities; whatever plague,
whatever sickness there is;
(29)whatever prayer, whatever
supplication is made by any man or by
all thy people Israel, each knowing
his own affliction,
and his own sorrow and
stretching out his hands toward this
house; (30)then hear thou from heaven
thy dwelling place, and forgive, and

render to each whose heart thou
knowest, according to all his ways
(for thou, thou only, knowest the
hearts of the children of men);
(31)that they may fear thee
and walk in thy ways
all the days that they live in the
land which thou gavest to our fathers.
(32)"Likewise when a foreigner,
who is not of thy people Israel,
comes from a far country for

the sake of

thy great name,
and thy mighty hand, and
thy outstretched arm, when he comes
and prays toward this house, (33)hear
thou from heaven thy dwelling place,
and do according to all for which the
foreigner calls to thee; in order
that all the peoples of the earth may
know thy name and fear thee, as do thy
people Israel, and that they may know
that this house which I have built is
called by thy name.
(34)"If thy people go out to

battle against their enemy, by
whatever way thou shalt send them,
and they pray to the LORD toward
the city which thou hast chosen and
the house which I have built for
thy name, (45)then hear thou in
heaven their prayer and their
supplication, and maintain their
cause.
   (46)"If they sin against thee—
for there is no man who does not sin—
and thou art angry with them, and
dost give them to an enemy, so that
they are carried away captive to
the land of the enemy,
far off or near;
(47)yet if they lay it to heart
in the land to which they have been
carried captive, and repent, and make
supplication to thee in the land of
their captors, saying, 'We have
sinned, and have acted perversely and
wickedly'; (48)if they repent with
all their mind and with all their
heart in the land of their enemies,
who carried them captive,
and pray to thee toward their land,
which thou gavest to their fathers,
the city which thou hast chosen, and
the house which I have built for thy
name; (49)then hear thou in heaven
thy dwelling place their prayer and
their supplication, and maintain
their cause (50)and forgive thy
people who have sinned against thee,
and all their transgressions which
they have committed against thee; and
grant them compassion in the sight of
those who carried them captive, that
they may have compassion on them
(51)(for they are thy people, and
thy heritage, which thou didst bring
out of Egypt, from the midst of the
iron furnace). (52)Let thy eyes be
open to the supplication of thy
servant, and to the supplication of
thy people Israel, giving ear to them

battle against their enemies, by
whatever way thou shalt send them,
and they pray to thee toward
this city which thou hast chosen and
the house which I have built for
thy name, (35)then hear thou from
heaven their prayer and their
supplication, and maintain their
cause.
   (36)"If they sin against thee—
for there is no man who does not sin—
and thou art angry with them, and
dost give them to an enemy, so that
they are carried away captive to
a land
far off or near;
(37)yet if they lay it to heart
in the land to which they have been
carried captive, and repent, and make
supplication to thee in the land of
their captivity, saying, 'We have
sinned, and have acted perversely and
wickedly'; (38)if they repent with
all their mind and with all their
heart in the land of their captivity,
to which they were carried captive,
and pray toward their land,
which thou gavest to their fathers,
the city which thou hast chosen, and
the house which I have built for thy
name; (39)then hear thou from heaven
thy dwelling place their prayer and
their supplications, and maintain
their cause and forgive thy
people who have sinned against thee.

whenever they call to thee. (53)For
thou didst separate them from among
all the peoples of the earth, to be
thy heritage, as thou didst declare
through Moses, thy servant, when thou
didst bring our fathers out of Egypt,
O LORD God."

(40)Now, O my God, let thy eyes be
open and thy ears attentive to a
prayer of this place.

Psalm 132:8–10, 1

(8)Arise, O Lord,
 and go to thy resting place,
 thou and the ark of thy might.
(9)Let thy priests
 be clothed with righteousness,
and let thy saints shout for joy.

(10)For thy servant David's sake

do not turn away the face of
 thy anointed one.
(1)Remember, O LORD,
 in David's favor,
all the hardships he endured.

(41)"And now arise, O LORD God,
 and go to thy resting place,
 thou and the ark of thy might.
Let thy priests, O LORD God,
 be clothed with salvation,
and let thy saints rejoice in
 thy goodness.

/42/O LORD God,
 do not turn away the face of
 thy anointed one.
Remember thy steadfast love
 for David thy servant."

I Kings 8:54–66

(54)Now as Solomon finished offering
all this prayer and supplication to
the LORD, he arose from before the
altar of the LORD, where he had knelt
with hands outstretched toward heaven;
(55)and he stood, and blessed all
the assembly of Israel with a loud
voice, saying, (56)"Blessed be the LORD
who has given rest to his people
Israel, according to all that he
promised; not one word has failed of
all his good promise, which he uttered
by Moses his servant. (57)The LORD
our God be with us, as he was with our
fathers; may he not leave us or
forsake us; (58)that he may incline
our hearts to him, to walk in all his
ways, and to keep his commandments,

(7:1)When Solomon had ended
his prayer,

his statutes, and his ordinances, which
he commanded our fathers. (59)Let
these words of mine, wherewith I have
made supplication before the LORD, be
near to the LORD our God day and
night, and may he maintain the cause
of his servant, and the cause of his
people Israel, as each day requires;
(60)that all the peoples of the
earth may know that the LORD is God;
there is no other. (61)Let your
heart therefore be wholly true to
the LORD our God, walking in his
statutes and keeping his commandments,
as at this day."

fire came down from heaven and
consumed the burnt offering and the
sacrifices, and the glory of the LORD
filled the temple. (2)And the priests
could not enter the house of
the LORD, because the glory of
the LORD filled the LORD's house.
(3)When all the children of Israel
saw the fire come down and the glory
of the LORD upon the temple, they
bowed down with their faces to the
earth on the pavement, and worshiped
and
gave thanks to the LORD, saying,

"For he is good,
  for his steadfast love endures
    for ever."*

(62)Then the king,
and all Israel with him,
offered sacrifice before the LORD.
(63)Solomon offered as
peace offerings to the LORD
twenty-two thousand oxen and
a hundred and twenty thousand sheep.
So the king and all the people
of Israel
dedicated the house of the LORD.

(4)Then the king
and all the people
offered sacrifice before the LORD.
(5)King Solomon offered as
a sacrifice
twenty-two thousand oxen and
a hundred and twenty thousand sheep.
So the king and all the people

dedicated the house of God.
(6)The priests stood at their posts;
the Levites also, with the instruments
for music to the LORD which King

*Cf. Ps. 136:1.

David had made for
giving thanks to the LORD—
for his steadfast love endures
for ever—*

whenever David offered praises by
their ministry; opposite them the
priests sounded trumpets; and all
Israel stood.

$^{(64)}$The same day the king
consecrated the middle of the court
that was before the house of the LORD;
for there he offered the burnt
offering and
the cereal offering and
the fat of the peace offerings,
because the bronze altar that
was before the LORD
was too small to receive
the burnt offering and
the cereal offering and
the fat of the peace offerings.

$^{(7)}$And Solomon
consecrated the middle of the court
that was before the house of the LORD;
for there he offered the burnt
offering and

the fat of the peace offerings,
because the bronze altar that
Solomon had made
could not hold
the burnt offering and
the cereal offering and
the fat.

$^{(65)}$So Solomon held the feast

at that time,
and all Israel with him,
a great assembly,
from the entrance of Hamath to
the Brook of Egypt,
before the LORD our God,
seven days and seven days,
fourteen days.
$^{(66)}$On the eighth day

$^{/8/}$At that time
Solomon held the feast
for seven days,

and all Israel with him,
a very great assembly,
from the entrance of Hamath to
the Brook of Egypt.

$^{(9)}$And on the eighth day
they held a solemn assembly; for
they had kept the dedication of the
altar seven days and the feast seven
days. $^{(10)}$On the twenty-third day
of the seventh month
he sent the people away

he sent the people away;
and they blessed the king, and went
to their homes joyful and glad of
heart for all the goodness that
the LORD had shown to
David his servant and

to their homes, joyful and glad of
heart for all the goodness that
the LORD had shown to
David and
to Solomon and
to Israel his people.

to Israel his people.

*Cf. Ps. 136:1.

123

66 The Lord's Appearance to Solomon

I Kings 9:1–9	*II Chronicles 7:11–22*

(1)When Solomon had finished
building
the house of the LORD
and the king's house
and all that Solomon
desired to build,

(11)Thus Solomon finished

the house of the LORD
and the king's house;
all that Solomon

had planned to do in the house of
the LORD and in his own house he
successfully accomplished.
(12)Then the LORD appeared to Solomon

(2)the LORD appeared to Solomon
a second time,
as he had appeared to him at Gibeon.

in the night
and said to him,

(3)And the LORD said to him,
"I have heard your prayer
and your supplication,
which you have made before me;

"I have heard your prayer,

and have chosen this place for myself
as a house of sacrifice. (13)When I
shut up the heavens so that there is
no rain, or command the locust to
devour the land, or send pestilence
among my people, (14)if my people
who are called by my name humble
themselves, and pray and seek my
face, and turn from their wicked
ways, then I will hear from heaven,
and will forgive their sin and heal
their land. (15)Now my eyes will be
open and my ears attentive to the
prayer that is made in this place.
(16)For now I have
chosen and

I have

consecrated this house
which you have built,
and put my name there for ever;
my eyes and my heart will be there
for all time. (4)And as for you,
if you will walk before me,
as David your father walked,
with integrity of heart
and uprightness,
doing according to all that I have

consecrated this house

that my name may be there for ever;
my eyes and my heart will be there
for all time. /17/And as for you,
if you will walk before me,
as David your father walked,

doing according to all that I have

commanded you, and keeping my statutes and my ordinances, (5)then I will establish your royal throne over Israel for ever,	commanded you, and keeping my statutes and my ordinances, (18)then I will establish your royal throne,
as I promised David your father, saying, 'There shall not fail you a man upon the throne of Israel.' (6)But if you turn aside from following me, you or your children, and do not keep my commandments and	as I covenanted with David your father, saying, 'There shall not fail you a man to rule Israel.' (19)"But if you turn aside
my statutes	and forsake my statutes and my commandments
which I have set before you, but go and serve other gods and worship them, (7)then I will cut off Israel	which I have set before you, but go and serve other gods and worship them, (20)then I will pluck them up
from the land which I have given them; and the house which I have consecrated for my name I will cast out of my sight; and Israel will become a proverb and a byword among all peoples. [8]And this house will become exalted* everyone passing by it will be astonished, and will hiss; and they will say, 'Why has the LORD done thus to this land and to this house?' (9)Then they will say, 'Because they forsook the LORD their God who brought their fathers out of the land of Egypt, and laid hold on other gods, and worshiped them and served them; therefore the LORD has brought all this evil upon them.' "	from the land which I have given them; and this house, which I have consecrated for my name, I will cast out of my sight, and will make it a proverb and a byword among all peoples. (21)And at this house, which is exalted, every one passing by will be astonished, and say, 'Why has the LORD done thus to this land and to this house?' (22)Then they will say, 'Because they forsook the LORD the God of their fathers who brought them out of the land of Egypt, and laid hold on other gods, and worshiped them and served them; therefore he has brought all this evil upon them.' "

*The Hebrew text has been disturbed.

125

67 Solomon's Enterprises

I Kings 9:10–28	II Chronicles 8:1–18

(10)At the end of twenty years,
in which Solomon had built
<u>the two houses,</u>
the house of the LORD and
the king's house,
(11)and Hiram king of Tyre had
supplied Solomon with cedar and
cypress timber and gold, as much as
he desired, King Solomon gave to Hiram
twenty cities in the land of Galilee.
(12)But when Hiram came from Tyre
to see the cities which Solomon had
given him, they did not please him.

(13)Therefore he said, "What kind
of cities are these which you have
given me, my brother?" So they are
called the land of Cabul to this day.
(14)Hiram had sent to the king one
hundred and twenty talents of gold.
(15)And this is the account of
the forced labor which King Solomon
levied to build the house of the LORD
and his own house and the Millo and
the wall of Jerusalem and Hazor and
Megiddo and Gezer (16)(Pharaoh king
of Egypt had gone up and captured
Gezer and burnt it with fire, and had
slain the Canaanites who dwelt in the
city, and had given it as dowry to his
daughter, Solomon's wife; (17)so
Solomon rebuilt Gezer)

and Lower Beth-horon

(18)and Baalath
and Tamar in the wilderness,

---

(1)At the end of twenty years,
in which Solomon had built

the house of the LORD and
his own house,

(2)Solomon rebuilt the cities which
Huram had given to him, and settled
the people of Israel in them.

(3)And Solomon went to Hamath-
zobah, and took it. (4)He built
Tadmor in the wilderness and all the
store-cities which he built in Hamath.
(5)He also built Upper Beth-horon
and Lower Beth-horon,
fortified cities with walls, gates,
and bars,
(6)and Baalath,

in the land of Judah,	
(19)and all the store-cities that	and all the store-cities that
Solomon had, and	Solomon had, and all
the cities for his chariots, and	the cities for his chariots, and
the cities for his horsemen, and	the cities for his horsemen, and
whatever Solomon desired to build	whatever Solomon desired to build
in Jerusalem, in Lebanon, and in	in Jerusalem, in Lebanon, and in
all the land of his dominion.	all the land of his dominion.
(20)All the people who were left of	(7)All the people who were left of
the Amorites, the Hittites,	the Hittites, the Amorites,
the Perizzites, the Hivites, and	the Perizzites, the Hivites, and
the Jebusites, who were not	the Jebusites, who were not
of the people of Israel—	of Israel,
(21)their descendants who were	(8)from their descendants who were
left after them in the land,	left after them in the land,
whom the people of Israel	whom the people of Israel
were unable to destroy utterly—	had not destroyed—
these Solomon made a forced levy	these Solomon made a forced levy
of slaves,	
and so they are to this day.	and so they are to this day.
/22/But of the people of Israel	/9/But of the people of Israel
Solomon made no slaves;	Solomon made no slaves
	for his work;
they were the soldiers,	they were soldiers,
and his servants,	
and his commanders, and his officers,	and commanders of his officers,
and his chariot commanders,	and his chariot commanders,
and his horsemen.	and his horsemen.
(23)These were the chief officers	(10)And these were the chief officers
who were over Solomon's work:	of King Solomon,
five hundred and fifty,	two hundred and fifty,
who had charge	who exercised authority
of the people	over the people.
who carried on the work.	
(24)But Pharaoh's	(11)Solomon brought Pharaoh's
daughter went up from	daughter up from
the city of David to her own house	the city of David to the house
which Solomon had built for her;	which he had built for her,
	for he said, "My wife shall not live
	in the house of David king of Israel,
	for the places to which the ark of
	the LORD has come are holy."
	(12)Then
then	
he built the Millo.	
(25)Three times a year	
Solomon used to offer up	Solomon offered up
burnt offerings	burnt offerings
and peace offerings	

upon the altar <u>which he built</u>	<u>to the LORD</u>
to the LORD,	upon the altar
	of the LORD
	<u>which he had built</u>
<u>burning incense</u>	
before	before
<u>the LORD.</u>	
<u>So he finished the house.</u>	
	the vestibule,
	(13)as the duty of each day
	required, offering according to the
	commandment of Moses for the
	sabbaths, the new moons, and the three
	annual feasts—the feast of
	unleavened bread, the feast of weeks,
	and the feast of tabernacles.
	(14)According to the ordinance of
	David his father, he appointed the
	divisions of the priests for their
	service, and the Levites for their
	offices of praise and ministry before
	the priests as the duty of each day
	required, and the gatekeepers in
	their divisions for the several gates;
	for so David the man of God had
	commanded. (15)And they did not
	turn aside from what the king had
	commanded the priests and Levites
	concerning any matter and concerning
	the treasuries.
	(16)Thus was accomplished all
	the work of Solomon from the day the
	foundation of the house of the LORD
	was laid until it was finished. So
	the house of the LORD was completed.
(26)<u>King</u> Solomon	(17)<u>Then</u> Solomon
<u>built a fleet of ships at</u>	
	went to
Ezion-geber,	Ezion-geber
<u>which is near</u>	
	and
Eloth on the shore of <u>the Red</u> Sea,	Eloth on the shore of <u>the</u> sea,
in the land of Edom.	in the land of Edom.
(27)And <u>Hiram</u> sent <u>with the fleet</u>	/18/And <u>Huram</u> sent <u>him</u>
his servants,	<u>by</u> his servants
	<u>ships and</u>
<u>seamen who were</u> familiar with the sea,	<u>servants</u> familiar with the sea,

128

together with the servants of Solomon;
(28)and they went to Ophir,

and brought from there
gold,
for the amount of
four hundred and twenty talents;

and they brought it to King Solomon.

and they went to Ophir
together with the servants of Solomon,
and brought from there

four hundred and fifty talents
of gold
and brought it to King Solomon.

68 The Visit of the Queen of Sheba

I Kings 10:1–13

(1)Now when the queen of Sheba
heard of the fame of Solomon
concerning the name of the LORD,
she came
to test him with hard questions.
(2)She came to Jerusalem
with
a very great retinue, with camels
bearing spices, and very much gold,
and precious stones; and when she
came to Solomon, she told him all
that was on her mind. (3)And
Solomon answered all her questions;
there was nothing hidden from the king
which he could not explain to her.
(4)And when the queen of Sheba had
seen all the wisdom of Solomon,
the house that he had built,
(5)the food of his table,
the seating of his officials,
and the attendance of his servants,
their clothing, his cupbearers, and

his burnt offerings which he offered
at the house of the LORD, there was
no more spirit in her.
(6)And she said to the king,
"The report was true which I heard
in my own land of your affairs and
of your wisdom, (7)but I did not
believe the reports until I came
and my own eyes had seen it; and,
behold, the half

II Chronicles 9:1–12

(1)Now when the queen of Sheba
heard of the fame of Solomon

she came to Jerusalem
to test him with hard questions,

having
a very great retinue and camels
bearing spices and very much gold
and precious stones. When she
came to Solomon, she told him all
that was on her mind. (2)And
Solomon answered all her questions;
there was nothing hidden from Solomon
which he could not explain to her.
(3)And when the queen of Sheba had
seen the wisdom of Solomon,
the house that he had built,
(4)the food of his table,
the seating of his officials,
and the attendance of his servants, and
their clothing, his cupbearers, and
their clothing, and
his burnt offerings which he offered
at the house of the LORD, there was
no more spirit in her.
(5)And she said to the king,
"The report was true which I heard
in my own land of your affairs and
of your wisdom, (6)but I did not
believe their reports until I came
and my own eyes had seen it; and
behold, half

<table>
<tr>
<td>

was not told me;
your wisdom and prosperity

surpass the report which I heard.
⁽⁸⁾Happy are your men!
Happy are these your servants, who
continually stand before you and
hear your wisdom! ⁽⁹⁾Blessed be
the LORD your God, who has delighted
in you and set you on
the throne of Israel!

Because the LORD loved Israel

for ever, he has made you king,

that you may execute justice and
righteousness." ⁽¹⁰⁾Then she
gave the king a hundred and twenty
talents of gold, and a very great
quantity of spices,
and precious stones;
never again came such an abundance
of spices

as these which the queen of Sheba
gave to King Solomon.
   ⁽¹¹⁾Moreover
the fleet of Hiram,

which brought gold from Ophir, brought
from Ophir a very great amount of
almug wood
and precious stones. ⁽¹²⁾And the
king made of the almug wood
supports
for the house of the LORD,
and for the king's house,
lyres also and harps for the singers;
no such almug wood has come or
been seen,
to this day.

</td>
<td>

the greatness of your wisdom
was not told me;

you
surpass the report which I heard.
⁽⁷⁾Happy are your men!
Happy are these your servants, who
continually stand before you and
hear your wisdom! ⁽⁸⁾Blessed be
the LORD your God, who has delighted
in you and set you on
his throne
as king for the LORD your God!
Because your God loved Israel
and would establish them
for ever, he has made you king
over them,
that you may execute justice and
righteousness." ⁽⁹⁾Then she
gave the king a hundred and twenty
talents of gold, and a very great
quantity of spices,
and precious stones:

there were no spices such
as those which the queen of Sheba
gave to King Solomon.
   ⁽¹⁰⁾Moreover

the servants of Huram and
the servants of Solomon,
who brought gold from Ophir, brought

algum wood
and precious stones. ⁽¹¹⁾And the
king made of the algum wood
. . .*
for the house of the LORD
and for the king's house,
lyres also and harps for the singers;

there never was seen

the like of them before
in the land of Judah.
*Hebrew word uncertain.

</td>
</tr>
</table>

⁽¹³⁾And King Solomon gave to
the queen of Sheba all that she
desired, whatever she asked besides
<u>what was given her by the bounty of
King Solomon.</u>

So she turned and went back to her
own land, with her servants.

⁽¹²⁾And King Solomon gave to
the queen of Sheba all that she
desired, whatever she asked besides

<u>what she had brought to the king.</u>
So she turned and went back to her
own land, with her servants.

69 Solomon's Wealth

I Kings 10:14–29; 4:21

I Kings 10:14–25

⁽¹⁴⁾Now the weight of gold that
came to Solomon in one year was
six hundred and sixty-six talents of
gold, ⁽¹⁵⁾besides that which
<u>came from</u> the traders and
<u>from the traffic of the</u> merchants,
and <u>from</u> all the kings of Arabia and
<u>from</u> the governors of the land.

⁽¹⁶⁾King Solomon made two hundred
large shields of beaten gold;
six hundred shekels of gold
went into each shield. ⁽¹⁷⁾And
he made three hundred shields of
beaten gold;
three <u>minas</u> of gold
went into each shield; and
the king put them in the House of
the Forest of Lebanon.
⁽¹⁸⁾The king also made a great ivory
throne, and overlaid it with
<u>the finest</u> gold.
⁽¹⁹⁾The throne had six steps, and
<u>at the back of the throne was a
calf's head,</u>

and on each side of the seat were
arm rests and two lions standing
beside the arm rests, ⁽²⁰⁾while
twelve lions stood there, one on each
end of a step on the six steps.

II Chronicles 9:13–28; 1:14–17

II Chronicles 9:13–24

⁽¹³⁾Now the weight of gold that
came to Solomon in one year was
six hundred and sixty-six talents of
gold, ⁽¹⁴⁾besides that which
the traders and
merchants <u>brought;</u>
and all the kings of Arabia and
the governors of the land
<u>brought gold and silver to Solomon.</u>
⁽¹⁵⁾King Solomon made two hundred
large shields of beaten gold;
six hundred shekels of <u>beaten</u> gold
went into each shield. ⁽¹⁶⁾And
he made three hundred shields of
beaten gold;
three <u>hundred</u> <u>shekels</u> of gold
went into each shield; and
the king put them in the House of
the Forest of Lebanon.
⁽¹⁷⁾The king also made a great ivory
throne, and overlaid it with
pure gold.
⁽¹⁸⁾The throne had six steps and

<u>a footstool of gold, which were
attached to the throne,</u>
and on each side of the seat were
arm rests and two lions standing
beside the arm rests, ⁽¹⁹⁾while
twelve lions stood there, one on each
end of a step on the six steps.

The like of it was never made
in any kingdom. (21)All King
Solomon's drinking vessels were
of gold, and all the vessels of
the House of the Forest of Lebanon
were of pure gold;
none were of silver, it
was not considered as anything in
the days of Solomon.
(22)For the king had a fleet of ships

of Tarshish
at sea
with the fleet of Hiram.
Once every three years the
fleet of
ships of Tarshish used to come
bringing gold, silver, ivory, apes,
and peacocks.
(23)Thus King Solomon excelled
all the kings of the earth in riches
and in wisdom.
(24)And the whole earth
sought the presence of Solomon to hear
his wisdom, which God had put into his
mind. (25)Every one of them brought
his present, articles of silver and
gold, garments, myrrh, spices, horses,
and mules, so much year by year.

The like of it was never made
in any kingdom. (20)All King
Solomon's drinking vessels were
of gold, and all the vessels of
the House of the Forest of Lebanon
were of pure gold;
silver
was not considered as anything in
the days of Solomon.
(21)For the king's ships
went
to Tarshish

with the servants of Huram;
once every three years the

ships of Tarshish used to come
bringing gold, silver, ivory, apes,
and peacocks.
(22)Thus King Solomon excelled
all the kings of the earth in riches
and in wisdom.
(23)And all the kings of the earth
sought the presence of Solomon to hear
his wisdom, which God had put into his
mind. (24)Every one of them brought
his present, articles of silver and of
gold, garments, myrrh, spices, horses,
and mules, so much year by year.

I Kings 10:26

(26)And Solomon
gathered together

chariots and horsemen;
he had fourteen hundred
chariots and
twelve thousand
horsemen, whom he
stationed in the chariot
cities and with the king
in Jerusalem.

I Kings 4:21

Solomon ruled
over all the kingdoms
from the Euphrates to

II Chronicles 1:14–17

(14)Solomon
gathered together

chariots and horsemen;
he had fourteen hundred
chariots and
twelve thousand
horsemen, whom he
stationed in the chariot
cities and with the king
in Jerusalem.

II Chronicles 9:25–28

(25)And Solomon

had four thousand stalls
for horses and chariots,

and
twelve thousand
horsemen, whom he
stationed in the chariot
cities and with the king
in Jerusalem.

(26)And he ruled
over all the kings
from the Euphrates to

132

the land of the
Philistines and to the
border of Egypt;
<u>they brought tribute
and served Solomon all
the days of his life.</u>

the land of the
Philistines, and to the
border of Egypt.

I Kings 10:27–29

(27)And the king made
silver
as common in Jerusalem
as stone, and he made
cedar as plentiful as
the sycamore of the
Shephelah. (28)And
<u>Solomon's import of</u>
horses <u>was</u>

(15)And the king made
silver and gold
as common in Jerusalem
as stone, and he made
cedar as plentiful as
the sycamore of the
Shephelah. /16/And
Solomon's import of
horses was

/27/And the king made
silver
as common in Jerusalem
as stone, and he made
cedar as plentiful as
the sycamore of the
Shephelah. (28)And

horses <u>were imported
for Solomon</u>
from Egypt
<u>and from all lands.</u>

from Egypt <u>and Kue,</u>

from Egypt and Kue,

and the king's traders
received them from Kue
at a price.
(29)A chariot could be
imported from Egypt
for six hundred shekels
of silver, and a horse
for a hundred and fifty;
and so through
the king's traders
they were exported to
all the kings of the
Hittites and the kings
of Syria.

and the king's traders
received them from Kue
at a price.
/17/They imported
a chariot from Egypt
for six hundred shekels
of silver, and a horse
for a hundred and fifty;
and so through
them
they were exported to
all the kings of the
Hittites and the kings
of Syria.

70 Solomon's Sins and Ahijah's Prophecy

I Kings 11:1–40

(1)Now King Solomon loved many foreign women: the daughter of Pharaoh, and Moabite, Ammonite, Edomite, Sidonian, and Hittite women, (2)from the nations concerning which the LORD had said to the people of Israel, "You shall not enter into marriage with them, neither shall they with you, for surely they will turn away your heart after their gods"; Solomon clung to these in love. (3)He had seven hundred wives, princesses, and three hundred concubines; and his wives turned away his heart. (4)For

133

when Solomon was old his wives turned away his heart after other gods; and his heart was not wholly true to the LORD his God, as was the heart of David his father. [5]For Solomon went after Ashtoreth the goddess of the Sidonians, and after Milcom the abomination of the Ammonites. [6]So Solomon did what was evil in the sight of the LORD, and did not wholly follow the LORD, as David his father had done. [7]Then Solomon built a high place for Chemosh the abomination of Moab, and for Molech the abomination of the Ammonites, on the mountain east of Jerusalem. [8]And so he did for all his foreign wives, who burned incense and sacrificed to their gods.

[9]And the LORD was angry with Solomon, because his heart had turned away from the LORD, the God of Israel, who had appeared to him twice, [10]and had commanded him concerning this thing, that he should not go after other gods; but he did not keep what the LORD commanded. [11]Therefore the LORD said to Solomon, "Since this has been your mind and you have not kept my covenant and my statutes which I have commanded you, I will surely tear the kingdom from you and will give it to your servant. [12]Yet for the sake of David your father I will not do it in your days, but I will tear it out of the hand of your son. [13]However I will not tear away all the kingdom; but I will give one tribe to your son, for the sake of David my servant and for the sake of Jerusalem which I have chosen."

[14]And the LORD raised up an adversary against Solomon, Hadad the Edomite; he was of the royal house in Edom. [15]For when David was in Edom, and Joab the commander of the army went up to bury the slain, he slew every male in Edom [16](for Joab and all Israel remained there six months, until he had cut off every male in Edom); [17]but Hadad fled to Egypt, together with certain Edomites of his father's servants, Hadad being yet a little child. [18]They set out from Midian and came to Paran, and took men with them from Paran and came to Egypt, to Pharaoh king of Egypt, who gave him a house, and assigned him an allowance of food, and gave him land. [19]And Hadad found great favor in the sight of Pharaoh, so that he gave him in marriage the sister of his own wife, the sister of Tahpenes the queen. [20]And the sister of Tahpenes bore him Genubath his son, whom Tahpenes weaned in Pharaoh's house; and Genubath was in Pharaoh's house among the sons of Pharaoh. [21]But when Hadad heard in Egypt that David slept with his fathers and that Joab the commander of the army was dead, Hadad said to Pharaoh, "Let me depart, that I may go to my own country." [22]But Pharaoh said to him, "What have you lacked with me that you are now seeking to go to your own country?" And he said to him, "Only let me go."

[23]God also raised up as an adversary to him, Rezon the son of Eliada, who had fled from his master Hadad-ezer king of Zobah. [24]And he gathered men about him and became leader of a marauding band, after the slaughter by David; and they went to Damascus, and dwelt there, and made him king in Damascus. [25]He was an adversary of Israel all the days of Solomon, doing mischief as Hadad did; and he abhorred Israel, and reigned over Syria.

[26]Jeroboam the son of Nebat, an Ephraimite of Zeredah, a servant of Solomon, whose mother's name was Zeruah, a widow, also lifted up his hand against the king. [27]And this was the reason why he lifted up his hand against the king. Solomon built the Millo, and closed up the breach of the city of David his father. [28]The man Jeroboam was very able, and when Solomon saw that the young man was industrious he gave him charge over all the forced labor of the house of Joseph. [29]And at that time, when Jeroboam went out of Jerusalem, the prophet Ahijah the Shilonite found him on the

road. Now Ahijah had clad himself with a new garment; and the two of them were alone in the open country. (30)Then Ahijah laid hold of the new garment that was on him, and tore it into twelve pieces. (31)And he said to Jeroboam, "Take for yourself ten pieces; for thus says the LORD, the God of Israel, 'Behold, I am about to tear the kingdom from the hand of Solomon, and will give you ten tribes (32)(but he shall have one tribe, for the sake of my servant David and for the sake of Jerusalem, the city which I have chosen out of all the tribes of Israel), (33)because he has forsaken me, and worshiped Ashtoreth the goddess of the Sidonians, Chemosh the god of Moab, and Milcom the god of the Ammonites, and has not walked in my ways, doing what is right in my sight and keeping my statutes and my ordinances, as David his father did. (34)Nevertheless I will not take the whole kingdom out of his hand; but I will make him ruler all the days of his life, for the sake of David my servant whom I chose, who kept my commandments and my statutes; (35)but I will take the kingdom out of his son's hand, and will give it to you, ten tribes. (36)Yet to his son I will give one tribe, that David my servant may always have a lamp before me in Jerusalem, the city where I have chosen to put my name. (37)And I will take you, and you shall reign over all that your soul desires, and you shall be king over Israel. (38)And if you will hearken to all that I command you, and will walk in my ways, and do what is right in my eyes by keeping my statutes and my commandments, as David my servant did, I will be with you, and will build you a sure house, as I built for David, and I will give Israel to you. (39)And I will for this afflict the descendants of David, but not for ever.' " (40)Solomon sought therefore to kill Jeroboam; but Jeroboam arose, and fled into Egypt, to Shishak king of Egypt, and was in Egypt until the death of Solomon.

71 The Death of Solomon

I Kings 11:41–43

(41)Now the rest of the acts of Solomon,
and all that he did, and his wisdom,

are they not written in the
book of the acts of Solomon?

(42)And the time that
Solomon reigned in Jerusalem over all
Israel was forty years. (43)And
Solomon slept with his fathers, and
was buried in the city of David his
father; and Rehoboam his son reigned
in his stead.

II Chronicles 9:29–31

(29)Now the rest of the acts of Solomon,

from first to last,
are they not written in the

history of Nathan the prophet,
and in the prophecy of Ahijah the Shilonite, and in the visions of Iddo the seer concerning Jeroboam the son of Nebat?

(30)Solomon reigned in Jerusalem over all Israel forty years. (31)And Solomon slept with his fathers, and was buried in the city of David his father; and Rehoboam his son reigned in his stead.

72 Israel's Rebellion

I Kings 12:1–24	*II Chronicles 10:1–11:4*
(1)Rehoboam went to Shechem, for all Israel had come to Shechem to make him king. (2)And when Jeroboam the son of Nebat heard of it (for he was <u>still</u> in Egypt, whither he had fled from King Solomon), then Jeroboam <u>dwelt in</u> Egypt. (3)And they sent and called him; and Jeroboam and all <u>the assembly of</u> Israel came and said to Rehoboam, (4)"Your father made our yoke heavy. Now therefore lighten the hard service of your father and his heavy yoke upon us, and we will serve you." (5)He said to them, <u>"Depart for three days,</u> <u>then</u> come <u>again</u> to me."	(1)Rehoboam went to Shechem, for all Israel had come to Shechem to make him king. (2)And when Jeroboam the son of Nebat heard of it (for he was in Egypt, whither he had fled from King Solomon), then Jeroboam <u>returned from</u> Egypt. (3)And they sent and called him; and Jeroboam and all Israel came and said to Rehoboam, (4)"Your father made our yoke heavy. Now therefore lighten the hard service of your father and his heavy yoke upon us, and we will serve you." (5)He said to them, "Come to me <u>again</u> <u>in</u> three <u>days."</u>
So the people went away. (6)Then King Rehoboam took counsel with the old men, who had stood before Solomon his father while he was yet alive, saying, "How do you advise me to answer this people?" (7)And they said to him, "If you will be <u>a servant to this people today</u> <u>and serve them,</u>	So the people went away. (6)Then King Rehoboam took counsel with the old men, who had stood before Solomon his father while he was yet alive, saying, "How do you advise me to answer this people?" (7)And they said to him, "If you will be <u>kind to this people</u> <u>and please them,</u>
and speak good words to them <u>when you answer them,</u> then they will be your servants for ever." (8)But he forsook the counsel which the old men gave him, and took counsel with the young men who had grown up with him and stood before him. (9)And he said to them, "What do you advise that we answer this people who have said to me, 'Lighten the yoke that your father put upon us'?" (10)And the	and speak good words to them, then they will be your servants for ever." (8)But he forsook the counsel which the old men gave him, and took counsel with the young men who had grown up with him and stood before him. (9)And he said to them, "What do you advise that we answer this people who have said to me, 'Lighten the yoke that your father put upon us'?" (10)And the

young men who had grown up with him
said to him, "Thus shall you speak to
this people who said to you, 'Your
father made our yoke heavy, but do
you lighten it for us'; thus shall
you say to them, 'My little finger
is thicker than my father's loins.
(11)And now, whereas my father laid
upon you a heavy yoke, I will add to
your yoke. My father chastised you
with whips, but I will chastise you
with scorpions.' "
(12)So Jeroboam and all the
people came to Rehoboam the third day,
as the king said, "Come to me again
the third day." (13)And the king
answered the people harshly, and
forsaking the counsel
which the old men had given him,
(14)he spoke to them
according to the counsel of the young
men, saying, "My father made your yoke
heavy, but I will add to your yoke;
my father chastised you with whips,
but I will chastise you with
scorpions." (15)So the king did not
hearken to the people; for it was a
turn of affairs brought about by
the LORD that he might fulfil his
word, which the LORD spoke by Ahijah
the Shilonite to Jeroboam the son
of Nebat.
(16)And when all Israel saw that
the king did not hearken to them,
the people answered the king,

"What portion have we in David?
  We have no inheritance in the
    son of Jesse.
To your tents, O Israel!
  Look now to your own house,
    David."

So Israel departed to their tents.
(17)But Rehoboam reigned over the
people of Israel who dwelt in the
cities of Judah. (18)Then King

young men who had grown up with him
said to him, "Thus shall you speak to
the people who said to you, 'Your
father made our yoke heavy, but do
you lighten it for us'; thus shall
you say to them, 'My little finger
is thicker than my father's loins.
(11)And now, whereas my father laid
upon you a heavy yoke, I will add to
your yoke. My father chastised you
with whips, but I will chastise you
with scorpions.' "
(12)So Jeroboam and all the
people came to Rehoboam the third day,
as the king said, "Come to me again
the third day." (13)And the king
answered them harshly, and
forsaking the counsel
of the old men,
(14)King Rehoboam spoke to them
according to the counsel of the young
men, saying, "My father made your yoke
heavy, but I will add to it;
my father chastised you with whips,
but I will chastise you with
scorpions." (15)So the king did not
hearken to the people; for it was a
turn of affairs brought about by
God that the LORD might fulfil his
word, which he spoke by Ahijah
the Shilonite to Jeroboam the son
of Nebat.
(16)And when all Israel saw that
the king did not hearken to them,
the people answered the king,

"What portion have we in David?
  We have no inheritance in the
    son of Jesse.
Each of you to your tents, O Israel!
  Look now to your own house,
    David."

So all Israel departed to their tents.
(17)But Rehoboam reigned over the
people of Israel who dwelt in the
cities of Judah. (18)Then King

Rehoboam sent <u>Ad</u>oram, who was
taskmaster over the forced labor,
and <u>all</u> Israel stoned him
to death with stones. And King
Rehoboam made haste to mount his
chariot, to flee to Jerusalem.
⁽¹⁹⁾So Israel has been in
rebellion against the house
of David to this day.
⁽²⁰⁾And when all Israel heard that
Jeroboam had returned, they sent and
called him to the assembly and made
him king over all Israel. There was
none that followed the house of David,
but the tribe of Judah only.
  ⁽²¹⁾When Rehoboam came to
Jerusalem, he assembled <u>all</u> the house
of Judah, and <u>the tribe of</u> Benjamin,
a hundred and eighty thousand chosen
warriors, to fight against <u>the house of</u>
Israel, to restore the kingdom to
Rehoboam
<u>the son of Solomon.</u>
⁽²²⁾But the word of <u>God</u> came
to Shemaiah the man of God:
⁽²³⁾"Say to Rehoboam the son of
Solomon, king of Judah, and to all
<u>the house of</u>
Judah and Benjamin,
<u>and to the rest of the people,</u>
⁽²⁴⁾'Thus says the LORD, You shall
not go up or fight against your
kinsmen <u>the people of Israel.</u>
Return every man to his home, for
this thing is from me.' " So they
hearkened to the word of the LORD,
and <u>went home again,</u>
<u>according to the word of the LORD.</u>

Rehoboam sent <u>Had</u>oram, who was
taskmaster over the forced labor,
and <u>the people of</u> Israel stoned him
to death with stones. And King
Rehoboam made haste to mount his
chariot, to flee to Jerusalem.
⁽¹⁹⁾So Israel has been in
rebellion against the house
of David to this day.

  ^(11:1)When Rehoboam came to
Jerusalem, he assembled the house
of Judah, and Benjamin,
a hundred and eighty thousand chosen
warriors, to fight against
Israel, to restore the kingdom to
Rehoboam.

⁽²⁾But the word of <u>the LORD</u> came
to Shemaiah the man of God:
⁽³⁾"Say to Rehoboam the son of
Solomon king of Judah, and to all
<u>Israel in</u>
Judah and Benjamin,

/4/'Thus says the LORD, You shall
not go up or fight against your
kinsmen.
Return every man to his home, for
this thing is from me.' " So they
hearkened to the word of the LORD,
and <u>returned</u>

<u>and did not go against Jeroboam.</u>

73 The Enterprises of Jeroboam

I Kings 12:25–33

⁽²⁵⁾Then Jeroboam built Shechem in the hill country of Ephraim, and dwelt there;
and he went out from there and built Penuel. ⁽²⁶⁾And Jeroboam said in his heart, "Now

the kingdom will turn back to the house of David; (27)if this people go up to offer sacrifices in the house of the LORD at Jerusalem, then the heart of this people will turn again to their lord, to Rehoboam king of Judah, and they will kill me and return to Rehoboam king of Judah." (28)So the king took counsel, and made two calves of gold. And he said to the people, "You have gone up to Jerusalem long enough. Behold your gods, O Israel, who brought you up out of the land of Egypt." (29)And he set one in Bethel, and the other he put in Dan. (30)And this thing became a sin, for the people went to the one at Bethel and to the other as far as Dan. (31)He also made houses on high places, and appointed priests from among all the people, who were not of the Levites. (32)And Jeroboam appointed a feast on the fifteenth day of the eighth month like the feast that was in Judah, and he offered sacrifices upon the altar; so he did in Bethel, sacrificing to the calves that he had made. And he placed in Bethel the priests of the high places that he had made. (33)He went up to the altar which he had made in Bethel on the fifteenth day in the eighth month, in the month which he had devised of his own heart; and he ordained a feast for the people of Israel, and went up to the altar to burn incense.

74 The Enterprises of Rehoboam

II Chronicles 11:5–23

(5)Rehoboam dwelt in Jerusalem, and he built cities for defense in Judah. (6)He built Bethlehem, Etam, Tekoa, (7)Beth-zur, Soco, Adullam, (8)Gath, Mareshah, Ziph, (9)Adoraim, Lachish, Azekah, (10)Zorah, Aijalon, and Hebron, fortified cities which are in Judah and in Benjamin. (11)He made the fortresses strong, and put commanders in them, and stores of food, oil, and wine. (12)And he put shields and spears in all the cities, and made them very strong. So he held Judah and Benjamin.

(13)And the priests and the Levites that were in all Israel resorted to him from all places where they lived. (14)For the Levites left their common lands and their holdings and came to Judah and Jerusalem, because Jeroboam and his sons cast them out from serving as priests of the LORD, (15)and he appointed his own priests for the high places, and for the satyrs, and for the calves which he had made. (16)And those who had set their hearts to seek the LORD God of Israel came after them from all the tribes of Israel to Jerusalem to sacrifice to the LORD, the God of their fathers. (17)They strengthened the kingdom of Judah, and for three years they made Rehoboam the son of Solomon secure, for they walked for three years in the way of David and Solomon.

(18)Rehoboam took as wife Mahalath the daughter of Jerimoth the son of David, and of Abihail the daughter of Eliab the son of Jesse; (19)and she bore him sons, Jeush, Shemariah, and Zaham. (20)After her he took Maacah the daughter of Absalom, who bore him Abijah, Attai, Ziza, and Shelomith. (21)Rehoboam loved Maacah the daughter of Absalom above all his wives and concubines (he took eighteen wives and sixty concubines, and had twenty-eight sons and sixty daughters); (22)and Rehoboam appointed Abijah the son of Maacah as chief prince among his brothers, for he intended to make him king. (23)And he dealt wisely, and distributed some of his sons through all the districts of Judah and Benjamin, in all the fortified cities; and he gave them abundant provisions, and procured wives for them.

75 The Tale of a Prophet From Judah

I Kings 13:1–34

(1)And behold, a man of God came out of Judah by the word of the LORD to Bethel. Jeroboam was standing by the altar to burn incense. (2)And the man cried against the altar by the word of the LORD, and said, "O altar, altar, thus says the LORD: 'Behold, a son shall be born to the house of David, Josiah by name; and he shall sacrifice upon you the priests of the high places who burn incense upon you, and men's bones shall be burned upon you.' " (3)And he gave a sign the same day, saying, "This is the sign that the LORD has spoken: 'Behold, the altar shall be torn down, and the ashes that are upon it shall be poured out.' " (4)And when the king heard the saying of the man of God, which he cried against the altar at Bethel, Jeroboam stretched out his hand from the altar, saying, "Lay hold of him." And his hand, which he stretched out against him, dried up, so that he could not draw it back to himself. (5)The altar also was torn down, and the ashes poured out from the altar, according to the sign which the man of God had given by the word of the LORD. (6)And the king said to the man of God, "Entreat now the favor of the LORD your God, and pray for me, that my hand may be restored to me." And the man of God entreated the LORD; and the king's hand was restored to him, and became as it was before. (7)And the king said to the man of God, "Come home with me, and refresh yourself, and I will give you a reward." (8)And the man of God said to the king, "If you give me half your house, I will not go in with you. And I will not eat bread or drink water in this place; (9)for so was it commanded me by the word of the LORD, saying, 'You shall neither eat bread, nor drink water, nor return by the way that you came.' " (10)So he went another way, and did not return by the way that he came to Bethel.

(11)Now there dwelt an old prophet in Bethel. And his sons came and told him all that the man of God had done that day in Bethel; the words also which he had spoken to the king, they told to their father. (12)And their father said to them, "Which way did he go?" And his sons showed him the way which the man of God who came from Judah had gone. (13)And he said to his sons, "Saddle the ass for me." So they saddled the ass for him and he mounted it. (14)And he went after the man of God, and found him sitting under an oak; and he said to him, "Are you the man of God who came from Judah?" And he said, "I am." (15)Then he said to him, "Come home with me and eat bread." (16)And he said, "I may not return with you, or go in with you; neither will I eat bread nor drink water with you in this place; (17)for it was said to me by the word of the LORD, 'You shall neither eat bread nor drink water there, nor return by the way that you came.' " (18)And he said to him, "I also am a prophet as you are, and an angel spoke to me by the word of the LORD, saying, 'Bring him back with you into your house that he may eat bread and drink water.' " But he lied to him. (19)So he went back with him, and ate bread in his house, and drank water.

(20)And as they sat at the table, the word of the LORD came to the prophet who had brought him back; (21)and he cried to the man of God who came from Judah, "Thus says the LORD, 'Because you have disobeyed the word of the LORD, and have not kept the commandment which the LORD your God commanded you, (22)but have come back, and have eaten bread and drunk water in the place of which he said to you, "Eat no bread, and drink no water"; your body shall not come to the tomb of your fathers.' "

(23)And after he had eaten bread and drunk, he saddled the ass for the prophet whom he had brought back. (24)And as he went away a lion met him on the road and killed him. And his body was thrown in the road, and the ass stood beside it; the lion also stood beside the body. (25)And behold, men passed by, and saw the body thrown in the road, and the lion standing by the body. And they came and told it in the city where the old prophet dwelt.

(26)And when the prophet who had brought him back from the way heard of it, he said, "It is the man of God, who disobeyed the word of the LORD; therefore the LORD has given him to the lion, which has torn him and slain him, according to the word which the LORD spoke to him." (27)And he said to his sons, "Saddle the ass for me." And they saddled it. (28)And he went and found his body thrown in the road, and the ass and the lion standing beside the body. The lion had not eaten the body or torn the ass. (29)And the prophet took up the body of the man of God and laid it upon the ass, and brought it back to the city, to mourn and to bury him. (30)And he laid the body in his own grave; and they mourned over him, saying, "Alas, my brother!" (31)And after he had buried him, he said to his sons, "When I die, bury me in the grave in which the man of God is buried; lay my bones beside his bones. (32)For the saying which he cried by the word of the LORD against the altar in Bethel, and against all the houses of the high places which are in the cities of Samaria, shall surely come to pass."

(33)After this thing Jeroboam did not turn from his evil way, but made priests for the high places again from among all the people; any who would, he consecrated to be priests of the high places. (34)And this thing became sin to the house of Jeroboam, so as to cut it off and to destroy it from the face of the earth.

76 Ahijah's Judgment Upon Jeroboam

I Kings 14:1–20

(1)At that time Abijah the son of Jeroboam fell sick. (2)And Jeroboam said to his wife, "Arise, and disguise yourself, that it be not known that you are the wife of Jeroboam, and go to Shiloh; behold, Ahijah the prophet is there, who said of me that I should be king over this people. (3)Take with you ten loaves, some cakes, and a jar of honey, and go to him; he will tell you what shall happen to the child."

(4)Jeroboam's wife did so; she arose, and went to Shiloh, and came to the house of Ahijah. Now Ahijah could not see, for his eyes were dim because of his age. (5)And the LORD said to Ahijah, "Behold, the wife of Jeroboam is coming to inquire of you concerning her son; for he is sick. Thus and thus shall you say to her."

When she came, she pretended to be another woman. (6)But when Ahijah heard the sound of her feet, as she came in at the door, he said, "Come in, wife of Jeroboam; why do you pretend to be another? For I am charged with heavy tidings for you. (7)Go, tell Jeroboam, 'Thus says the LORD, the God of Israel: "Because I exalted you from among the people, and made you leader over my people Israel, (8)and tore the kingdom away from the house of David and gave it to you; and yet you have not been like my servant David, who kept my commandments, and followed me with all his heart, doing only that which was right in my eyes, (9)but you have done evil above all that were before you and have gone and made for yourself other gods, and molten images, provoking me to anger, and have cast me behind your back; [10]therefore behold, I will bring evil upon the house of Jeroboam, and will cut off from Jeroboam every male, both bond and free in Israel, and will utterly consume the house of Jeroboam, as a man burns up dung until it is all gone. [11]Any one belonging to Jeroboam who dies in the city the dogs shall eat; and any one who dies in the open country the birds of the air shall eat; for the LORD has spoken it." ' [12]Arise therefore, go to your house. When your feet enter the city, the child shall die. [13]And all Israel shall mourn for him, and bury him; for he only of Jeroboam shall come to the grave, because in him there is found something pleasing to the LORD, the God of Israel, in the house of Jeroboam. [14]Moreover the LORD will raise up for himself a king over Israel, who shall cut off the house of Jeroboam today. And henceforth [15]the LORD will smite Israel, as a reed is shaken in the water, and root up Israel out of this good land which he gave to their fathers, and scatter them beyond the Euphrates, because they have made their Asherim, provoking the LORD to anger. [16]And he will give Israel up because of the sins of Jeroboam, which he sinned and which he made Israel to sin."

[17]Then Jeroboam's wife arose, and departed, and came to Tirzah. And as she came to the threshold of the house, the child died. [18]And all Israel buried him and mourned for him, according to the word of the LORD, which he spoke by his servant Ahijah the prophet. [19]Now the rest of the acts of Jeroboam, how he warred and how he reigned, behold, they are written in the Book of the Chronicles of the Kings of Israel. [20]And the time that Jeroboam reigned was twenty-two years; and he slept with his fathers, and Nadab his son reigned in his stead.

77 Judah Under Rehoboam

I Kings 14:21-31   II Chronicles 12:1-16

[21]Now Rehoboam the son of Solomon reigned in Judah. Rehoboam was forty-one years old when he began to reign, and he reigned seventeen years in Jerusalem, the city which the LORD had chosen out of all the tribes of Israel, to put his name there. His mother's name was Naamah the Ammonitess. [22]And Judah did what was evil in the sight of the LORD, and they provoked him to jealousy with their sins which they committed, more than all that their fathers had done. [23]For they also built for themselves high places, and pillars, and Asherim on every high hill and under every green tree; [24]and there were also male cult prostitutes in the land. They did

according to all the abominations of
the nations which the LORD drove out
before the people of Israel.

(1)When the rule of Rehoboam was
established and was strong, he forsook
the law of the LORD, and all Israel
with him.

(25)In the fifth year of King
Rehoboam,

(2)In the fifth year of King
Rehoboam,
because they had been unfaithful
to the LORD,

Shishak king of Egypt came up against
Jerusalem;

Shishak king of Egypt came up against
Jerusalem
(3)with twelve hundred chariots and
sixty thousand horsemen. And the
people were without number who came
with him from Egypt—Libyans, Sukkiim,
and Ethiopians. (4)And he took the
fortified cities of Judah and came as
far as Jerusalem. (5)Then Shemaiah
the prophet came to Rehoboam and to
the princes of Judah, who had gathered
at Jerusalem because of Shishak, and
said to them, "Thus says the LORD,
'You abandoned me, so I have
abandoned
you to the hand of Shishak.' "
(6)Then the princes of Israel and
the king humbled themselves and said,
"The LORD is righteous." (7)When
the LORD saw that they humbled
themselves, the word of the LORD came
to Shemaiah: "They have humbled
themselves; I will not destroy them,
but I will grant them some
deliverance, and my wrath shall not
be poured out upon Jerusalem by the
hand of Shishak. (8)Nevertheless
they shall be servants to him, that
they may know my service and the
service of the kingdoms of the
countries."
(9)So Shishak king of Egypt came
up against Jerusalem;

(26)he took away the treasures of
the house of the LORD and the
treasures of the king's house;

he took away the treasures of
the house of the LORD and the
treasures of the king's house;

he took away everything. He also
took away all the shields of gold
which Solomon had made; (27)and
King Rehoboam made in their stead
shields of bronze, and committed
them to the hands of the officers
of the guard, who kept the door of
the king's house. (28)And as often
as the king went into the house of
the LORD, the guard
bore them and brought them back to
the guardroom.

(29)Now the rest of the acts
of Rehoboam,
and all that he did,

are they not written in the
Book of the Chronicles of
the Kings of Judah?

(30)And there was war
between Rehoboam and Jeroboam
continually.
(31)And Rehoboam slept with his
fathers and was buried
with his fathers
in the city of David.

he took away everything. He also
took away the shields of gold
which Solomon had made; (10)and
King Rehoboam made in their stead
shields of bronze, and committed
them to the hands of the officers
of the guard, who kept the door of
the king's house. (11)And as often
as the king went into the house of
the LORD, the guard came and
bore them, and brought them back to
the guardroom.
(12)And when he humbled himself
the wrath of the LORD turned from him,
so as not to make a complete
destruction; moreover, conditions
were good in Judah.
(13)So King Rehoboam established
himself in Jerusalem and reigned.
Rehoboam was forty-one years old when
he began to reign, and he reigned
seventeen years in Jerusalem, the
city which the LORD had chosen out
of all the tribes of Israel to put
his name there. His mother's name
was Naamah the Ammonitess.* (14)And
he did evil, for he did not set his
heart to seek the LORD.
(15)Now the acts
of Rehoboam,

from first to last,
are they not written in the
chronicles of

Shemaiah the prophet and of
Iddo the seer?
There were continual wars
between Rehoboam and Jeroboam.

(16)And Rehoboam slept with his
fathers, and was buried

in the city of David;

*Cf. I Kings 14:21.

His mother's name was Naamah
the Ammonitess.
And Abijam his son reigned
in his stead.

and Abijah his son reigned
in his stead.

78 The Reign of Abijam/Abijah Begins

I Kings 15:1–6

(1)Now in the eighteenth year
of King Jeroboam
the son of Nebat,
Abijam began to reign over Judah.
(2)He reigned for three years in
Jerusalem. His mother's name was
Maacah the daughter of Abishalom.

(3)And he walked in all the sins
which his father did before him; and
his heart was not wholly true to the
LORD his God, as the heart of David
his father. (4)Nevertheless for
David's sake the LORD his God gave
him a lamp in Jerusalem, setting up
his son after him, and establishing
Jerusalem; (5)because David did
what was right in the eyes of the
LORD, and did not turn aside from
anything that he commanded him all
the days of his life, except in the
matter of Uriah the Hittite.
(6)Now there was war between
Rehoboam and Jeroboam all the days
of his life.

II Chronicles 13:1–2

(1)In the eighteenth year
of King Jeroboam

Abijah began to reign over Judah.
(2)He reigned for three years in
Jerusalem. His mother's name was
Micaiah the daughter of Uriel of
Gibe-ah.

Now there was war between Abijah
and Jeroboam.*

79 Abijam/Abijah Struggles Against Jeroboam

II Chronicles 13:3–21

(3)Abijah went out to battle having an army of valiant men of war, four hundred
thousand picked men; and Jeroboam drew up his line of battle against him with eight
hundred thousand picked mighty warriors. (4)Then Abijah stood up on Mount Zemaraim
which is in the hill country of Ephraim, and said, "Hear me, O Jeroboam and all Israel!

*Cf. I Kings 15:7.

(5)Ought you not to know that the LORD God of Israel gave the kingship over Israel for ever to David and his sons by a covenant of salt? (6)Yet Jeroboam the son of Nebat, a servant of Solomon the son of David, rose up and rebelled against his lord; (7)and certain worthless scoundrels gathered about him and defied Rehoboam the son of Solomon, when Rehoboam was young and irresolute and could not withstand them.

(8)"And now you think to withstand the kingdom of the LORD in the hand of the sons of David, because you are a great multitude and have with you the golden calves which Jeroboam made you for gods. (9)Have you not driven out the priests of the LORD, the sons of Aaron, and the Levites, and made priests for yourselves like the peoples of other lands? Whoever comes to consecrate himself with a young bull or seven rams becomes a priest of what are no gods. (10)But as for us, the LORD is our God, and we have not forsaken him. We have priests ministering to the LORD who are sons of Aaron, and Levites for their service. (11)They offer to the LORD every morning and every evening burnt offerings and incense of sweet spices, set out the showbread on the table of pure gold, and care for the golden lampstand that its lamps may burn every evening; for we keep the charge of the LORD our God, but you have forsaken him. (12)Behold, God is with us at our head, and his priests with their battle trumpets to sound the call to battle against you. O sons of Israel, do not fight against the LORD, the God of your fathers; for you cannot succeed."

(13)Jeroboam had sent an ambush around to come on them from behind; thus his troops were in front of Judah, and the ambush was behind them. (14)And when Judah looked, behold, the battle was before and behind them; and they cried to the LORD, and the priests blew the trumpets. (15)Then the men of Judah raised the battle shout. And when the men of Judah shouted, God defeated Jeroboam and all Israel before Abijah and Judah. (16)The men of Israel fled before Judah, and God gave them into their hand. (17)Abijah and his people slew them with a great slaughter; so there fell slain of Israel five hundred thousand picked men. (18)Thus the men of Israel were subdued at that time, and the men of Judah prevailed, because they relied upon the LORD, the God of their fathers. (19)And Abijah pursued Jeroboam, and took cities from him, Bethel with its villages and Jeshanah with its villages and Ephron with its villages. (20)Jeroboam did not recover his power in the days of Abijah; and the LORD smote him, and he died. (21)But Abijah grew mighty. And he took fourteen wives, and had twenty-two sons and sixteen daughters.

80 The Reign of Abijam/Abijah Concludes

I Kings 15:7–8	*II Chronicles 13:22–14:1*
(7)The rest of the acts of Abijam, and all that he did,	(22)The rest of the acts of Abijah,
	his ways and his sayings,
are they not written in the Book of the Chronicles of the Kings of Judah?	are written in
	the story of the prophet Iddo.
And there was war between Abijam	

146

_and Jeroboam.⊛

⁽⁸⁾And Abijam slept with his
fathers; and they buried him in
the city of David. And Asa his son
reigned in his stead.

/14:1/And Abijah slept with his
fathers; and they buried him in
the city of David. And Asa his son
reigned in his stead.
In his days the land had rest for
ten years.

81 Asa's Reign Begins

I Kings 15:9–12   *II Chronicles 14:2–5*

⁽⁹⁾In the twentieth year of
Jeroboam king of Israel Asa began to
reign over Judah, ⁽¹⁰⁾and he reigned
forty-one years in Jerusalem. His
mother's name was Maacah the daughter
of Abishalom.

⁽¹¹⁾And Asa did what was

right in the eyes of the LORD,
as David his father had done.

⁽¹²⁾He put away the male cult
prostitutes out of the land, and
removed all the idols that his
fathers had made.

⁽²⁾And Asa did what was
good and
right in the eyes of the LORD

his God.

⁽³⁾He took away the foreign altars
and the high places, and broke down the
pillars and hewed down
the Asherim, ⁽⁴⁾and commanded Judah
to seek the LORD, the God of their
fathers, and to keep the law and the
commandment. ⁽⁵⁾He also took out of
all the cities of Judah the high
places and the incense altars. And
the kingdom had rest under him.

82 Military Affairs of Asa

II Chronicles 14:6–15

⁽⁶⁾He built fortified cities in Judah, for the land had rest. He had no war in those
years, for the LORD gave him peace. ⁽⁷⁾And he said to Judah, "Let us build these cities,

*Cf. II Chron. 13:2.

and surround them with walls and towers, gates and bars; the land is still ours, because we have sought the LORD our God; we have sought him, and he has given us peace on every side." So they built and prospered. (8)And Asa had an army of three hundred thousand from Judah, armed with bucklers and spears, and two hundred and eighty thousand men from Benjamin, that carried shields and drew bows; all these were mighty men of valor.

(9)Zerah the Ethiopian came out against them with an army of a million men and three hundred chariots, and came as far as Mareshah. (10)And Asa went out to meet him, and they drew up their lines of battle in the valley of Zephathah at Mareshah. (11)And Asa cried to the LORD his God, "O LORD, there is none like thee to help, between the mighty and the weak. Help us, O LORD our God, for we rely on thee, and in thy name we have come against this multitude. O LORD, thou art our God; let not man prevail against thee." (12)So the LORD defeated the Ethiopians before Asa and before Judah, and the Ethiopians fled. (13)Asa and the people that were with him pursued them as far as Gerar, and the Ethiopians fell until none remained alive; for they were broken before the LORD and his army. The men of Judah carried away very much booty. (14)And they smote all the cities round about Gerar, for the fear of the LORD was upon them. They plundered all the cities, for there was much plunder in them. (15)And they smote the tents of those who had cattle, and carried away sheep in abundance and camels. Then they returned to Jerusalem.

83 Asa Responds to Azariah's Prophecy

II Chronicles 15:1–15

(1)The Spirit of God came upon Azariah the son of Oded, (2)and he went out to meet Asa, and said to him, "Hear me, Asa, and all Judah and Benjamin: The LORD is with you, while you are with him. If you seek him, he will be found by you, but if you forsake him, he will forsake you. (3)For a long time Israel was without the true God, and without a teaching priest, and without law; (4)but when in their distress they turned to the LORD, the God of Israel, and sought him, he was found by them. (5)In those times there was no peace to him who went out or to him who came in, for great disturbances afflicted all the inhabitants of the lands. (6)They were broken in pieces, nation against nation and city against city, for God troubled them with every sort of distress. (7)But you, take courage! Do not let your hands be weak, for your work shall be rewarded."

(8)When Asa heard these words, the prophecy of Azariah the son of Oded, he took courage, and put away the abominable idols from all the land of Judah and Benjamin and from the cities which he had taken in the hill country of Ephraim, and he repaired the altar of the LORD that was in front of the vestibule of the house of the LORD. (9)And he gathered all Judah and Benjamin, and those from Ephraim, Manasseh, and Simeon who were sojourning with them, for great numbers had deserted to him from Israel when they saw that the LORD his God was with him. (10)They were gathered at Jerusalem in the third month of the fifteenth year of the reign of Asa. (11)They sacrificed to the LORD on that day, from the spoil which they had brought, seven hundred oxen and seven thousand sheep. (12)And they entered into a covenant to seek the LORD, the God of their fathers, with all their heart and with all their soul; (13)and that whoever would not seek the LORD, the God of Israel, should be put to death, whether young or old, man or woman. (14)They took oath to the LORD with a loud voice, and with shouting, and with trumpets, and with horns. (15)And all Judah rejoiced over the oath; for they had sworn with all their heart, and had sought him with their whole desire, and he was found by them, and the LORD gave them rest round about.

84 Asa's Goodness

I Kings 15:13–15

(13)He also removed
Maacah his mother

from being queen mother because
she had an abominable image made for
Asherah; and Asa cut down her image

and burned it at the brook Kidron.
(14)But the high places were not
taken away. Nevertheless
the heart of Asa was wholly true
to the LORD
all his days. (15)And he brought
into the house of the LORD the votive
gifts of his father and his own votive
gifts, silver, and gold, and vessels.

II Chronicles 15:16–19

(16)Even Maacah, his mother,
King Asa removed
from being queen mother because
she had made an abominable image for
Asherah. And Asa cut down her image,
crushed it,
and burned it at the brook Kidron.
/17/But the high places were not
taken out of Israel. Nevertheless
the heart of Asa was wholly true

all his days. (18)And he brought
into the house of God the votive
gifts of his father and his own votive
gifts, silver, and gold, and vessels.
(19)And there was no more war until
the thirty-fifth year of the reign
of Asa.

85 The War of Asa and Baasha

I Kings 15:16–24

(16)And there was war between
Asa and Baasha king of Israel all
their days.

(17)Baasha king of Israel went up
against Judah, and built Ramah, that
he might permit no one to go out or
come in to Asa king of Judah.
(18)Then Asa took all the silver
and the gold that were left in
the treasures of the house of the LORD
and the treasures of the king's house,

II Chronicles 16:1–17:1

(1)In the thirty-sixth year
of the reign of Asa,
Baasha king of Israel went up
against Judah, and built Ramah, that
he might permit no one to go out or
come in to Asa king of Judah.
(2)Then Asa took silver
and gold from
the treasures of the house of the LORD
and the king's house,

149

and gave them into the hands
of his servants;
and King Asa sent them to Ben-hadad
the son of Tabrimmon,
the son of Hezi-on,
king of Syria, who dwelt in Damascus,
saying, (19)"Let there be a league
between me and you, as between my
father and your father: behold, I am
sending to you a present of silver and
gold; go, break your league with
Baasha king of Israel, that he may
withdraw from me." (20)And Ben-hadad
hearkened to King Asa, and sent the
commanders of his armies against the
cities of Israel, and conquered
Ijon, Dan, Abel-beth-maacah, and all
Chinneroth, with all the land of

Naphtali. (21)And when Baasha heard
of it, he stopped building Ramah, and
he dwelt in Tirzeh.

(22)Then King Asa
made a proclamation to

all Judah,
none was exempt,
and they carried away the stones
of Ramah and its timber, with which
Baasha had been building; and with
them King Asa built Geba of Benjamin
and Mizpah.

and sent them to Ben-hadad

king of Syria, who dwelt in Damascus,
saying, (3)"Let there be a league
between me and you, as between my
father and your father: behold, I am
sending to you silver and
gold; go, break your league with
Baasha king of Israel, that he may
withdraw from me." (4)And Ben-hadad
hearkened to King Asa, and sent the
commanders of his armies against the
cities of Israel, and they conquered
Ijon, Dan, Abel-maim, and all

the store-cities of
Naphtali. (5)And when Baasha heard
of it, he stopped building Ramah, and

let his work cease.
/6/Then King Asa

took
all Judah,

and they carried away the stones
of Ramah and its timber, with which
Baasha had been building; and with
them he built Geba
and Mizpah.
(7)At that time Hanani the seer
came to Asa king of Judah, and said
to him, "Because you relied on the
king of Syria, and did not rely on
the LORD your God, the army of the
king of Syria has escaped you.
(8)Were not the Ethiopians and the
Libyans a huge army with exceedingly
many chariots and horsemen? Yet
because you relied on the LORD, he
gave them into your hand. (9)For
the eyes of the LORD run to and fro
throughout the whole earth, to show
his might in behalf of those whose

heart is blameless toward him. You have done foolishly in this; for from now on you will have wars." (10)Then Asa was angry with the seer, and put him in the stocks, in prison, for he was in a rage with him because of this. And Asa inflicted cruelties upon some of the people at the same time.

(23)Now the rest of all the acts of Asa, all his might, and all that he did, and the cities which he built,

(11)The acts of Asa,

are they not written in the Book of the Chronicles of the Kings of Judah? But in his old age

from first to last, are written in the Book of the Kings of Judah and Israel.

(12)In the thirty-ninth year of his reign Asa was diseased in his feet, and his disease became severe; yet even in his disease he did not seek the LORD, but sought help from physicians.

he was diseased in his feet.

(24)And Asa slept with his fathers,

(13)And Asa slept with his fathers, dying in the forty-first year of his reign.
(14)They buried him

and was buried with his fathers

in the tomb which he had hewn out for himself

in the city of David his father;

in the city of David.

They laid him on a bier which had been filled with various kinds of spices prepared by the perfumer's art; and they made a very great fire in his honor.

and Jehoshaphat his son reigned in his stead.

(17:1)Jehoshaphat his son reigned in his stead, and strengthened himself against Israel.

86 The Reign of Nadab

I Kings 15:25–31

(25)Nadab the son of Jeroboam began to reign over Israel in the second year of Asa king of Judah; and he reigned over Israel two years. (26)He did what was evil in the sight

151

of the LORD, and walked in the way of his father, and in his sin which he made Israel to sin. (27)Baasha the son of Ahijah, of the house of Issachar, conspired against him; and Baasha struck him down at Gibbethon, which belonged to the Philistines; for Nadab and all Israel were laying siege to Gibbethon. (28)So Baasha killed him in the third year of Asa king of Judah, and reigned in his stead. (29)And as soon as he was king, he killed all the house of Jeroboam; he left to the house of Jeroboam not one that breathed, until he had destroyed it, according to the word of the LORD which he spoke by his servant Ahijah the Shilonite; (30)it was for the sins of Jeroboam which he sinned and which he made Israel to sin, and because of the anger to which he provoked the LORD, the God of Israel.

(31)Now the rest of the acts of Nadab, and all that he did, are they not written in the Book of the Chronicles of the Kings of Israel?

87 The Reign of Baasha

I Kings 15:32–16:7

(32)And there was war between Asa and Baasha king of Israel all their days.

(33)In the third year of Asa king of Judah, Baasha the son of Ahijah began to reign over all Israel at Tirzah, and he reigned twenty-four years. (34)He did what was evil in the sight of the LORD, and walked in the way of Jeroboam and in his sin which he made Israel to sin.

(16:1)And the word of the LORD came to Jehu the son of Hanani against Baasha, saying, (2)"Since I exalted you out of the dust and made you leader over my people Israel, and you have walked in the way of Jeroboam, and have made my people Israel to sin, provoking me to anger with their sins, (3)behold, I will utterly sweep away Baasha and his house, and I will make your house like the house of Jeroboam the son of Nebat. (4)Any one belonging to Baasha who dies in the city the dogs shall eat; and any one of his who dies in the field the birds of the air shall eat."

(5)Now the rest of the acts of Baasha, and what he did, and his might, are they not written in the Book of the Chronicles of the Kings of Israel? (6)And Baasha slept with his fathers, and was buried at Tirzah; and Elah his son reigned in his stead. (7)Moreover the word of the LORD came by the prophet Jehu the son of Hanani against Baasha and his house, both because of all the evil that he did in the sight of the LORD, provoking him to anger with the work of his hands, in being like the house of Jeroboam, and also because he destroyed it.

88 The Reign of Elah

I Kings 16:8–10

(8)In the twenty-sixth year of Asa king of Judah, Elah the son of Baasha began to reign over Israel in Tirzah, and reigned two years. (9)But his servant Zimri, commander of half his chariots, conspired against him. When he was at Tirzah, drinking himself drunk in the house of Arza, who was over the household in Tirzah, (10)Zimri came in and struck him down and killed him, in the twenty-seventh year of Asa king of Judah, and reigned in his stead.

89 The Reign of Zimri

I Kings 16:11–20

(11)When he began to reign, as soon as he had seated himself on his throne, he killed all the house of Baasha; he did not leave him a single male of his kinsmen or his friends. (12)Thus Zimri destroyed all the house of Baasha, according to the word of the LORD, which he spoke against Baasha by Jehu the prophet, (13)for all the sins of Baasha and the sins of Elah his son which they sinned, and which they made Israel to sin, provoking the LORD God of Israel to anger with their idols. (14)Now the rest of the acts of Elah, and all that he did, are they not written in the Book of the Chronicles of the Kings of Israel?

(15)In the twenty-seventh year of Asa king of Judah, Zimri reigned seven days in Tirzah. Now the troops were encamped against Gibbethon, which belonged to the Philistines, (16)and the troops who were encamped heard it said, "Zimri has conspired, and he has killed the king"; therefore all Israel made Omri, the commander of the army, king over Israel that day in the camp. (17)So Omri went up from Gibbethon, and all Israel with him, and they besieged Tirzah. (18)And when Zimri saw that the city was taken, he went into the citadel of the king's house, and burned the king's house over him with fire, and died, (19)because of his sins which he committed, doing evil in the sight of the LORD, walking in the way of Jeroboam, and for his sin which he committed, making Israel to sin. (20)Now the rest of the acts of Zimri, and the conspiracy which he made, are they not written in the Book of the Chronicles of the Kings of Israel?

90 The Reign of Omri

I Kings 16:21–28

(21)Then the people of Israel were divided into two parts; half of the people followed Tibni the son of Ginath, to make him king, and half followed Omri. (22)But the people who followed Omri overcame the people who followed Tibni the son of Ginath; so Tibni died, and Omri became king. (23)In the thirty-first year of Asa king of Judah, Omri began to reign over Israel, and reigned for twelve years; six years he reigned in Tirzah. (24)He bought the hill of Samaria from Shemer for two talents of silver; and he fortified the hill, and called the name of the city which he built, Samaria, after the name of Shemer, the owner of the hill.

(25)Omri did what was evil in the sight of the LORD, and did more evil than all who were before him. (26)For he walked in all the way of Jeroboam the son of Nebat, and in the sins which he made Israel to sin, provoking the LORD, the God of Israel, to anger by their idols. (27)Now the rest of the acts of Omri which he did, and the might that he showed, are they not written in the Book of the Chronicles of the Kings of Israel? (28)And Omri slept with his fathers, and was buried in Samaria; and Ahab his son reigned in his stead.

91 Ahab's Reign Begins

I Kings 16:29–34

(29)In the thirty-eighth year of Asa king of Judah, Ahab the son of Omri began to reign over Israel, and Ahab the son of Omri reigned over Israel in Samaria twenty-two years. (30)And Ahab the son of Omri did evil in the sight of the LORD more than all that were before him. (31)And as if it had been a light thing for him to walk in the sins of Jeroboam the son of Nebat, he took for wife Jezebel the daughter of Ethbaal king of the Sidonians, and went and served Baal, and worshiped him. (32)He erected an altar for Baal in the house of Baal, which he built in Samaria. (33)And Ahab made an Asherah. Ahab did more to provoke the LORD, the God of Israel, to anger than all the kings of Israel who were before him. (34)In his days Hiel of Bethel built Jericho; he laid its foundation at the cost of Abiram his first-born, and set up its gates at the cost of his youngest son Segub, according to the word of the LORD, which he spoke by Joshua the son of Nun.

92 Elijah Fed by the Ravens

I Kings 17:1–7

(1)Now Elijah the Tishbite, of Tishbe in Gilead, said to Ahab, "As the LORD the God of Israel lives, before whom I stand, there shall be neither dew nor rain these years, except by my word." (2)And the word of the LORD came to him. (3)"Depart from here and turn eastward, and hide yourself by the brook Cherith, that is east of the Jordan. (4)You shall drink from the brook, and I have commanded the ravens to feed you there." (5)So he went and did according to the word of the LORD; he went and dwelt by the brook Cherith that is east of the Jordan. (6)And the ravens brought him bread and meat in the morning, and bread and meat in the evening; and he drank from the brook. (7)And after a while the brook dried up, because there was no rain in the land.

93 Two Miracles of Elijah

I Kings 17:8–24

(8)Then the word of the LORD came to him. (9)"Arise, go to Zarephath, which belongs to Sidon, and dwell there. Behold, I have commanded a widow there to feed you." (10)So he arose and went to Zarephath; and when he came to the gate of the city, behold, a widow was there gathering sticks; and he called to her and said, "Bring me a little water in a vessel, that I may drink." (11)And as she was going to bring it, he called to her and said, "Bring me a morsel of bread in your hand." (12)And she said, "As the LORD your God lives, I have nothing baked, only a handful of meal in a jar, and a little oil in a cruse; and now, I am gathering a couple of sticks, that I may go in and prepare it for myself and my son, that we may eat it, and die." (13)And Elijah said to her, "Fear not; go and do as you have said; but first make me a little cake of it and bring it to me, and afterward make for yourself and your son. (14)For thus says the LORD the God of

Israel, 'The jar of meal shall not be spent, and the cruse of oil shall not fail, until the day that the LORD sends rain upon the earth.' " (15)And she went and did as Elijah said; and she, and he, and her household ate for many days. (16)The jar of meal was not spent, neither did the cruse of oil fail, according to the word of the LORD which he spoke by Elijah.

(17)After this the son of the woman, the mistress of the house, became ill; and his illness was so severe that there was no breath left in him. (18)And she said to Elijah, "What have you against me, O man of God? You have come to me to bring my sin to remembrance, and to cause the death of my son!" (19)And he said to her, "Give me your son." And he took him from her bosom, and carried him up into the upper chamber, where he lodged, and laid him upon his own bed. (20)And he cried to the LORD, "O LORD my God, hast thou brought calamity even upon the widow with whom I sojourn, by slaying her son?" (21)Then he stretched himself upon the child three times, and cried to the LORD, "O LORD my God, let this child's soul come into him again." (22)And the LORD hearkened to the voice of Elijah; and the soul of the child came into him again, and he revived. (23)And Elijah took the child, and brought him down from the upper chamber into the house, and delivered him to his mother; and Elijah said, "See, your son lives." (24)And the woman said to Elijah, "Now I know that you are a man of God, and that the word of the LORD in your mouth is truth."

94 The Contest on Mount Carmel

I Kings 18:1–46

(1)After many days the word of the LORD came to Elijah, in the third year, saying, "Go, show yourself to Ahab; and I will send rain upon the earth." (2)So Elijah went to show himself to Ahab. Now the famine was severe in Samaria. (3)And Ahab called Obadiah, who was over the household. (Now Obadiah revered the LORD greatly; (4)and when Jezebel cut off the prophets of the LORD, Obadiah took a hundred prophets and hid them by fifties in a cave, and fed them with bread and water.) (5)And Ahab said to Obadiah, "Go through the land to all the springs of water and to all the valleys; perhaps we may find grass and save the horses and mules alive, and not lose some of the animals." (6)So they divided the land between them to pass through it; Ahab went in one direction by himself, and Obadiah went in another direction by himself.

(7)And as Obadiah was on the way, behold, Elijah met him; and Obadiah recognized him, and fell on his face, and said, "Is it you, my lord Elijah?" (8)And he answered him, "It is I. Go, tell your lord, 'Behold, Elijah is here.' " (9)And he said, "Wherein have I sinned, that you would give your servant into the hand of Ahab, to kill me? (10)As the LORD your God lives, there is no nation or kingdom whither my lord has not sent to seek you; and when they would say, 'He is not here,' he would take an oath of the kingdom or nation, that they had not found you. (11)And now you say, 'Go, tell your lord, "Behold, Elijah is here." ' " (12)And as soon as I have gone from you, the Spirit of the LORD will carry you whither I know not; and so, when I come and tell Ahab and he cannot find you, he will kill me, although I your servant have revered the LORD from my youth. (13)Has it not been told my lord what I did when Jezebel killed the prophets of the LORD, how I hid a hundred men of the LORD's prophets by fifties in a cave, and fed them with bread and water? (14)And now you say, 'Go, tell your lord, "Behold, Elijah is here" '; and he will kill me." (15)And Elijah said, "As the LORD of hosts lives, before whom I stand, I will surely show myself to him today." (16)So Obadiah went to meet Ahab, and told him; and Ahab went to meet Elijah.

(17)When Ahab saw Elijah, Ahab said to him, "Is it you, you troubler of Israel?" (18)And he answered, "I have not troubled Israel; but you have, and your father's house, because you have forsaken the commandments of the LORD and followed the Baals. (19)Now therefore send and gather all Israel to me at Mount Carmel, and the four hundred and fifty prophets of Baal and the four hundred prophets of Asherah, who eat at Jezebel's table."

(20)So Ahab sent to all the people of Israel, and gathered the prophets together at Mount Carmel. (21)And Elijah came near to all the people, and said, "How long will you go limping with two different opinions? If the LORD is God, follow him; but if Baal, then follow him." And the people did not answer him a word. (22)Then Elijah said to the people, "I, even I only, am left a prophet of the LORD; but Baal's prophets are four hundred and fifty men. (23)Let two bulls be given to us; and let them choose one bull for themselves, and cut it in pieces and lay it on the wood, but put no fire to it; and I will prepare the other bull and lay it on the wood, and put no fire to it. (24)And you call on the name of your god and I will call on the name of the LORD; and the God who answers by fire, he is God." And all the people answered, "It is well spoken." (25)Then Elijah said to the prophets of Baal, "Choose for yourselves one bull and prepare it first, for you are many; and call on the name of your god, but put no fire to it." (26)And they took the bull which was given them, and they prepared it, and called on the name of Baal from morning until noon, saying, "O Baal, answer us!" But there was no voice, and no one answered. And they limped about the altar which they had made. (27)And at noon Elijah mocked them, saying, "Cry aloud, for he is a god; either he is musing, or he has gone aside, or he is on a journey, or perhaps he is asleep and must be awakened." (28)And they cried aloud, and cut themselves after their custom with swords and lances, until the blood gushed out upon them. (29)And as midday passed, they raved on until the time of the offering of the oblation, but there was no voice; no one answered, no one heeded.

(30)Then Elijah said to all the people, "Come near to me"; and all the people came near to him. And he repaired the altar of the LORD that had been thrown down; (31)Elijah took twelve stones, according to the number of the tribes of the sons of Jacob, to whom the word of the LORD came, saying, "Israel shall be your name"; (32)and with the stones he built an altar in the name of the LORD. And he made a trench about the altar, as great as would contain two measures of seed. (33)And he put the wood in order, and cut the bull in pieces and laid it on the wood. And he said, "Fill four jars with water, and pour it on the burnt offering, and on the wood." (34)And he said, "Do it a second time"; and they did it a second time. And he said, "Do it a third time"; and they did it a third time. (35)And the water ran round about the altar, and filled the trench also with water.

(36)And at the time of the offering of the oblation, Elijah the prophet came near and said, "O LORD, God of Abraham, Isaac, and Israel, let it be known this day that thou art God in Israel, and that I am thy servant, and that I have done all these things at thy word. (37)Answer me, O LORD, answer me, that this people may know that thou, O LORD, art God, and that thou hast turned their hearts back." (38)Then the fire of the LORD fell, and consumed the burnt offering, and the wood, and the stones, and the dust, and licked up the water that was in the trench. [39]And when all the people saw it, they fell on their faces; and they said, "The LORD, he is God; the LORD, he is God." [40]And Elijah said to them, "Seize the prophets of Baal; let not one of them escape." And they seized them; and Elijah brought them down to the brook Kishon, and killed them there.

[41]And Elijah said to Ahab, "Go up, eat and drink; for there is a sound of the rushing of rain." [42]So Ahab went up to eat and to drink. And Elijah went up to the top of Carmel; and he bowed himself down upon the earth, and put his face between his knees. [43]And he said to his servant, "Go up now, look toward the sea." And he went up and looked, and said, "There is nothing." And he said, "Go again seven times." [44]And at the seventh time he said, "Behold, a little cloud like a man's hand is rising out of the sea." And he said, "Go up, say to Ahab, 'Prepare your chariot and go down, lest the rain stop you.'" [45]And in a little while the heavens grew black with clouds and wind, and there was a great rain. And Ahab rode and went to Jezreel. [46]And the hand of the LORD was on Elijah; and he girded up his loins and ran before Ahab to the entrance of Jezreel.

95 The Theophany on Mount Horeb

I Kings 19:1–18

[1]Ahab told Jezebel all that Elijah had done, and how he had slain all the prophets with the sword. [2]Then Jezebel sent a messenger to Elijah, saying, "So may the gods do to me, and more also, if I do not make your life as the life of one of them by this time tomorrow." [3]Then he was afraid, and he arose and went for his life, and came to Beer-sheba, which belongs to Judah, and left his servant there.

[4]But he himself went a day's journey into the wilderness, and came and sat down under a broom tree; and he asked that he might die, saying, "It is enough; now, O LORD, take away my life; for I am no better than my fathers." [5]And he lay down and slept under a broom tree; and behold, an angel touched him, and said to him, "Arise and eat." [6]And he looked, and behold, there was at his head a cake baked on hot stones and a jar of water. And he ate and drank, and lay down again. [7]And the angel of the LORD came again a second time, and touched him, and said, "Arise and eat, else the journey will be too great for you." [8]And he arose, and ate and drank, and went in the strength of that food forty days and forty nights to Horeb the mount of God.

[9]And there he came to a cave, and lodged there; and behold, the word of the LORD came to him, and he said to him, "What are you doing here, Elijah?" [10]He said, "I have been very jealous for the LORD, the God of hosts; for the people of Israel have forsaken thy covenant, thrown down thy altars, and slain thy prophets with the sword; and I, even I only, am left; and they seek my life, to take it away." [11]And he said, "Go forth, and stand upon the mount before the LORD." And behold, the LORD passed by, and a great and strong wind rent the mountains, and broke in pieces the rocks before the LORD, but the LORD was not in the wind; and after the wind an earthquake, but the LORD was not in the earthquake; [12]and after the earthquake a fire, but the LORD was not in the fire; and after the fire a still small voice. [13]And when Elijah heard it, he wrapped his face in his mantle and went out and stood at the entrance of the cave. And

behold, there came a voice to him, and said, "What are you doing here, Elijah?" [14]He said, "I have been very jealous for the LORD, the God of hosts; for the people of Israel have forsaken thy covenant, thrown down thy altars, and slain thy prophets with the sword; and I, even I only, am left; and they seek my life, to take it away." [15]And the LORD said to him, "Go, return on your way to the wilderness of Damascus; and when you arrive, you shall anoint Hazael to be king over Syria; [16]and Jehu the son of Nimshi you shall anoint to be king over Israel; and Elisha the son of Shaphat of Abel-meholah you shall anoint to be prophet in your place. [17]And him who escapes from the sword of Hazael shall Jehu slay; and him who escapes from the sword of Jehu shall Elisha slay. [18]Yet I will leave seven thousand in Israel, all the knees that have not bowed to Baal, and every mouth that has not kissed him."

96 The Call of Elisha

I Kings 19:19–21

[19]So he departed from there, and found Elisha the son of Shaphat, who was plowing, with twelve yoke of oxen before him, and he was with the twelfth. Elijah passed by him and cast his mantle upon him. [20]And he left the oxen, and ran after Elijah, and said, "Let me kiss my father and my mother, and then I will follow you." And he said to him, "Go back again; for what have I done to you?" [21]And he returned from following him, and took the yoke of oxen, and slew them, and boiled their flesh with the yokes of the oxen, and gave it to the people, and they ate. Then he arose and went after Elijah, and ministered to him.

97 The Struggles of Ahab With Ben-hadad

I Kings 20:1–34

[1]Ben-hadad the king of Syria gathered all his army together; thirty-two kings were with him, and horses and chariots; and he went up and besieged Samaria, and fought against it. [2]And he sent messengers into the city of Ahab king of Israel, and said to him, "Thus says Ben-hadad: [3]'Your silver and your gold are mine; your fairest wives and children also are mine.' " [4]And the king of Israel answered, "As you say, my lord, O king, I am yours, and all that I have." [5]The messengers came again, and said, "Thus says Ben-hadad: 'I sent to you, saying, "Deliver to me your silver and your gold, your wives and your children"; [6]nevertheless I will send my servants to you tomorrow about this time, and they shall search your house and the houses of your servants, and lay hands on whatever pleases them, and take it away.' "

[7]Then the king of Israel called all the elders of the land, and said, "Mark, now, and see how this man is seeking trouble; for he sent to me for my wives and my children, and for my silver and my gold, and I did not refuse him." [8]And all the elders and all the people said to him, "Do not heed or consent." [9]So he said to the messengers of Ben-hadad, "Tell my lord the king, 'All that you first demanded of your servant I will do; but this thing I cannot do.' " And the messengers departed and brought him word again. [10]Ben-hadad sent to him and said, "The gods do so to me, and more also, if the

dust of Samaria shall suffice for handfuls for all the people who follow me." (11)And the king of Israel answered, "Tell him, 'Let not him that girds on his armor boast himself as he that puts it off.' " (12)When Ben-hadad heard this message as he was drinking with the kings in the booths, he said to his men, "Take your positions." And they took their positions against the city.

(13)And behold, a prophet came near to Ahab king of Israel and said, "Thus says the LORD, Have you seen all this great multitude? Behold, I will give it into your hand this day; and you shall know that I am the LORD." (14)And Ahab said, "By whom?" He said, "Thus says the LORD, By the servants of the governors of the districts." Then he said, "Who shall begin the battle?" He answered, "You." (15)Then he mustered the servants of the governors of the districts, and they were two hundred and thirty-two; and after them he mustered all the people of Israel, seven thousand.

(16)And they went out at noon, while Ben-hadad was drinking himself drunk in the booths, he and the thirty-two kings who helped him. (17)The servants of the governors of the districts went out first. And Ben-hadad sent out scouts, and they reported to him, "Men are coming out from Samaria." (18)He said, "If they have come out for peace, take them alive; or if they have come out for war, take them alive."

(19)So these went out of the city, the servants of the governors of the districts, and the army which followed them. (20)And each killed his man; the Syrians fled and Israel pursued them, but Ben-hadad king of Syria escaped on a horse with horsemen. (21)And the king of Israel went out, and captured the horses and chariots, and killed the Syrians with a great slaughter.

(22)Then the prophet came near to the king of Israel, and said to him, "Come, strengthen yourself, and consider well what you have to do; for in the spring the king of Syria will come up against you."

(23)And the servants of the king of Syria said to him, "Their gods are gods of the hills, and so they were stronger than we; but let us fight against them in the plain, and surely we shall be stronger than they. (24)And do this: remove the kings, each from his post, and put commanders in their places; (25)and muster an army like the army that you have lost, horse for horse, and chariot for chariot; then we will fight against them in the plain, and surely we shall be stronger than they." And he hearkened to their voice, and did so.

(26)In the spring Ben-hadad mustered the Syrians, and went up to Aphek, to fight against Israel. (27)And the people of Israel were mustered, and were provisioned, and went against them; the people of Israel encamped before them like two little flocks of goats, but the Syrians filled the country. (28)And a man of God came near and said to the king of Israel, "Thus says the LORD, 'Because the Syrians have said, "The LORD is a god of the hills but he is not a god of the valleys," therefore I will give all this great multitude into your hand, and you shall know that I am the LORD.' " (29)And they encamped opposite one another seven days. Then on the seventh day the battle was joined; and the people of Israel smote of the Syrians a hundred thousand foot soldiers in one day. (30)And the rest fled into the city of Aphek; and the wall fell upon twenty-seven thousand men that were left.

Ben-hadad also fled, and entered an inner chamber in the city. (31)And his servants said to him, "Behold now, we have heard that the kings of the house of Israel are merciful kings; let us put sackcloth on our loins and ropes upon our heads, and go out to the king of Israel; perhaps he will spare your life." (32)So they girded sackcloth on their loins, and put ropes on their heads, and went to the king of Israel and said, "Your servant Ben-hadad says, 'Pray, let me live.' " And he said, "Does he still live? He is my brother." (33)Now the men were watching for an omen, and they quickly took it up from him and said, "Yes, your brother Ben-hadad." Then he said, "Go and bring him." Then Ben-hadad came forth to him; and he caused him to come up into the chariot. (34)And Ben-hadad said to him, "The cities which my father took from your father I will restore; and you may establish bazaars for yourself in Damascus, as my father did in Samaria." And Ahab said, "I will let you go on these terms." So he made a covenant with him and let him go.

98 Ahab Condemned by an Unnamed Prophet

I Kings 20:35–43

(35)And a certain man of the sons of the prophets said to his fellow at the command of the LORD, "Strike me, I pray." But the man refused to strike him. (36)Then he said to him, "Because you have not obeyed the voice of the LORD, behold, as soon as you have gone from me, a lion shall kill you." And as soon as he had departed from him, a lion met him and killed him. (37)Then he found another man, and said, "Strike me, I pray." And the man struck him, smiting and wounding him. (38)So the prophet departed, and waited for the king by the way, disguising himself with a bandage over his eyes. (39)And as the king passed, he cried to the king and said, "Your servant went out into the midst of the battle; and behold, a soldier turned and brought a man to me, and said, 'Keep this man; if by any means he be missing, your life shall be for his life, or else you shall pay a talent of silver.' (40)And as your servant was busy here and there, he was gone." The king of Israel said to him, "So shall your judgment be; you yourself have decided it." (41)Then he made haste to take the bandage away from his eyes; and the king of Israel recognized him as one of the prophets. (42)And he said to him, "Thus says the LORD, 'Because you have let go out of your hand the man whom I had devoted to destruction, therefore your life shall go for his life, and your people for his people.' " (43)And the king of Israel went to his house resentful and sullen, and came to Samaria.

99 The Story of Naboth

I Kings 21:1–29

(1)Now Naboth the Jezreelite had a vineyard in Jezreel, beside the palace of Ahab king of Samaria. (2)And after this Ahab said to Naboth, "Give me your vineyard, that I may have it for a vegetable garden, because it is near my house; and I will give you a better vineyard for it; or, if it seems good to you, I will give you its value in money." (3)But Naboth said to Ahab, "The LORD forbid that I should give you the inheritance of my fathers." (4)And Ahab went into his house vexed and sullen because of what Naboth the Jezreelite had said to him; for he had said, "I will not give you the inheritance of my fathers." And he lay down on his bed, and turned away his face, and would eat no food.

(5)But Jezebel his wife came to him, and said to him, "Why is your spirit so vexed that you eat no food?" (6)And he said to her, "Because I spoke to Naboth the Jezreelite, and said to him, 'Give me your vineyard for money; or else, if it please you, I will give you another vineyard for it'; and he answered, 'I will not give you my vineyard.' "
(7)And Jezebel his wife said to him, "Do you now govern Israel? Arise, and eat bread, and let your heart be cheerful; I will give you the vineyard of Naboth the Jezreelite."

(8)So she wrote letters in Ahab's name and sealed them with his seal, and she sent the letters to the elders and the nobles who dwelt with Naboth in his city. (9)And she wrote in the letters, "Proclaim a fast, and set Naboth on high among the people; (10)and set two base fellows opposite him, and let them bring a charge against him, saying, 'You have cursed God and the king.' Then take him out, and stone him to death." (11)And the men of his city, the elders and the nobles who dwelt in his city, did as Jezebel had sent word to them. As it was written in the letters which she had sent to them, (12)they proclaimed a fast, and set Naboth on high among the people. (13)And the two base fellows came in and sat opposite him; and the base fellows brought a charge against Naboth, in the presence of the people, saying, "Naboth cursed God and the king." So they took him outside the city, and stoned him to death with stones. (14)Then they sent to Jezebel, saying, "Naboth has been stoned; he is dead."

(15)As soon as Jezebel heard that Naboth had been stoned and was dead, Jezebel said to Ahab, "Arise, take possession of the vineyard of Naboth the Jezreelite, which he refused to give you for money; for Naboth is not alive, but dead." (16)And as soon as Ahab heard that Naboth was dead, Ahab arose to go down to the vineyard of Naboth the Jezreelite, to take possession of it.

(17)Then the word of the LORD came to Elijah the Tishbite, saying, (18)"Arise, go down to meet Ahab king of Israel, who is in Samaria; behold, he is in the vineyard of Naboth, where he has gone to take possession. (19)And you shall say to him, 'Thus says the LORD, "Have you killed, and also taken possession?" ' And you shall say to him, 'Thus says the LORD: "In the place where dogs licked up the blood of Naboth shall dogs lick your own blood." ' "

(20)Ahab said to Elijah, "Have you found me, O my enemy?" He answered, "I have found you, because you have sold yourself to do what is evil in the sight of the LORD. (21)Behold, I will bring evil upon you; I will utterly sweep you away, and will cut off from Ahab every male, bond or free, in Israel; (22)and I will make your house like the house of Jeroboam the son of Nebat, and like the house of Baasha the son of Ahijah, for the anger to which you have provoked me, and because you have made Israel to sin. (23)And of Jezebel the LORD also said, 'The dogs shall eat Jezebel within the bounds of Jezreel.' (24)Any one belonging to Ahab who dies in the city the dogs shall eat; and any one of his who dies in the open country the birds of the air shall eat."

(25)(There was none who sold himself to do what was evil in the sight of the LORD like Ahab, whom Jezebel his wife incited. (26)He did very abominably in going after idols, as the Amorites had done, whom the LORD cast out before the people of Israel.)

(27)And when Ahab heard those words, he rent his clothes, and put sackcloth upon his flesh, and fasted and lay in sackcloth, and went about dejectedly. (28)And the word of the LORD came to Elijah the Tishbite, saying, (29)"Have you seen how Ahab has humbled himself before me? Because he has humbled himself before me, I will not bring evil in his days; but in his son's days I will bring the evil upon his house."

100 Events During the Reign of Jehoshaphat

II Chronicles 17:1–19

[1]Jehoshaphat his son reigned in his stead, and strengthened himself against Israel. [2]He placed forces in all the fortified cities of Judah, and set garrisons in the land of Judah, and in the cities of Ephraim which Asa his father had taken. [3]The LORD was with Jehoshaphat, because he walked in the earlier ways of his father; he did not seek the Baals, [4]but sought the God of his father and walked in his commandments, and not according to the ways of Israel. [5]Therefore the LORD established the kingdom in his hand; and all Judah brought tribute to Jehoshaphat; and he had great riches and honor. [6]His heart was courageous in the ways of the LORD; and furthermore he took the high places and the Asherim out of Judah.

[7]In the third year of his reign he sent his princes, Ben-hail, Obadiah, Zechariah, Nethanel, and Micaiah, to teach in the cities of Judah; [8]and with them the Levites, Shemaiah, Nethaniah, Zebadiah, Asahel, Shemiramoth, Jehonathan, Adonijah, Tobijah, and Tobadonijah; and with these Levites, the priests Elishama and Jehoram. [9]And they taught in Judah, having the book of the law of the LORD with them; they went about through all the cities of Judah and taught among the people.

[10]And the fear of the LORD fell upon all the kingdoms of the lands that were round about Judah, and they made no war against Jehoshaphat. [11]Some of the Philistines brought Jehoshaphat presents, and silver for tribute; and the Arabs also brought him seven thousand seven hundred rams and seven thousand seven hundred he-goats. [12]And Jehoshaphat grew steadily greater. He built in Judah fortresses and store-cities, [13]and he had great stores in the cities of Judah. He had soldiers, mighty men of valor, in Jerusalem. [14]This was the muster of them by fathers' houses: Of Judah, the commanders of thousands: Adnah the commander, with three hundred thousand mighty men of valor, [15]and next to him Jeho-hanan the commander, with two hundred and eighty thousand, [16]and next to him Amasiah the son of Zichri, a volunteer for the service of the LORD, with two hundred thousand mighty men of valor. [17]Of Benjamin: Eliada, a mighty man of valor, with two hundred thousand men armed with bow and shield, [18]and next to him Jehozabad with a hundred and eighty thousand armed for war. [19]These were in the service of the king, besides those whom the king had placed in the fortified cities throughout all Judah.

101 The Affair of the Prophet Micaiah, the Death of Ahab

I Kings 22:1–40   II Chronicles 18:1–34

[1]For three years Syria and Israel continued without war.

[1]Now Jehoshaphat had great riches and honor; and he made a marriage alliance with Ahab.

[2]But in the third year

Jehoshaphat the king of Judah
came down to
the king of Israel.

(2)After some years
he
went down to

Ahab in Samaria.
And Ahab killed an abundance of sheep
and oxen for him and for the people
who were with him, and induced him
to go up against

(3)And the king of Israel said to
his servants, "Do you know that
Ramoth-gilead
belongs to us, and we keep quiet and
do not take it out of the hand of
the king of Syria?"
(4)And he said
to Jehoshaphat,
"Will you go with me to battle at
Ramoth-gilead?"
And Jehoshaphat said to
the king of Israel,
"I am as you are, my people as your
people,
my horses as your horses."

Ramoth-gilead.

(3)Ahab king of Israel said
to Jehoshaphat king of Judah,
"Will you go with me to
Ramoth-gilead?"
He answered
him,
"I am as you are, my people as your
people.

(5)And Jehoshaphat said to
the king of Israel, "Inquire first
for the word of the LORD." (6)Then
the king of Israel gathered the
prophets together, about four hundred
men, and said to them, "Shall I go to
battle against Ramoth-gilead, or
shall I forbear?" And they said,
"Go up; for the LORD will give it
into the hand of the king."
(7)But Jehoshaphat said, "Is there
not here another prophet of the LORD
of whom we may inquire?" (8)And the
king of Israel said to Jehoshaphat,
"There is yet one man by whom we may
inquire of the LORD, Micaiah the son
of Imlah; but I hate him, for he
never prophesies good concerning me,
but evil." And Jehoshaphat
said, "Let not the king say so."
(9)Then the king of Israel summoned
an officer and said, "Bring quickly

We will be with you in the war."
(4)And Jehoshaphat said to
the king of Israel, "Inquire first
for the word of the LORD." (5)Then
the king of Israel gathered the
prophets together, four hundred
men, and said to them, "Shall we go to
battle against Ramoth-gilead, or
shall I forbear?" And they said,
"Go up; for God will give it
into the hand of the king."
(6)But Jehoshaphat said, "Is there
not here another prophet of the LORD
of whom we may inquire?" (7)And the
king of Israel said to Jehoshaphat,
"There is yet one man by whom we may
inquire of the LORD, Micaiah the son
of Imlah; but I hate him, for he
never prophesies good concerning me,
but always evil." And Jehoshaphat
said, "Let not the king say so."
(8)Then the king of Israel summoned
an officer and said, "Bring quickly

163

Micaiah the son of Imlah." (10)Now
the king of Israel and Jehoshaphat
the king of Judah were sitting on
their thrones, arrayed in their robes,

at the threshing floor at the entrance
of the gate of Samaria; and all the
prophets were prophesying before them.
(11)And Zedekiah the son of
Chenaanah made for himself horns of
iron, and said, "Thus says the LORD,
'With these you shall push the Syrians
until they are destroyed.' " (12)And
all the prophets prophesied so, and
said, "Go up to Ramoth-gilead and
triumph; the LORD will give it into
the hand of the king."
(13)And the messenger who went
to summon Micaiah said to him,
"Behold, the words of the prophets
with one accord are favorable to the
king; let your word be like the word
of one of them, and speak favorably."
(14)But Micaiah said, "As the LORD
lives, what the LORD says to me, that
I will speak." (15)And when he had
come to the king, the king said to
him, "Micaiah, shall we go to Ramoth-
gilead to battle, or shall we
forbear?" And he answered him,
"Go up and triumph;
the LORD will give it into the hand
of the king."
(16)But the king said to him,
"How many times shall I adjure you
that you speak to me nothing but the
truth in the name of the LORD?"
(17)And he said, "I saw all Israel
scattered upon the mountains, as
sheep that have no shepherd; and
the LORD said, 'These have no master;
let each return to his home
in peace.' " (18)And the king of
Israel said to Jehoshaphat, "Did I not
tell you that he would not prophesy
good concerning me, but evil?"
(19)And Micaiah said, "Therefore

Micaiah the son of Imlah." (9)Now
the king of Israel and Jehoshaphat
the king of Judah were sitting on
their thrones, arrayed in their robes;
and they were sitting
at the threshing floor at the entrance
of the gate of Samaria; and all the
prophets were prophesying before them.
(10)And Zedekiah the son of
Chenaanah made for himself horns of
iron, and said, "Thus says the LORD,
'With these you shall push the Syrians
until they are destroyed.' " (11)And
all the prophets prophesied so, and
said, "Go up to Ramoth-gilead and
triumph; the LORD will give it into
the hand of the king."
(12)And the messenger who went
to summon Micaiah said to him,
"Behold, the words of the prophets
with one accord are favorable to the
king; let your word be like the word
of one of them, and speak favorably."
(13)But Micaiah said, "As the LORD
lives, what my God says, that
I will speak." (14)And when he had
come to the king, the king said to
him, "Micaiah, shall we go to Ramoth-
gilead to battle, or shall I
forbear?" And he answered,
"Go up and triumph;
they will be given into your hand."

(15)But the king said to him,
"How many times shall I adjure you
that you speak to me nothing but the
truth in the name of the LORD?"
(16)And he said, "I saw all Israel
scattered upon the mountains, as
sheep that have no shepherd; and
the LORD said, 'These have no master;
let each return to his home
in peace.' " (17)And the king of
Israel said to Jehoshaphat, "Did I not
tell you that he would not prophesy
good concerning me, but evil?"
(18)And Micaiah said, "Therefore

hear the word of the LORD: I saw the LORD sitting on his throne, and all the host of heaven standing _beside him_ on his right hand and on his left; (20)and the LORD said, 'Who will entice Ahab, that he may go up and fall at Ramoth-gilead?' And one said one thing, and another said another. (21)Then a spirit came forward and stood before the LORD, saying, 'I will entice him.' (22)And the LORD said to him, 'By what means?' And he said, 'I will go forth, and will be a lying spirit in the mouth of all his prophets.' And he said, 'You are to entice him, and you shall succeed; go forth and do so.' (23)Now therefore behold, the LORD has put a lying spirit in the mouth of all these your prophets; the LORD has spoken evil concerning you."

(24)Then Zedekiah the son of Chenaanah came near and struck Micaiah on the cheek, and said, "How did the Spirit of the LORD go from me to speak to you?" (25)And Micaiah said, "Behold, you shall see on that day when you go into an inner chamber to hide yourself." (26)And the king of Israel said, "Seize Micaiah, and take him back to Amon the governor of the city and to Joash the king's son; (27)and say, 'Thus says the king, "Put this fellow in prison, and feed him with scant fare of bread and water, until I come in peace." ' " (28)And Micaiah said, "If you return in peace, the LORD has not spoken by me." And he said, "Hear, all you peoples!"

(29)So the king of Israel and Jehoshaphat the king of Judah went up to Ramoth-gilead. (30)And the king of Israel said to Jehoshaphat, "I will disguise myself and go into battle,

hear the word of the LORD: I saw the LORD sitting on his throne, and all the host of heaven standing on his right hand and on his left; (19)and the LORD said, 'Who will entice Ahab _the king of Israel,_ that he may go up and fall at Ramoth-gilead?' And one said one thing, and another said another. (20)Then a spirit came forward and stood before the LORD, saying, 'I will entice him.' And the LORD said to him, 'By what means?' (21)And he said, 'I will go forth, and will be a lying spirit in the mouth of all his prophets.' And he said, 'You are to entice him, and you shall succeed; go forth and do so.' (22)Now therefore behold, the LORD has put a lying spirit in the mouth of these your prophets; the LORD has spoken evil concerning you."

(23)Then Zedekiah the son of Chenaanah came near and struck Micaiah on the cheek, and said, "Which way did the Spirit of the LORD go from me to speak to you?" (24)And Micaiah said, "Behold, you shall see on that day when you go into an inner chamber to hide yourself." (25)And the king of Israel said, "Seize Micaiah, and take him back to Amon the governor of the city and to Joash the king's son; /26/and say, 'Thus says the king, "Put this fellow in prison, and feed him with scant fare of bread and water, until I return in peace." ' " (27)And Micaiah said, "If you return in peace, the LORD has not spoken by me." And he said, "Hear, all you peoples!"

(28)So the king of Israel and Jehoshaphat the king of Judah went up to Ramoth-gilead. (29)And the king of Israel said to Jehoshaphat, "I will disguise myself and go into battle,

but you wear your robes." And the
king of Israel disguised himself and
went into battle. (31)Now the
king of Syria had commanded the
thirty-two
captains of his chariots, "Fight with
neither small nor great, but only with
the king of Israel." (32)And when
the captains of the chariots saw
Jehoshaphat, they said, "It is surely
the king of Israel." So they turned
to fight against him; and
Jehoshaphat cried out.

(33)And when the captains of the
chariots saw that it was not the king
of Israel, they turned back from
pursuing him. (34)But a certain man
drew his bow at a venture, and struck
the king of Israel between the scale
armor and the breastplate; therefore
he said to the driver of his chariot,
"Turn about, and carry me out of the
battle, for I am wounded." (35)And
the battle grew hot that day, and
the king was propped up
in his chariot facing the Syrians,
until at evening

he died;
and the blood of the wound flowed
into the bottom of the chariot.
(36)And about sunset a cry went
through the army, "Every man to his
city, and every man to his country!"
(37)So the king died, and was
brought to Samaria; and they buried
the king in Samaria. (38)And they
washed the chariot by the pool of
Samaria, and the dogs licked up his
blood, and the harlots washed
themselves in it, according to the
word of the LORD which he had spoken.
(39)Now the rest of the acts of
Ahab, and all that he did, and the
ivory house which he built, and all

but you wear your robes." And the
king of Israel disguised himself; and
they went into battle. (30)Now the
king of Syria had commanded the

captains of his chariots, "Fight with
neither small nor great, but only with
the king of Israel." (31)And when
the captains of the chariots saw
Jehoshaphat, they said, "It is
the king of Israel." So they turned
to fight against him; and
Jehoshaphat cried out,
and the LORD helped him.
God drew them away from him,
(32)and when the captains of the
chariots saw that it was not the king
of Israel, they turned back from
pursuing him. (33)But a certain man
drew his bow at a venture, and struck
the king of Israel between the scale
armor and the breastplate; therefore
he said to the driver of his chariot,
"Turn about, and carry me out of the
battle, for I am wounded." (34)And
the battle grew hot that day, and
the king of Israel propped himself up
in his chariot facing the Syrians
until evening,
then at sunset
he died.

the cities that he built, are they
not written in the Book of the
Chronicles of the Kings of Israel?
(40)So Ahab slept with his fathers;
and Ahaziah his son reigned
in his stead.

102 Reforms of Jehoshaphat

II Chronicles 19:1–11

(1)Jehoshaphat the king of Judah returned in safety to his house in Jerusalem. (2)But Jehu the son of Hanani the seer went out to meet him, and said to king Jehoshaphat, "Should you help the wicked and love those who hate the LORD? Because of this, wrath has gone out against you from the LORD. (3)Nevertheless some good is found in you, for you destroyed the Asherahs out of the land, and have set your heart to seek God."

(4)Jehoshaphat dwelt at Jerusalem; and he went out again among the people, from Beer-sheba to the hill country of Ephraim, and brought them back to the LORD, the God of their fathers. (5)He appointed judges in the land in all the fortified cities of Judah, city by city, (6)and said to the judges, "Consider what you do, for you judge not for man but for the LORD; he is with you in giving judgment. (7)Now then, let the fear of the LORD be upon you; take heed what you do, for there is no perversion of justice with the LORD our God, or partiality, or taking bribes."

(8)Moreover in Jerusalem Jehoshaphat appointed certain Levites and priests and heads of families of Israel, to give judgment for the LORD and to decide disputed cases. They had their seat at Jerusalem. (9)And he charged them: "Thus you shall do in the fear of the LORD, in faithfulness, and with your whole heart: (10)whenever a case comes to you from your brethren who live in their cities, concerning bloodshed, law or commandment, statutes or ordinances, then you shall instruct them, that they may not incur guilt before the LORD and wrath may not come upon you and your brethren. Thus you shall do, and you will not incur guilt. (11)And behold, Amariah the chief priest is over you in all matters of the LORD; and Zebadiah the son of Ishmael, the governor of the house of Judah, in all the king's matters; and the Levites will serve you as officers. Deal courageously, and may the LORD be with the upright!"

103 Jehoshaphat's Prayer and Judah's Deliverance

II Chronicles 20:1–30

(1)After this the Moabites and Ammonites, and with them some of the Meunites, came against Jehoshaphat for battle. (2)Some men came and told Jehoshaphat, "A great multitude is coming against you from Edom, from beyond the sea; and, behold, they are in Hazazon-tamar" (that is, En-gedi). (3)Then Jehoshaphat feared, and set himself to seek the LORD, and proclaimed a fast throughout all Judah. (4)And Judah assembled to seek help from the LORD; from all the cities of Judah they came to seek the LORD.

(5)And Jehoshaphat stood in the assembly of Judah and Jerusalem, in the house of the LORD, before the new court, (6)and said, "O LORD, God of our fathers, art thou not God in heaven? Dost thou not rule over all the kingdoms of the nations? In thy hand are power and might, so that none is able to withstand thee. (7)Didst thou not, O our God, drive out the inhabitants of this land before thy people Israel, and give it for ever to the descendants of Abraham thy friend? (8)And they have dwelt in it, and have built thee in it a sanctuary for thy name, saying, (9)'If evil comes upon us, the sword, judgment, or pestilence, or famine, we will stand before this house, and before thee, for thy name is in this house, and cry to thee in our affliction, and thou wilt hear and save.' (10)And now behold, the men of Ammon and Moab and Mount Seir, whom thou wouldest not let Israel invade when they came from the land of Egypt, and whom they avoided and did not destroy—(11)behold, they reward us by coming to drive us out of thy possession, which thou hast given us to inherit. (12)O our God, wilt thou not execute judgment upon them? For we are powerless against this great multitude that is coming against us. We do not know what to do, but our eyes are upon thee."

(13)Meanwhile all the men of Judah stood before the LORD, with their little ones, their wives, and their children. (14)And the Spirit of the LORD came upon Jahaziel the son of Zechariah, son of Benaiah, son of Je-iel, son of Mattaniah, a Levite of the sons of Asaph, in the midst of the assembly. (15)And he said, "Hearken, all Judah and inhabitants of Jerusalem, and King Jehoshaphat: Thus says the LORD to you, 'Fear not, and be not dismayed at this great multitude; for the battle is not yours but God's. (16)Tomorrow go down against them; behold, they will come up by the ascent of Ziz; you will find them at the end of the valley, east of the wilderness of Jeruel. (17)You will not need to fight in this battle; take your position, stand still, and see the victory of the LORD on your behalf, O Judah and Jerusalem.' Fear not, and be not dismayed; tomorrow go out against them, and the LORD will be with you."

(18)Then Jehoshaphat bowed his head with his face to the ground, and all Judah and the inhabitants of Jerusalem fell down before the LORD, worshiping the LORD. (19)And the Levites, of the Kohathites and the Korahites, stood up to praise the LORD, the God of Israel, with a very loud voice.

(20)And they rose early in the morning and went out into the wilderness of Tekoa; and as they went out, Jehoshaphat stood and said, "Hear me, Judah and inhabitants of Jerusalem! Believe in the LORD your God, and you will be established; believe his prophets, and you will succeed." (21)And when he had taken counsel with the people, he appointed those who were to sing to the LORD and praise him in holy array, as they went before the army, and say,

"Give thanks to the LORD,
for his steadfast love endures for ever."

(22)And when they began to sing and praise, the LORD set an ambush against the men of Ammon, Moab, and Mount Seir, who had come against Judah, so that they were routed. (23)For the men of Ammon and Moab rose against the inhabitants of Mount Seir, destroying them utterly, and when they had made an end of the inhabitants of Seir, they all helped to destroy one another.

(24)When Judah came to the watchtower of the wilderness, they looked toward the multitude; and behold, they were dead bodies lying on the ground; none had escaped. (25)When Jehoshaphat and his people came to take the spoil from them, they found cattle in great numbers, goods, clothing, and precious things, which they took for themselves until they could carry no more. They were three days in taking the spoil, it was so much. (26)On the fourth day they assembled in the Valley of Beracah, for there they blessed the LORD; therefore the name of that place has been called the Valley of Beracah to this day. (27)Then they returned, every man of Judah and Jerusalem, and Jehoshaphat at their head, returning to Jerusalem with joy, for the LORD had made them rejoice over their enemies. (28)They came to Jerusalem, with harps and lyres and trumpets, to the house of the LORD. (29)And the fear of God came on all the kingdoms of the countries when they heard that the LORD had fought against the enemies of Israel. (30)So the realm of Jehoshaphat was quiet, for his God gave him rest round about.

104 Summary of Jehoshaphat's Reign

I Kings 22:41–50	*II Chronicles 20:31–21:1*
(41)Jehoshaphat the son of Asa began to reign over Judah in the fourth year of Ahab king of Israel.	
	(31)Thus Jehoshaphat reigned over Judah.
(42)Jehoshaphat was thirty-five years old when he began to reign, and he reigned twenty-five years in Jerusalem. His mother's name was Azubah the daughter of Shilhi. (43)He walked in all the way of Asa his father; he did not turn aside from it, doing what was right in the sight of the LORD; yet the high places were not taken away, and the people still sacrificed and burned incense on the high places.	He was thirty-five years old when he began to reign, and he reigned twenty-five years in Jerusalem. His mother's name was Azubah the daughter of Shilhi. /32/He walked in the way of Asa his father; and did not turn aside from it, doing what was right in the sight of the LORD. /33/Yet the high places were not taken away, and the people had not yet set their hearts upon the God of their fathers.
(44)Jehoshaphat also made peace with the king of Israel.	
(45)Now the rest of the acts of Jehoshaphat, and his might that he showed, and how he warred, are they not written	(34)Now the rest of the acts of Jehoshaphat, from first to last, are written in the chronicles of Jehu the son of Hanani, which are recorded in the Book of the Kings of Israel.
in the Book of the Chronicles of the Kings of Judah? (46)And the remnant of the male cult prostitutes who remained in the	

days of his father Asa, he
exterminated from the land.
(47)There was no king in Edom; a
deputy was king.

(35)After this Jehoshaphat king
of Judah joined with Ahaziah king of
Israel, who did wickedly.

(48)Jehoshaphat made

(36)He joined him in building

ships of Tarshish
to go to Ophir for gold;

ships to go to Tarshish,

and they built the ships in
Ezion-geber.

(37)Then Eliezer the son of
Dodavahu of Maresha prophesied
against Jehoshaphat, saying,
"Because you have joined with
Ahaziah, the LORD will destroy what
you have made."

but they did not go,

for the ships were wrecked
at Ezion-geber.

And the ships were wrecked

and were not able to go to Tarshish.

(49)Then Ahaziah the son of Ahab
said to Jehoshaphat, "Let my servants
go with your servants in the ships,"
but Jehoshaphat was not willing.
(50)And Jehoshaphat slept with
his fathers, and was buried with his
fathers in the city of David
his father;
and Jehoram his son reigned in his
stead.

/21:1/And Jehoshaphat slept with
his fathers, and was buried with his
fathers in the city of David;

and Jehoram his son reigned in his
stead.

105 The Reign of Ahaziah of Israel

I Kings 22:51–II Kings 1:18

(51)Ahaziah the son of Ahab began to reign over Israel in Samaria in the seventeenth
year of Jehoshaphat king of Judah, and he reigned two years over Israel. (52)He did
what was evil in the sight of the LORD, and walked in the way of his father, and in the
way of his mother, and in the way of Jeroboam the son of Nebat, who made Israel to
sin. (53)He served Baal and worshiped him, and provoked the LORD, the God of Israel,
to anger in every way that his father had done.
(II Kings 1:1)After the death of Ahab, Moab rebelled against Israel.
(2)Now Ahaziah fell through the lattice in his upper chamber in Samaria, and lay

sick; so he sent messengers, telling them, "Go, inquire of Baal-zebub, the god of Ekron, whether I shall recover from this sickness." (3)But the angel of the LORD said to Elijah the Tishbite, "Arise, go up to meet the messengers of the king of Samaria, and say to them, 'Is it because there is no God in Israel that you are going to inquire of Baal-zebub, the god of Ekron?' (4)Now therefore thus says the LORD, 'You shall not come down from the bed to which you have gone, but you shall surely die.' " So Elijah went.

(5)The messengers returned to the king, and he said to them, "Why have you returned?" (6)And they said to him, "There came a man to meet us, and said to us, 'Go back to the king who sent you, and say to him, Thus says the LORD, Is it because there is no God in Israel that you are sending to inquire of Baal-zebub, the god of Ekron? Therefore you shall not come down from the bed to which you have gone, but shall surely die.' " (7)He said to them, "What kind of man was he who came to meet you and told you these things?" (8)They answered him, "He wore a garment of haircloth, with a girdle of leather about his loins." And he said, "It is Elijah the Tishbite."

(9)Then the king sent to him a captain of fifty men with his fifty. He went up to Elijah, who was sitting on the top of a hill, and said to him, "O man of God, the king says, 'Come down.' " (10)But Elijah answered the captain of fifty, "If I am a man of God, let fire come down from heaven and consume you and your fifty." Then fire came down from heaven, and consumed him and his fifty.

(11)Again the king sent to him another captain of fifty men with his fifty. And he went up and said to him, "O man of God, this is the king's order, 'Come down quickly!' " (12)But Elijah answered them, "If I am a man of God, let fire come down from heaven and consume you and your fifty." Then the fire of God came down from heaven and consumed him and his fifty.

(13)Again the king sent the captain of a third fifty with his fifty. And the third captain of fifty went up, and came and fell on his knees before Elijah, and entreated him, "O man of God, I pray you, let my life, and the life of these fifty servants of yours, be precious in your sight. (14)Lo, fire came down from heaven, and consumed the two former captains of fifty men with their fifties; but now let my life be precious in your sight." (15)Then the angel of the LORD said to Elijah, "Go down with him; do not be afraid of him." So he arose and went down with him to the king, (16)and said to him, "Thus says the LORD, 'Because you have sent messengers to inquire of Baal-zebub, the god of Ekron,—is it because there is no God in Israel to inquire of his word?— therefore you shall not come down from the bed to which you have gone, but you shall surely die.' "

(17)So he died according to the word of the LORD which Elijah had spoken. Jehoram, his brother, became king in his stead in the second year of Jehoram the son of Jehoshaphat, king of Judah, because Ahaziah had no son. (18)Now the rest of the acts of Ahaziah which he did, are they not written in the Book of the Chronicles of the Kings of Israel?

106 The Translation of Elijah, the Ministry of Elisha Begins

II Kings 2:1–25

(1)Now when the LORD was about to take Elijah up to heaven by a whirlwind, Elijah and Elisha were on their way from Gilgal. (2)And Elijah said to Elisha, "Tarry here, I pray you; for the LORD has sent me as far as Bethel." But Elisha said, "As the LORD lives, and as you yourself live, I will not leave you." So they went down to Bethel. (3)And the sons of the prophets who were in Bethel came out to Elisha, and said to him, "Do you know that today the LORD will take away your master from over you?" And he said, "Yes, I know it; hold your peace."

(4)Elijah said to him, "Elisha, tarry here, I pray you; for the LORD has sent me to Jericho." But he said, "As the LORD lives, and as you yourself live, I will not leave you." So they came to Jericho. (5)The sons of the prophets who were at Jericho drew near to Elisha, and said to him, "Do you know that today the LORD will take away your master from over you?" And he answered, "Yes, I know it; hold your peace."

(6)Then Elijah said to him, "Tarry here, I pray you; for the LORD has sent me to the Jordan." But he said, "As the LORD lives, and as you yourself live, I will not leave you." So the two of them went on. (7)Fifty men of the sons of the prophets also went, and stood at some distance from them, as they both were standing by the Jordan. (8)Then Elijah took his mantle, and rolled it up, and struck the water, and the water was parted to the one side and to the other, till the two of them could go over on dry ground.

(9)When they had crossed, Elijah said to Elisha, "Ask what I shall do for you, before I am taken from you." And Elisha said, "I pray you, let me inherit a double share of your spirit." (10)And he said, "You have asked a hard thing; yet, if you see me as I am being taken from you, it shall be so for you; but if you do not see me, it shall not be so." (11)And as they still went on and talked, behold, a chariot of fire and horses of fire separated the two of them. And Elijah went up by a whirlwind into heaven. (12)And Elisha saw it and cried, "My father, my father! the chariots of Israel and its horsemen!" And he saw him no more.

Then he took hold of his own clothes and rent them in two pieces. (13)And he took up the mantle of Elijah that had fallen from him, and went back and stood on the bank of the Jordan. (14)Then he took the mantle of Elijah that had fallen from him, and struck the water, saying, "Where is the LORD, the God of Elijah?" And when he had struck the water, the water was parted to the one side and to the other; and Elisha went over.

(15)Now when the sons of the prophets who were at Jericho saw him over against them, they said, "The spirit of Elijah rests on Elisha." And they came to meet him, and bowed to the ground before him. (16)And they said to him, "Behold now, there are with your servants fifty strong men; pray, let them go, and seek your master; it may be that the Spirit of the LORD has caught him up and cast him upon some mountain or into some valley." And he said, "You shall not send." (17)But when they urged him till he was ashamed, he said, "Send." They sent therefore fifty men; and for three days they sought him but did not find him. (18)And they came back to him, while he tarried at Jericho, and he said to them, "Did I not say to you, Do not go?"

(19)Now the men of the city said to Elisha, "Behold, the situation of this city is pleasant, as my lord sees; but the water is bad, and the land is unfruitful." (20)He said, "Bring me a new bowl, and put salt in it." So they brought it to him. (21)Then he went to the spring of water and threw salt in it, and said, "Thus says the LORD, I have made this water wholesome; henceforth neither death nor miscarriage shall come from it." (22)So the water has been wholesome to this day, according to the word which Elisha spoke.

(23)He went up from there to Bethel; and while he was going up on the way, some small boys came out of the city and jeered at him, saying, "Go up, you baldhead! Go up, you baldhead!'' (24)And he turned around, and when he saw them, he cursed them in the name of the LORD. And two she-bears came out of the woods and tore forty-two of the boys. (25)From there he went on to Mount Carmel, and thence he returned to Samaria.

107 Elisha's Miracle of Water as Judah and Israel Campaign Against Moab

II Kings 3:1–27

(1)In the eighteenth year of Jehoshaphat king of Judah, Jehoram the son of Ahab became king over Israel in Samaria, and he reigned twelve years. (2)He did what was evil in the sight of the LORD, though not like his father and mother, for he put away the pillar of Baal which his father had made. (3)Nevertheless he clung to the sin of Jeroboam the son of Nebat, which he made Israel to sin; he did not depart from it.

(4)Now Mesha king of Moab was a sheep breeder; and he had to deliver annually to the king of Israel a hundred thousand lambs, and the wool of a hundred thousand rams. (5)But when Ahab died, the king of Moab rebelled against the king of Israel. (6)So King Jehoram marched out of Samaria at that time and mustered all Israel. (7)And he went and sent word to Jehoshaphat king of Judah, "The king of Moab has rebelled against me; will you go with me to battle against Moab?" And he said, "I will go; I am as you are, my people as your people, my horses as your horses." (8)Then he said, "By which way shall we march?" Jehoram answered, "By the way of the wilderness of Edom."

(9)So the king of Israel went with the king of Judah and the king of Edom. And when they had made a circuitous march of seven days, there was no water for the army or for the beasts which followed them. (10)Then the king of Israel said, "Alas! The LORD has called these three kings to give them into the hand of Moab." (11)And Jehoshaphat said, "Is there no prophet of the LORD here, through whom we may inquire of the LORD?" Then one of the king of Israel's servants answered, "Elisha the son of Shaphat is here, who poured water on the hands of Elijah." (12)And Jehoshaphat said, "The word of the LORD is with him." So the king of Israel and Jehoshaphat and the king of Edom went down to him.

(13)And Elisha said to the king of Israel, "What have I to do with you? Go to the prophets of your father and the prophets of your mother." But the king of Israel said to him, "No; it is the LORD who has called these three kings to give them into the hand of Moab." (14)And Elisha said, "As the LORD of hosts lives, whom I serve, were it not that I have regard for Jehoshaphat the king of Judah, I would neither look at you, nor see you. (15)But now bring me a minstrel." And when the minstrel played, the power of the LORD came upon him. (16)And he said, "Thus says the LORD, 'I will make this dry stream-bed full of pools.' (17)For thus says the LORD, 'You shall not see wind or rain, but that stream-bed shall be filled with water, so that you shall drink, you, your cattle, and your beasts.' (18)This is a light thing in the sight of the LORD; he will also give the Moabites into your hand, (19)and you shall conquer every fortified city, and every choice city, and shall fell every good tree, and stop up all springs of water, and ruin every good piece of land with stones." (20)The next morning, about the time of offering the sacrifice, behold, water came from the direction of Edom, till the country was filled with water.

(21)When all the Moabites heard that the kings had come up to fight against them, all who were able to put on armor, from the youngest to the oldest, were called out, and were drawn up at the frontier. (22)And when they rose early in the morning, and the sun shone upon the water, the Moabites saw the water opposite them as red as blood. (23)And they said, "This is blood; the kings have surely fought together, and slain one another. Now then, Moab, to the spoil!" (24)But when they came to the camp of Israel, the Israelites rose and attacked the Moabites, till they fled before them; and they went forward, slaughtering the Moabites as they went. (25)And they overthrew the cities, and on every good piece of land every man threw a stone, until it was covered; they stopped every spring of water, and felled all the good trees; till only its stones were left in Kir-hareseth, and the slingers surrounded and conquered it. (26)When the king of Moab saw that the battle was going against him, he took with him seven hundred swordsmen to break through, opposite the king of Edom; but they could not. (27)Then he took his eldest son who was to reign in his stead, and offered him for a burnt offering upon the wall. And there came great wrath upon Israel; and they withdrew from him and returned to their own land.

108 Elisha and the Widow's Oil

II Kings 4:1–7

(1)Now the wife of one of the sons of the prophets cried to Elisha, "Your servant my husband is dead; and you know that your servant feared the LORD, but the creditor has come to take my two children to be his slaves." (2)And Elisha said to her, "What shall I do for you? Tell me; what have you in the house?" And she said, "Your maidservant has nothing in the house, except a jar of oil." (3)Then he said, "Go outside, borrow vessels of all your neighbors, empty vessels and not too few. (4)Then go in, and shut the door upon yourself and your sons, and pour into all these vessels; and when one is full, set it aside." (5)So she went from him and shut the door upon herself and her sons; and as she poured they brought the vessels to her. (6)When the vessels were full, she said to her son, "Bring me another vessel." And he said to her, "There is not another." Then the oil stopped flowing. (7)She came and told the man of God, and he said, "Go, sell the oil and pay your debts, and you and your sons can live on the rest."

109 Elisha Raises the Shunammite Woman's Son

II Kings 4:8–37

(8)One day Elisha went on to Shunem, where a wealthy woman lived, who urged him to eat some food. So whenever he passed that way, he would turn in there to eat food. (9)And she said to her husband, "Behold now, I perceive that this is a holy man of God, who is continually passing our way. (10)Let us make a small roof chamber with walls, and put there for him a bed, a table, a chair, and a lamp, so that whenever he comes to us, he can go in there."

(11)One day he came there, and he turned into the chamber and rested there. (12)And he said to Gehazi his servant, "Call this Shunammite." When he had called her, she stood before him. (13)And he said to him, "Say now to her, See, you have taken all this trouble for us; what is to be done for you? Would you have a word spoken on your behalf to the king or to the commander of the army?" She answered, "I dwell among my own people." (14)And he said, "What then is to be done for her?" Gehazi answered, "Well, she has no son, and her husband is old." (15)He said, "Call her." And when he had called her, she stood in the doorway. (16)And he said, "At this season, when the time comes round, you shall embrace a son." And she said, "No, my lord, O man of God; do not lie to your maidservant." (17)But the woman conceived, and she bore a son about that time the following spring, as Elisha had said to her.

(18)When the child had grown, he went out one day to his father among the reapers. (19)And he said to his father, "Oh, my head, my head!" The father said to his servant, "Carry him to his mother." (20)And when he had lifted him, and brought him to his mother, the child sat on her lap till noon, and then he died. (21)And she went up and laid him on the bed of the man of God, and shut the door upon him, and went out. (22)Then she called to her husband, and said, "Send me one of the servants and one of the asses, that I may quickly go to the man of God, and come back again." (23)And he said, "Why will you go to him today? It is neither new moon nor sabbath." She said, "It will be well." (24)Then she saddled the ass, and she said to her servant, "Urge the beast on; do not slacken the pace for me unless I tell you." (25)So she set out, and came to the man of God at Mount Carmel.

When the man of God saw her coming, he said to Gehazi his servant, "Look, yonder is the Shunammite; (26)run at once to meet her, and say to her, Is it well with you? Is it well with your husband? Is it well with the child?" And she answered, "It is well." (27)And when she came to the mountain to the man of God, she caught hold of his feet. And Gehazi came to thrust her away. But the man of God said, "Let her alone, for she is in bitter distress; and the LORD has hidden it from me, and has not told me." (28)Then she said, "Did I ask my lord for a son? Did I not say, Do not deceive me?" (29)He said to Gahazi, "Gird up your loins, and take my staff in your hand, and go. If you meet any one, do not salute him; and if any one salutes you, do not reply; and lay my staff upon the face of the child." (30)Then the mother of the child said, "As the LORD lives, and as you yourself live, I will not leave you." So he arose and followed her. (31)Gehazi went on ahead and laid the staff upon the face of the child, but there was no sound or sign of life. Therefore he returned to meet him, and told him, "The child has not awaked."

(32)When Elisha came into the house, he saw the child lying dead on his bed. (33)So he went in and shut the door upon the two of them, and prayed to the LORD. (34)Then he went up and lay upon the child, putting his mouth upon his mouth, his eyes upon his eyes, and his hands upon his hands; and as he stretched himself upon him, the flesh of the child became warm. (35)Then he got up again, and walked once to and fro in the house, and went up, and stretched himself upon him; the child sneezed seven times, and the child opened his eyes. (36)Then he summoned Gehazi and said, "Call this Shunammite." So he called her. And when she came to him, he said, "Take up your son." (37)She came and fell at his feet, bowing to the ground; then she took up her son and went out.

110 Two Miracles Concerning Food

II Kings 4:38–44

(38)And Elisha came again to Gilgal when there was a famine in the land. And as the sons of the prophets were sitting before him, he said to his servant, "Set on the great pot, and boil pottage for the sons of the prophets." (39)One of them went out into the field to gather herbs, and found a wild vine and gathered from it his lap full of wild gourds, and came and cut them up into the pot of pottage, not knowing what they were. (40)And they poured out for the men to eat. But while they were eating of the pottage, they cried out, "O man of God, there is death in the pot!" And they could not eat it. (41)He said, "Then bring meal." And he threw it into the pot, and said, "Pour out for the men, that they may eat." And there was no harm in the pot.

(42)A man came from Baal-shalishah, bringing the man of God bread of the first fruits, twenty loaves of barley, and fresh ears of grain in his sack. And Elisha said, "Give to the men, that they may eat." (43)But his servant said, "How am I to set this before a hundred men?" So he repeated, "Give them to the men, that they may eat, for thus says the LORD, 'They shall eat and have some left.' " (44)So he set it before them. And they ate, and had some left, according to the word of the LORD.

111 Elisha Heals Naaman

II Kings 5:1–27

(1)Naaman, commander of the army of the king of Syria, was a great man with his master and in high favor, because by him the LORD had given victory to Syria. He was a mighty man of valor, but he was a leper. (2)Now the Syrians on one of their raids had carried off a little maid from the land of Israel, and she waited on Naaman's wife. (3)She said to her mistress, "Would that my lord were with the prophet who is in Samaria! He would cure him of his leprosy." (4)So Naaman went in and told his lord, "Thus and so spoke the maiden from the land of Israel." (5)And the king of Syria said, "Go now, and I will send a letter to the king of Israel."

So he went, taking with him ten talents of silver, six thousand shekels of gold, and ten festal garments. (6)And he brought the letter to the king of Israel, which read, "When this letter reaches you, know that I have sent to you Naaman my servant, that you may cure him of his leprosy." (7)And when the king of Israel read the letter, he rent his clothes and said, "Am I God, to kill and to make alive, that this man sends word to me to cure a man of his leprosy? Only consider, and see how he is seeking a quarrel with me."

(8)But when Elisha the man of God heard that the king of Israel had rent his clothes, he sent to the king, saying, "Why have you rent your clothes? Let him come now to me, that he may know that there is a prophet in Israel." (9)So Naaman came with his horses and chariots, and halted at the door of Elisha's house. (10)And Elisha sent a messenger to him, saying, "Go and wash in the Jordan seven times, and your flesh shall be restored, and you shall be clean." (11)But Naaman was angry, and went away, saying, "Behold, I thought that he would surely come out to me, and stand, and call on the name of the LORD his God, and wave his hand over the place, and cure the leper. [12]Are not Abana and Pharpar, the rivers of Damascus, better than all the waters of Israel? Could I not wash in them, and be clean?" So he turned and went away in a rage. [13]But his servants came near and said to him, "My father, if the prophet had commanded you to do some great thing, would you not have done it? How much rather, then, when he says to you, 'Wash, and be clean'?" [14]So he went down and dipped himself seven times in the Jordan, according to the word of the man of God; and his flesh was restored like the flesh of a little child, and he was clean.

[15]Then he returned to the man of God, he and all his company, and he came and stood before him; and he said, "Behold, I know that there is no God in all the earth but in Israel; so accept now a present from your servant." [16]But he said, "As the LORD lives, whom I serve, I will receive none." And he urged him to take it, but he refused. [17]Then Naaman said, "If not, I pray you, let there be given to your servant two mules' burden of earth; for henceforth your servant will not offer burnt offering or sacrifice to any god but the LORD. [18]In this matter may the LORD pardon your servant: when my master goes into the house of Rimmon to worship there, leaning on my arm, and I bow myself in the house of Rimmon, when I bow myself in the house of Rimmon, the LORD pardon your servant in this matter." [19]He said to him, "Go in peace."

But when Naaman had gone from him a short distance, [20]Gehazi, the servant of Elisha the man of God, said, "See, my master has spared this Naaman the Syrian, in not accepting from his hand what he brought. As the LORD lives, I will run after him, and get something from him." [21]So Gehazi followed Naaman. And when Naaman saw some one running after him, he alighted from the chariot to meet him, and said, "Is all well?" [22]And he said, "All is well. My master has sent me to say, 'There have just now come to me from the hill country of Ephraim two young men of the sons of the prophets; pray, give them a talent of silver and two festal garments.' " [23]And Naaman said, "Be pleased to accept two talents." And he urged him, and tied up two talents of silver in two bags, with two festal garments, and laid them upon two of his servants; and they carried them before Gehazi. [24]And when he came to the hill, he took them from their hand, and put them in the house; and he sent the men away, and they departed. [25]He went in, and stood before his master, and Elisha said to him, "Where have you been, Gehazi?" And he said, "Your servant went nowhere." [26]But he said to him, "Did I not go with you in spirit when the man turned from his chariot to meet you? Was it a time to accept money and garments, olive orchards and vineyards, sheep and oxen, menservants and maidservants? [27]Therefore the leprosy of Naaman shall cleave to you, and to your descendants for ever." So he went out from his presence a leper, as white as snow.

112 The Miracle of the Floating Axe Head

II Kings 6:1–7

[1]Now the sons of the prophets said to Elisha, "See, the place where we dwell under your charge is too small for us. [2]Let us go to the Jordan and each of us get there a log, and let us make a place for us to dwell there." And he answered, "Go." [3]Then one

of them said, "Be pleased to go with your servants." And he answered, "I will go." (4)So he went with them. And when they came to the Jordan, they cut down trees. (5)But as one was felling a log, his axe head fell into the water; and he cried out, "Alas, my master! It was borrowed." (6)Then the man of God said, "Where did it fall?" When he showed him the place, he cut off a stick, and threw it in there, and made the iron float. (7)And he said, "Take it up." So he reached out his hand and took it.

113 The Syrians Miraculously Captured

II Kings 6:8–23

(8)Once when the king of Syria was warring against Israel, he took counsel with his servants, saying, "At such and such a place shall be my camp." (9)But the man of God sent word to the king of Israel, "Beware that you do not pass this place, for the Syrians are going down there." (10)And the king of Israel sent to the place of which the man of God told him. Thus he used to warn him, so that he saved himself there more than once or twice.

(11)And the mind of the king of Syria was greatly troubled because of this thing; and he called his servants and said to them, "Will you not show me who of us is for the king of Israel?" (12)And one of his servants said, "None, my lord, O king; but Elisha, the prophet who is in Israel, tells the king of Israel the words that you speak in your bedchamber." (13)And he said, "Go and see where he is, that I may send and seize him." It was told him, "Behold, he is in Dothan." (14)So he sent there horses and chariots and a great army; and they came by night, and surrounded the city.

(15)When the servant of the man of God rose early in the morning and went out, behold, an army with horses and chariots was round about the city. And the servant said, "Alas, my master! What shall we do?" (16)He said, "Fear not, for those who are with us are more than those who are with them." (17)Then Elisha prayed, and said, "O LORD, I pray thee, open his eyes that he may see." So the LORD opened the eyes of the young man, and he saw; and behold, the mountain was full of horses and chariots of fire round about Elisha. (18)And when the Syrians came down against him, Elisha prayed to the LORD, and said, "Strike this people, I pray thee, with blindness." So he struck them with blindness in accordance with the prayer of Elisha. (19)And Elisha said to them, "This is not the way, and this is not the city; follow me, and I will bring you to the man whom you seek." And he led them to Samaria.

(20)As soon as they entered Samaria, Elisha said, "O LORD, open the eyes of these men, that they may see." So the LORD opened their eyes, and they saw; and lo, they were in the midst of Samaria. (21)When the king of Israel saw them he said to Elisha, "My father, shall I slay them? Shall I slay them?" (22)He answered, "You shall not slay them. Would you slay those whom you have taken captive with your sword and with your bow? Set bread and water before them, that they may eat and drink and go to their master." (23)So he prepared for them a great feast; and when they had eaten and drunk, he sent them away, and they went to their master. And the Syrians came no more on raids into the land of Israel.

114 The Lifting of the Siege of Samaria

II Kings 6:24–7:20

(24)Afterward Ben-hadad king of Syria mustered his entire army, and went up, and besieged Samaria. (25)And there was a great famine in Samaria, as they besieged it, until an ass's head was sold for eighty shekels of silver, and the fourth part of a kab of dove's dung for five shekels of silver. (26)Now as the king of Israel was passing by upon the wall, a woman cried out to him, saying, "Help, my lord, O king!" (27)And he said, "If the LORD will not help you, whence shall I help you? From the threshing floor, or from the wine press?" (28)And the king asked her, "What is your trouble?" She answered, "This woman said to me, 'Give your son, that we may eat him today, and we will eat my son tomorrow.' (29)So we boiled my son, and ate him. And on the next day I said to her, 'Give your son, that we may eat him'; but she has hidden her son." (30)When the king heard the words of the woman he rent his clothes—now he was passing by upon the wall—and the people looked, and behold, he had sackcloth beneath upon his body—(31)and he said, "May God do so to me, and more also, if the head of Elisha the son of Shaphat remains on his shoulders today."

(32)Elisha was sitting in his house, and the elders were sitting with him. Now the king had dispatched a man from his presence; but before the messenger arrived Elisha said to the elders, "Do you see how this murderer has sent to take off my head? Look, when the messenger comes, shut the door, and hold the door fast against him. Is not the sound of his master's feet behind him?" (33)And while he was still speaking with them, the king came down to him and said, "This trouble is from the LORD! Why should I wait for the LORD any longer?" (7:1)But Elisha said, "Hear the word of the LORD: thus says the LORD, Tomorrow about this time a measure of fine meal shall be sold for a shekel, and two measures of barley for a shekel, at the gate of Samaria." (2)Then the captain on whose hand the king leaned said to the man of God, "If the LORD himself should make windows in heaven, could this thing be?" But he said, "You shall see it with your own eyes, but you shall not eat of it."

(3)Now there were four men who were lepers at the entrance to the gate; and they said to one another, "Why do we sit here till we die? (4)If we say, 'Let us enter the city,' the famine is in the city, and we shall die there; and if we sit here, we die also. So now come, let us go over to the camp of the Syrians; if they spare our lives we shall live, and if they kill us we shall but die." (5)So they arose at twilight to go to the camp of the Syrians; but when they came to the edge of the camp of the Syrians, behold, there was no one there. (6)For the LORD had made the army of the Syrians hear the sound of chariots, and of horses, the sound of a great army, so that they said to one another, "Behold, the king of Israel has hired against us the kings of the Hittites and the kings of Egypt to come upon us." (7)So they fled away in the twilight and forsook their tents, their horses, and their asses, leaving the camp as it was, and fled for their lives. (8)And when these lepers came to the edge of the camp, they went into a tent, and ate and drank, and they carried off silver and gold and clothing, and went and hid them; then they came back, and entered another tent, and carried off things from it, and went and hid them.

(9)Then they said to one another, "We are not doing right. This day is a day of good

179

news; if we are silent and wait until the morning light, punishment will overtake us; now therefore come, let us go and tell the king's household." (10)So they came and called to the gatekeepers of the city, and told them, "We came to the camp of the Syrians, and behold, there was no one to be seen or heard there, nothing but the horses tied, and the asses tied, and the tents as they were." (11)Then the gatekeepers called out, and it was told within the king's household. (12)And the king rose in the night, and said to his servants, "I will tell you what the Syrians have prepared against us. They know that we are hungry; therefore they have gone out of the camp to hide themselves in the open country, thinking, 'When they come out of the city, we shall take them alive and get into the city.' " (13)And one of his servants said, "Let some men take five of the remaining horses, seeing that those who are left here will fare like the whole multitude of Israel that have already perished; let us send and see." (14)So they took two mounted men, and the king sent them after the army of the Syrians, saying, "Go and see." (15)So they went after them as far as the Jordan; and, lo, all the way was littered with garments and equipment which the Syrians had thrown away in their haste. And the messengers returned, and told the king.

(16)Then the people went out, and plundered the camp of the Syrians. So a measure of fine meal was sold for a shekel, and two measures of barley for a shekel, according to the word of the LORD. (17)Now the king had appointed the captain on whose hand he leaned to have charge of the gate; and the people trod upon him in the gate, so that he died, as the man of God had said when the king came down to him. (18)For when the man of God had said to the king, "Two measures of barley shall be sold for a shekel, and a measure of fine meal for a shekel, about this time tomorrow in the gate of Samaria," (19)the captain had answered the man of God, "If the LORD himself should make windows in heaven, could such a thing be?" And he had said, "You shall see it with your own eyes, but you shall not eat of it." (20)And so it happened to him, for the people trod upon him in the gate and he died.

115 The Restoration of Property to the Shunammite Woman

II Kings 8:1–6

(1)Now Elisha had said to the woman whose son he had restored to life, "Arise, and depart with your household, and sojourn wherever you can; for the LORD has called for a famine, and it will come upon the land for seven years." (2)So the woman arose, and did according to the word of the man of God; she went with her household and sojourned in the land of the Philistines seven years. (3)And at the end of the seven years, when the woman returned from the land of the Philistines, she went forth to appeal to the king for her house and her land. (4)Now the king was talking with Gehazi the servant of the man of God, saying, "Tell me all the great things that Elisha has done." (5)And while he was telling the king how Elisha had restored the dead to life, behold, the woman whose son he had restored to life appealed to the king for her house and her land. And Gehazi said, "My lord, O king, here is the woman, and here is her son whom Elisha restored to life." (6)And when the king asked the woman, she told him. So the king appointed an official for her, saying, "Restore all that was hers, together with all the produce of the fields from the day that she left the land until now."

116 Elisha Predicts Hazael's Reign as King of Syria

II Kings 8:7–15

(7)Now Elisha came to Damascus. Ben-hadad the king of Syria was sick; and when it was told him, "The man of God has come here," (8)the king said to Hazael, "Take a present with you and go to meet the man of God, and inquire of the LORD through him, saying, 'Shall I recover from this sickness?' " (9)So Hazael went to meet him, and took a present with him, all kinds of goods of Damascus, forty camel loads. When he came and stood before him, he said, "Your son Ben-hadad king of Syria has sent me to you, saying, 'Shall I recover from this sickness?' " (10)And Elisha said to him, "Go, say to him, 'You shall certainly recover'; but the LORD has shown me that he shall certainly die." (11)And he fixed his gaze and stared at him, until he was ashamed. And the man of God wept. (12)And Hazael said, "Why does my lord weep?" He answered, "Because I know the evil that you will do to the people of Israel; you will set on fire their fortresses, and you will slay their young men with the sword, and dash in pieces their little ones, and rip up their women with child." (13)And Hazael said, "What is your servant, who is but a dog, that he should do this great thing?" Elisha answered, "The LORD has shown me that you are to be king over Syria." (14)Then he departed from Elisha, and came to his master, who said to him, "What did Elisha say to you?" And he answered, "He told me that you would certainly recover." (15)But on the morrow he took the coverlet and dipped it in water and spread it over his face, till he died. And Hazael became king in his stead.

117 The Reign of Jehoram/Joram of Judah Begins

II Kings 8:16–22   II Chronicles 21:2–10

(16)In the fifth year of Joram
the son of Ahab, king of Israel,
Jehoram the son of Jehoshaphat, king
of Judah, began to reign.

(2)He had brothers, the sons of
Jehoshaphat: Azariah, Jehiel,
Zechariah, Azariah, Michael, and
Shephatiah; all these were the sons
of Jehoshaphat king of Judah.
(3)Their father gave them great
gifts, of silver, gold, and valuable
possessions, together with fortified
cities in Judah; but he gave the
kingdom to Jehoram, because he was
the first-born. (4)When Jehoram
had ascended the throne of his father
and was established, he slew all his
brothers with the sword, and also some
of the princes of Israel.

(17)He was thirty-two years old
when he became king, and he reigned
eight years in Jerusalem. (18)And
he walked in the way of the kings of
Israel, as the house of Ahab had
done, for the daughter of Ahab was
his wife. And he did what was evil
in the sight of the LORD. (19)Yet
the LORD would not destroy
Judah, for the sake of David his
servant,

since he promised to give
a lamp to him and to his sons
for ever.
(20)In his days Edom revolted
from the rule of Judah, and set up a
king of their own. (21)Then Joram
passed over
to Zair
with

all his chariots,
and rose by night, and
he and his chariot commanders
smote the Edomites who had surrounded
him;

but his army fled home.
(22)So Edom revolted from the rule
of Judah to this day. Then Libnah
revolted
at the same time.

(5)Jehoram was thirty-two years old
when he became king, and he reigned
eight years in Jerusalem. (6)And
he walked in the way of the kings of
Israel, as the house of Ahab had
done; for the daughter of Ahab was
his wife. And he did what was evil
in the sight of the LORD. (7)Yet
the LORD would not destroy

the house of David, because of the
covenant which he had made with David,
and since he had promised to give
a lamp to him and to his sons
for ever.
(8)In his days Edom revolted
from the rule of Judah, and set up a
king of their own. (9)Then Jehoram
passed over

with
his commanders and
all his chariots,
and he rose by night and

smote the Edomites who had surrounded
him
and his chariot commanders.

/10/So Edom revolted from the rule
of Judah to this day. Then Libnah
revolted from his rule
at the same time,
because he had forsaken the LORD,
the God of his fathers.

118 The Sin and Punishment of Jehoram/Joram of Judah

II Chronicles 21:11-17

(11)Moreover he made high places in the hill country of Judah, and led the inhabitants of Jerusalem into unfaithfulness, and made Judah go astray. (12)And a letter came to him from Elijah the prophet saying, "Thus says the LORD, the God of David your father, 'Because you have not walked in the ways of Jehoshaphat your father, or in the ways of Asa king of Judah, (13)but have walked in the way of the kings of Israel, and have led

Judah and the inhabitants of Jerusalem into unfaithfulness, as the house of Ahab led Israel into unfaithfulness, and also you have killed your brothers, of your father's house, who were better than yourself; (14)behold, the LORD will bring a great plague on your people, your children, your wives, and all your possessions, (15)and you yourself will have a severe sickness with a disease of your bowels, until your bowels come out because of the disease, day by day.' "

(16)And the LORD stirred up against Jehoram the anger of the Philistines and of the Arabs who are near the Ethiopians; (17)and they came up against Judah, and invaded it, and carried away all the possessions they found that belonged to the king's house, and also his sons and his wives, so that no son was left to him except Jehoahaz, his youngest son.

119 The Reign of Jehoram/Joram of Judah Concludes

II Kings 8:23-24a   *II Chronicles 21:18-20*

(18)And after all this the LORD smote him in his bowels with an incurable disease. (19)In the course of time, at the end of two years, his bowels came out because of the disease, and he died in great agony. His people made no fire in his honor, like the fires made for his fathers. (20)He was thirty-two years old when he began to reign, and he reigned eight years in Jerusalem; and he departed with no one's regret.

(23)Now the rest of the acts of Joram, and all that he did, are they not written in the Book of the Chronicles of the Kings of Judah? (24)So Joram slept with his fathers, and was buried   They buried him
with his fathers
in the city of David;   in the city of David,
                                             but not in the tombs of the kings.

120 The Reign of Ahaziah of Judah Begins

II Kings 8:24b-29   *II Chronicles 22:1-6*

(1)And the inhabitants of
                                             Jerusalem made
and Ahaziah his son reigned   Ahaziah his youngest son king
in his stead.   in his stead;

183

for the band of men that came with
the Arabs to the camp had slain all
the older sons.

(25)In the twelfth year of Joram
the son of Ahab, king of Israel,
Ahaziah the son of Jehoram, king of
Judah, began to reign.

So Ahaziah the son of Jehoram king of
Judah reigned.

(26)Ahaziah was twenty-two years old
when he began to reign, and he reigned
one year in Jerusalem. His mother's
name was Athaliah; she was a grand-
daughter of Omri king of Israel.

/2/Ahaziah was forty-two years old
when he began to reign, and he reigned
one year in Jerusalem. His mother's
name was Athaliah; she was a grand-
daughter of Omri.

(27)He also walked in the way of
the house of Ahab,

(3)He also walked in the ways of
the house of Ahab,
for his mother was his counselor
in doing wickedly.

and did what was evil in the sight
of the LORD, as the house of Ahab
had done,
for he was son-in-law to the
house of Ahab.

(4)He did what was evil in the sight
of the LORD, as the house of Ahab
had done;

for after the death of his father
they were his counselors, to his
undoing. (5)He even followed their
counsel, and

(28)He went with Joram the son
of Ahab

went with Jehoram the son
of Ahab king of Israel

to make war against Hazael
king of Syria at Ramoth-gilead,
where the Syrians wounded Joram.

to make war against Hazael
king of Syria at Ramoth-gilead.
And the Syrians wounded Joram,

(29)And King Joram returned to be
healed in Jezreel of the wounds which
the Syrians had given him at Ramah,
when he fought against Hazael king
of Syria. And Ahaziah the son of
Jehoram king of Judah went down to
see Joram the son of Ahab in Jezreel,
because he was sick.

(6)and he returned to be
healed in Jezreel of the wounds which
he had received at Ramah,
when he fought against Hazael king
of Syria. And Ahaziah the son of
Jehoram king of Judah went down to
see Joram the son of Ahab in Jezreel,
because he was sick.

121 Jehu Anointed King of Israel

II Kings 9:1–13

(1)Then Elisha the prophet called one of the sons of the prophets and said to him,
"Gird up your loins, and take this flask of oil in your hand, and go to Ramoth-gilead.
(2)And when you arrive, look there for Jehu the son of Jehoshaphat, son of Nimshi;

and go in and bid him rise from among his fellows, and lead him to an inner chamber. ⁽³⁾Then take the flask of oil, and pour it on his head, and say, 'Thus says the LORD, I anoint you king over Israel.' Then open the door and flee; do not tarry."

⁽⁴⁾So the young man, the prophet, went to Ramoth-gilead. ⁽⁵⁾And when he came, behold, the commanders of the army were in council; and he said, "I have an errand to you, O commander." And Jehu said, "To which of us all?" And he said, "To you, O commander." ⁽⁶⁾So he arose, and went into the house; and the young man poured the oil on his head, saying to him, "Thus says the LORD the God of Israel, I anoint you king over the people of the LORD, over Israel. ⁽⁷⁾And you shall strike down the house of Ahab your master, that I may avenge on Jezebel the blood of my servants the prophets, and the blood of all the servants of the LORD. ⁽⁸⁾For the whole house of Ahab shall perish; and I will cut off from Ahab every male, bond or free, in Israel. ⁽⁹⁾And I will make the house of Ahab like the house of Jeroboam the son of Nebat, and like the house of Baasha the son of Ahijah. ⁽¹⁰⁾And the dogs shall eat Jezebel in the territory of Jezreel, and none shall bury her." Then he opened the door, and fled.

⁽¹¹⁾When Jehu came out to the servants of his master, they said to him, "Is all well? Why did this mad fellow come to you?" And he said to them, "You know the fellow and his talk." ⁽¹²⁾And they said, "That is not true; tell us now." And he said, "Thus and so he spoke to me, saying, 'Thus says the LORD, I anoint you king over Israel.' " ⁽¹³⁾Then in haste every man of them took his garment, and put it under him on the bare steps, and they blew the trumpet, and proclaimed, "Jehu is king."

122 Jehu Kills Joram of Israel and Ahaziah of Judah

II Kings 9:14–29	II Chronicles 22:7, 9

⁽¹⁴⁾Thus Jehu the son of Jehoshaphat the son of Nimshi conspired against Joram. (Now Joram with all Israel had been on guard at Ramoth-gilead against Hazael king of Syria; ⁽¹⁵⁾but King Joram had returned to be healed in Jezreel of the wounds which the Syrians had given him, when he fought with Hazael king of Syria.) So Jehu said, "If this is your mind, then let no one slip out of the city to go and tell the news in Jezreel." ⁽¹⁶⁾Then Jehu mounted his chariot, and went to Jezreel, for Joram lay there. And Ahaziah king of Judah had come down to visit Joram.

⁽¹⁷⁾Now the watchman was standing on the tower in Jezreel, and he spied the company of Jehu as he came, and

said, "I see a company." And Joram
said, "Take a horseman, and send to
meet them, and let him say, 'Is it
peace?' " (18)So a man on horseback
went to meet him, and said, "Thus
says the king, 'Is it peace?' " And
Jehu said, "What have you to do with
peace? Turn round and ride behind
me." And the watchman reported,
saying, "The messenger reached them,
but he is not coming back." (19)Then
he sent out a second horseman, who
came to them, and said, "Thus the king
has said, 'Is it peace?' " And Jehu
answered, "What have you to do with
peace? Turn round and ride behind
me." (20)Again the watchman
reported, "He reached them, but he is
not coming back. And the driving is
like the driving of Jehu the son of
Nimshi; for he drives furiously."

(7)But it was ordained by God
that the downfall of Ahaziah should
come about through his going to visit
Joram. For when he came there

(21)Joram said, "Make ready."
And they made ready his chariot.
Then Joram king of Israel and
Ahaziah king of Judah set out,
each in his chariot,
and went to meet Jehu,

he went out with Jehoram to meet Jehu
the son of Nimshi,
whom the LORD had anointed to destroy
the house of Ahab.

and met him at the property of Naboth
the Jezreelite. (22)And when Joram
saw Jehu, he said, "Is it peace,
Jehu?' " He answered, "What peace can
there be, so long as the harlotries
and the sorceries of your mother
Jezebel are so many?" (23)Then Joram
reined about and fled, saying to
Ahaziah, "Treachery, O Ahaziah!"
(24)And Jehu drew his bow with his
full strength, and shot Joram between
the shoulders, so that the arrow
pierced his heart, and he sank in his

chariot. (25)Jehu said to Bidkar his aide, "Take him up, and cast him on the plot of ground belonging to Naboth the Jezreelite; for remember, when you and I rode side by side behind Ahab his father, how the LORD uttered this oracle against him: (26)'As surely as I saw yesterday the blood of Naboth and the blood of his sons—says the LORD—I will requite you on this plot of ground.' Now therefore take him up and cast him on the plot of ground, in accordance with the word of the LORD."

(27)When Ahaziah the king of Judah saw this, he fled in the direction of Beth-haggan. And Jehu pursued him,

(9)He searched for Ahaziah,

and said, "Shoot him also"; and they shot him in the chariot at the ascent of Gur, which is by Ibleam. And he fled to Megiddo, and died there.

and he was captured while hiding in Samaria, and he was brought to Jehu and put to death.

(28)His servants carried him in a chariot to Jerusalem, and buried him in his tomb with his fathers in the city of David.

They buried him,

for they said, "He is the grandson of Jehoshaphat, who sought the LORD with all his heart." And the house of Ahaziah had no one able to rule the kingdom.

(29)In the eleventh year of Joram the son of Ahab, Ahaziah began to reign over Judah.

123 The Death of Jezebel

II Kings 9:30-37

(30)When Jehu came to Jezreel, Jezebel heard of it; and she painted her eyes, and adorned her head, and looked out of the window. (31)And as Jehu entered the gate, she said, "Is it peace, you Zimri, murderer of your master?" (32)And he lifted up his face to the window, and said, "Who is on my side? Who?" Two or three eunuchs looked out at him. (33)He said, "Throw her down." So they threw her down; and some of her blood spattered on the wall and on the horses, and they trampled on her. (34)Then he went in and ate and drank; and he said, "See now to this cursed woman, and bury her; for she is a king's daughter." (35)But when they went to bury her, they found no more of her than the skull and the feet and the palms of her hands. (36)When they came back and told him, he said, "This is the word of the LORD, which he spoke by his servant Elijah the Tishbite, 'In the territory of Jezreel the dogs shall eat the flesh of Jezebel; (37)and the corpse of Jezebel shall be as dung upon the face of the field in the territory of Jezreel, so that no one can say, This is Jezebel.' "

124 The Killing of Ahab's Sons

II Kings 10:1–11

(1)Now Ahab had seventy sons in Samaria. So Jehu wrote letters, and sent them to Samaria, to the rulers of the city, to the elders, and to the guardians of the sons of Ahab, saying, (2)"Now then, as soon as this letter comes to you, seeing your master's sons are with you, and there are with you chariots and horses, fortified cities also, and weapons, (3)select the best and fittest of your master's sons and set him on his father's throne, and fight for your master's house." (4)But they were exceedingly afraid, and said, "Behold, the two kings could not stand before him; how then can we stand?" (5)So he who was over the palace, and he who was over the city, together with the elders and the guardians, sent to Jehu, saying, "We are your servants, and we will do all that you bid us. We will not make any one king; do whatever is good in your eyes." (6)Then he wrote to them a second letter, saying, "If you are on my side, and if you are ready to obey me, take the heads of your master's sons, and come to me at Jezreel tomorrow at this time." Now the king's sons, seventy persons, were with the great men of the city, who were bringing them up. (7)And when the letter came to them, they took the king's sons, and slew them, seventy persons, and put their heads in baskets, and sent them to him at Jezreel. (8)When the messenger came and told him, "They have brought the heads of the king's sons," he said, "Lay them in two heaps at the entrance of the gate until the morning." (9)Then in the morning, when he went out, he stood, and said to all the people, "You are innocent. It was I who conspired against my master, and slew him; but who struck down all these? (10)Know then that there shall fall to the earth nothing of the word of the LORD, which the LORD spoke concerning the house of Ahab; for the LORD has done what he said by his servant Elijah." (11)So Jehu slew all that remained of the house of Ahab in Jezreel, all his great men, and his familiar friends, and his priests, until he left him none remaining.

125 The Killing of the Kin of Ahaziah of Judah

II Kings 10:12–14   II Chronicles 22:8

(12)Then he set out and went to
Samaria. On the way, when he was at
Beth-eked of the Shepherds,

188

	⁽⁸⁾And when Jehu was executing judgment upon the house of Ahab,

⁽¹³⁾Jehu met <u>the kinsmen of Ahaziah king</u> of Judah,

he met <u>the princes</u>
of Judah
and the sons of Ahaziah's brothers,
who attended Ahaziah,

and he said, "Who are you?" And they answered, "We are the kinsmen of Ahaziah, and we came down to visit the royal princes and the sons of the queen mother." ⁽¹⁴⁾He said, "Take them alive." And they took them alive,
and <u>slew</u> them
at the pit of Beth-eked, forty-two persons, and he spared none of them.

and <u>he killed</u> them.

126 Jehu Kills the Last Ahabites

II Kings 10:15-17

⁽¹⁵⁾And when he departed from there, he met Jehonadab the son of Rechab coming to meet him; and he greeted him, and said to him, "Is your heart true to my heart as mine is to yours?" And Jehonadab answered, "It is." Jehu said, "If it is, give me your hand." So he gave him his hand. And Jehu took him up with him into the chariot. ⁽¹⁶⁾And he said, "Come with me, and see my zeal for the LORD." So he had him ride in his chariot. ⁽¹⁷⁾And when he came to Samaria, he slew all that remained to Ahab in Samaria, till he had wiped them out, according to the word of the LORD which he spoke to Elijah.

127 Jehu Exterminates Baal Worship

II Kings 10:18-28

⁽¹⁸⁾Then Jehu assembled all the people, and said to them, "Ahab served Baal a little; but Jehu will serve him much. ⁽¹⁹⁾Now therefore call to me all the prophets of Baal, all his worshipers and all his priests; let none be missing, for I have a great sacrifice to offer to Baal; whoever is missing shall not live." But Jehu did it with cunning in order to destroy the worshipers of Baal. ⁽²⁰⁾And Jehu ordered, "Sanctify a solemn assembly for Baal." So they proclaimed it. ⁽²¹⁾And Jehu sent throughout all Israel; and all the worshipers of Baal came, so that there was not a man left who did not come. And they entered the house of Baal, and the house of Baal was filled from one end to the other. ⁽²²⁾He said to him who was in charge of the wardrobe, "Bring out the vestments for all the worshipers of Baal." So he brought out the vestments for them. ⁽²³⁾Then Jehu went into the house of Baal with Jehonadab the son of Rechab; and he said to the worshipers

of Baal, 'Search, and see that there is no servant of the LORD here among you, but only the worshipers of Baal.'' (24)Then he went in to offer sacrifices and burnt offerings.

Now Jehu had stationed eighty men outside, and said, "The man who allows any of those whom I give into your hands to escape shall forfeit his life." (25)So as soon as he had made an end of offering the burnt offering, Jehu said to the guard and to the officers, "Go in and slay them; let not a man escape." So when they put them to the sword, the guard and the officers cast them out and went into the inner room of the house of Baal (26)and they brought out the pillar that was in the house of Baal, and burned it. (27)And they demolished the pillar of Baal, and demolished the house of Baal, and made it a latrine to this day.

(28)Thus Jehu wiped out Baal from Israel.

128 Jehu's Sin and Death

II Kings 10:29–36

(29)But Jehu did not turn aside from the sins of Jeroboam the son of Nebat, which he made Israel to sin, the golden calves that were in Bethel, and in Dan. (30)And the LORD said to Jehu, "Because you have done well in carrying out what is right in my eyes, and have done to the house of Ahab according to all that was in my heart, your sons of the fourth generation shall sit on the throne of Israel." (31)But Jehu was not careful to walk in the law of the LORD the God of Israel with all his heart; he did not turn from the sins of Jeroboam, which he made Israel to sin.

(32)In those days the LORD began to cut off parts of Israel. Hazael defeated them throughout the territory of Israel: (33)from the Jordan eastward, all the land of Gilead, the Gadites, and the Reubenites, and the Manassites, from Aroer, which is by the valley of the Arnon, that is, Gilead and Bashan. (34)Now the rest of the acts of Jehu, and all that he did, and all his might, are they not written in the Book of the Chronicles of the Kings of Israel? (35)So Jehu slept with his fathers, and they buried him in Samaria. And Jehoahaz his son reigned in his stead. (36)The time that Jehu reigned over Israel in Samaria was twenty-eight years.

129 The Overthrow of Athaliah

II Kings 11:1–20	II Chronicles 22:10–23:21
(1)Now when Athaliah the mother of Ahaziah saw that her son was dead, she arose and destroyed all the royal family.	(10)Now when Athaliah the mother of Ahaziah saw that her son was dead, she arose and destroyed all the royal family of the house of Judah.
[2]But Jehosheba, the daughter of King Joram, sister of Ahaziah, took Joash the son of Ahaziah, and stole him away from among the king's sons who were about to be slain,*	(11)But Jeho-shabe-ath, the daughter of the king, took Joash the son of Ahaziah, and stole him away from among the king's sons who were about to be slain, and she put
*Hebrew lacks "and she put."	

him and his nurse in a bedchamber. Thus	him and his nurse in a bedchamber. Thus Jeho-shabe-ath, the daughter of King Jehoram and wife of Jehoiada the priest, because she was a sister of Ahaziah,
they hid him from Athaliah, so that he was not slain; (3)and he remained with her six years, hid in the house of the LORD, while Athaliah reigned over the land. (4)But in the seventh year Jehoiada sent and brought	hid him from Athaliah, so that she did not slay him; (12)and he remained with them six years, hid in the house of God, while Athaliah reigned over the land. /23:1/But in the seventh year Jehoiada took courage, and entered into a compact with the captains,
the captains of the Carites and of the guards,	Azariah the son of Jeroham, Ishmael the son of Jeho-hanan, Azariah the son of Obed, Ma-aseiah the son of Adaiah, and Elishaphat the son of Zichri. (2)And they went about through Judah and gathered the Levites from all the cities of Judah, and the heads of fathers' houses of Israel,
and had them come to him in the house of the LORD; and he made a covenant with them and put them under oath in the house of the LORD, and he showed them	and they came to Jerusalem. (3)And all the assembly made a covenant with the king in the house of God. And he
the king's son.	said to them, "Behold, the king's son! Let him reign, as the LORD spoke concerning the sons of David.
(5)And he commanded them, "This is the thing that you shall do: one third of you, those who come off duty on the sabbath and guard	(4)This is the thing that you shall do: of you priests and Levites who come off duty on the sabbath,

the king's house	one third shall be gatekeepers,
(6)(another third being at the	(5)and one third shall be at
gate Sur	the king's house
and a third at the gate behind the	and one third at the
guards), shall guard the palace;	Gate of the Foundation;
(7)and the two divisions of you,	
which come on duty in force on the	
sabbath and guard	
	and all the people shall be in
	the courts of
the house of the LORD	the house of the LORD.
to the king,	
	(6)Let no one enter the house
	of the LORD except the priests and
	ministering Levites; they may enter,
	for they are holy, but all the people
	shall keep the charge of the LORD.
	(7)The Levites
(8)shall surround the king, each with	shall surround the king, each with
his weapons in his hand; and whoever	his weapons in his hand; and whoever
approaches the ranks	
	enters the house
is to be slain. Be with the king	shall be slain. Be with the king
when he goes out and	when he comes in, and
when he comes in."	when he goes out."
(9)The captains	
	(8)The Levites and all Judah
did according to all that Jehoiada	did according to all that Jehoiada
the priest commanded, and each	the priest commanded. They each
brought his men who were to go off	brought his men, who were to go off
duty on the sabbath, with those who	duty on the sabbath, with those who
were to come on duty on the sabbath,	were to come on duty on the sabbath;
and came to	
	for
Jehoiada the priest.	Jehoiada the priest
	did not dismiss the divisions.
(10)And the priest delivered	(9)And Jehoiada the priest delivered
to the captains the spears and	to the captains the spears and
shields that had	the large and small shields that had
been King David's, which were in the	been King David's, which were in the
house of the LORD;	house of God;
	(10)and he set all the people as
(11)and the guards	a guard
	for the king,
stood,	

every man with his weapons in his
hand, from the south side of the house
to the north side of the house,
around the altar and the house
to the king.`
(12)Then he brought out the king's
son, and put the crown upon him, and
gave him the testimony; and they
proclaimed him king, and

anointed him;
and they clapped their hands,
and said,
"Long live the king!"
    (13)When Athaliah heard the
noise of the guard and
of the people,

she went into the house of the LORD
to the people; (14)and when she
looked, there was the king standing
by the pillar,
according to the custom,

and the captains and the trumpeters
beside the king, and all the people
of the land rejoicing and blowing
trumpets.

And Athaliah rent her clothes, and
cried, "Treason! Treason!" /15/Then
Jehoiada the priest commanded the
captains who were set over the army,
saying to them,
"Bring her out between the ranks; and
slay with the sword
any one who follows her."

For the priest said,
"Let her not be slain
in the house of the LORD."
(16)So they laid hands on her; and
she went through
the horses' entrance to
the king's house,

---

every man with his weapon in his
hand, from the south side of the house
to the north side of the house,
around the altar and the house.

⟨11⟩Then they brought out the king's
son, and put the crown upon him, and
gave him the testimony; and they
proclaimed him king, and
Jehoiada and his sons
anointed him,

and they said,
"Long live the king!"
    (12)When Athaliah heard the
noise
of the people
running and praising the king,
she went into the house of the LORD
to the people; (13)and when she
looked, there was the king standing
by his pillar

at the entrance,
and the captains and the trumpeters
beside the king, and all the people
of the land rejoicing and blowing
trumpets,
and the singers with their musical
instruments leading in the
celebration.
And Athaliah rent her clothes, and
cried, "Treason! Treason!" (14)Then
Jehoiada the priest brought out the
captains who were set over the army,
saying to them,
"Bring her out between the ranks;

any one who follows her
is to be slain with the sword."
For the priest said,
"Do not slay her
in the house of the LORD."
(15)So they laid hands on her; and
she went into
the entrance of the horse gate of
the king's house,

and there she was slain.

$^{(17)}$And Jehoiada made a covenant
between the LORD and
the king and people,
that they should be the LORD's people;
and also between the king and
the people.
$^{(18)}$Then all the people of the land
went to the house of Baal, and tore
it down; his altars and his images
they broke in pieces, and they slew
Mattan the priest of Baal before the
altars. And the priest posted
watchmen over the house of the LORD.

| | |

and they slew her there.

$^{(16)}$And Jehoiada made a covenant
between himself and
all the people and the king
that they should be the LORD's people.

$^{(17)}$Then all the people
went to the house of Baal, and tore
it down; his altars and his images
they broke in pieces, and they slew
Mattan the priest of Baal before the
altars. $^{(18)}$And Jehoiada posted
watchmen for the house of the LORD
under the direction of the Levitical
priests and the Levites whom David
had organized to be in charge of the
house of the LORD, to offer burnt
offerings to the LORD, as it is
written in the law of Moses, with
rejoicing and with singing, according
to the order of David. $^{(19)}$He
stationed the gatekeepers at the gates
of the house of the LORD so that no
one should enter who was in any way
unclean.

$^{(19)}$And he took the captains,
the Carites,
the guards,
and all the people of the land; and
they brought the king down from the
house of the LORD, marching through
the gate of the guards
to the king's house.
And he took his seat
on the throne of the kings.
$^{(20)}$So all the people of the land
rejoiced; and the city was quiet
after Athaliah had been slain
with the sword
at the king's house.

$^{(20)}$And he took the captains,
the nobles,
the governors of the people,
and all the people of the land; and
they brought the king down from the
house of the LORD, marching through
the upper gate
to the king's house.
And they set the king
upon the royal throne.
$^{(21)}$So all the people of the land
rejoiced; and the city was quiet,
after Athaliah had been slain
with the sword.

130 Jehoash/Joash of Judah Repairs the Temple

II Kings 11:21–12:16

$^{(21)}$Jehoash was seven years old
when he began to reign.

II Chronicles 24:1–14

$^{(1)}$Joash was seven years old
when he began to reign,

194

(12:1)In the seventh year of Jehu
Jehoash began to reign,
and he reigned forty years in   and he reigned forty years in
Jerusalem. His mother's name was   Jerusalem; his mother's name was
Zibiah of Beer-sheba. (2)And   Zibiah of Beer-sheba. (2)And
Jehoash did what was right in the   Joash did what was right in the
eyes of the LORD all his days,   eyes of the LORD all the days
because   of
Jehoiada the priest   Jehoiada the priest.
instructed him.
(3)Nevertheless the high places were
not taken away; the people continued
to sacrifice and burn incense on the
high places.

                                                 (3)Jehoiada got for him two wives,
                                                 and he had sons and daughters.
                                                      (4)After this Joash decided to
                                                 restore the house of the LORD.
                                                 (5)And he gathered the priests
                                                 and the Levites,
(4)Jehoash said to the priests,   and said to them,
"All the money of the holy things
which is brought into the house of
the LORD, the money for which each
man is assessed—the money from the
assessment of persons—and the money
which a man's heart prompts him to
bring into the house of the LORD,
(5)let the priests take, each from
his acquaintance; and let them

                                                 "Go out to the cities of Judah,
                                                 and gather from all Israel money
repair the house   to repair the house of your God
wherever any need of repairs is
discovered."

                                                 from year to year; and
                                                 see that you hasten the matter."

(6)But by the twenty-third year of
King Jehoash the priests had made no
repairs on the house.
                                                 But the Levites did not hasten it.
(7)Therefore King Jehoash summoned   (6)So the king summoned
Jehoiada the priest   Jehoiada the chief,
and the other priests
and said to them, "Why   and said to him, "Why
are you not repairing the house?
Now therefore take no more money
from your acquaintances, but hand it

over for the repair of the house."
(8)So the priests agreed that they
should take no more money from the
people, and that they should not
repair the house.

have you not required the Levites to
bring in from Judah and Jerusalem the
tax levied by Moses, the servant of
the LORD, on the congregation of
Israel for the tent of testimony?"
(7)For the sons of Athaliah, that
wicked woman, had broken into the
house of God; and had also used all
the dedicated things of the house of
the LORD for the Baals.

(9)Then Jehoiada the priest took

(8)So the king commanded,
and they made
a chest,

a chest,
and bored a hole in the lid of it,
and set it
beside the altar on the right side
as one entered

and set it

outside the gate of
the house of the LORD.

the house of the LORD;
and the priests who guarded the
threshold put in it all the money
that was brought into the house of
the LORD. (10)And

(9)A proclamation was made throughout
Judah and Jerusalem, to bring in for
the LORD the tax that Moses the
servant of God laid upon Israel in
the wilderness. (10)And all the
princes and all the people rejoiced
and brought their tax and dropped it
into the chest until they had
finished. (11)And whenever the
chest was brought to the king's
officers by the Levites,

whenever they saw that there was much
money in the chest, the king's
secretary and the
high priest
came up and
they counted and tied up in bags the
money that was found in the house
of the LORD.

when they saw that there was much
money in it, the king's
secretary and the
officer of the chief priest
would come and

	empty the chest and take it and return it to its place. Thus they did day after day, and collected money in abundance.
(11)Then they would give the money that was weighed out into the hands of the workmen who had the oversight of the house of the LORD; and they paid it out to	(12)And the king and Jehoiada gave it to those who had charge of the work of the house of the LORD,
the carpenters and the builders who worked upon	and they hired masons and carpenters
the house of the LORD, (12)and to the masons and the stonecutters,	to restore the house of the LORD,
as well as to buy timber and quarried stone for making repairs on the house of the LORD, and for any outlay upon the repairs of the house.	and also workers in iron and bronze to repair the house of the LORD.
	(13)So those who were engaged in the work labored, and the repairing went forward in their hands, and they restored the house of God to its proper condition and strengthened it. (14)And when they had finished, they brought the rest of the money before the king and Jehoiada, and with it were made
(13)But there were not made for the house of the LORD	utensils for the house of the LORD, both for the service and for the burnt offerings, and dishes for incense, and
basins of silver, snuffers, bowls, trumpets, or any vessels of gold, or of silver, from the money that was brought into the house of the LORD, (14)for that was given to the workmen who were repairing the house of the LORD with it. (15)And they did not ask an accounting from the men into whose hand they delivered the money to pay	vessels of gold and silver.

197

out to the workmen, for they dealt
honestly. (16)The money from the
guilt offerings and the money from
the sin offerings was not brought
into the house of the LORD; it
belonged to the priests.

                    And they offered burnt offerings in
                    the house of the LORD continually
                    all the days of Jehoiada.

131 The Deaths of Jehoiada and Zechariah

II Chronicles 24:15–22

(15)But Jehoiada grew old and full of days, and died; he was a hundred and thirty years old at his death. (16)And they buried him in the city of David among the kings, because he had done good in Israel, and toward God and his house.

(17)Now after the death of Jehoiada the princes of Judah came and did obeisance to the king; then the king hearkened to them. (18)And they forsook the house of the LORD, the God of their fathers, and served the Asherim and the idols. And wrath came upon Judah and Jerusalem for this their guilt. (19)Yet he sent prophets among them to bring them back to the LORD; these testified against them, but they would not give heed.

(20)Then the Spirit of God took possession of Zechariah the son of Jehoiada the priest; and he stood above the people, and said to them, "Thus says God, 'Why do you transgress the commandments of the LORD, so that you cannot prosper? Because you have forsaken the LORD, he has forsaken you.' " (21)But they conspired against him, and by command of the king they stoned him with stones in the court of the house of the LORD. (22)Thus Joash the king did not remember the kindness which Jehoiada, Zechariah's father, had shown him, but killed his son. And when he was dying, he said, "May the LORD see and avenge!"

132 The Death of Jehoash/Joash of Judah

II Kings 12:17–21	*II Chronicles 24:23–27*
(17)At that time	
	(23)At the end of the year
Hazael king of	
	the army of
Syria <u>went</u> up	<u>the</u> Syrians <u>came</u> up
and fought against Gath, and took it.	
But when Hazael set his face to go up	
against	against
	Joash. They came to Judah and
Jerusalem,	Jerusalem,

(18)Jehoash king of Judah took all
the votive gifts that Jehoshaphat and
Jehoram and Ahaziah, his fathers, the
kings of Judah, had dedicated, and his
own votive gifts, and all the gold
that was found in the treasuries of
the house of the LORD and of the
king's house, and sent these to
Hazael king of Syria. Then Hazael
went away from Jerusalem.

and destroyed all the princes of the
people from among the people, and sent
all their spoil to the king of
Damascus. (24)Though the army of
the Syrians had come with few men,
the LORD delivered into their hand a
very great army, because they had
forsaken the LORD, the God of their
fathers. Thus they executed judgment
on Joash.

(19)Now the rest of the acts of
Joash, and all that he did, are they
not written in the Book of the
Chronicles of the Kings of Judah?

(20)His servants arose and made a
conspiracy,

(25)When they had departed from him,
leaving him severely wounded,
his servants
conspired against him
because of the blood of the son of
Jehoiada the priest,
and slew him

and slew Joash
in the house of Millo, on the
way that goes down to Silla.

on his bed.

(21)It was Jozacar the son of
Shime-ath and Jehozabad the son of
Shomer, his servants, who struck him
down,
so that he died. And they buried him
with his fathers
in the city of David,

So he died; and they buried him

in the city of David,
but they did not bury him in the
tombs of the kings. (26)Those who
conspired against him were Zabad the
son of Shime-ath the Ammonitess, and
Jehozabad the son of Shimrith the
Moabitess. (27)Accounts of his sons,

199

and of the many oracles against him,
and of the rebuilding of the house of God
are written in the Commentary on the
Book of the Kings.

and Amaziah his son reigned in
his stead.

And Amaziah his son reigned in
his stead.

133 The Reign of Jehoahaz of Israel

II Kings 13:1–9

[1]In the twenty-third year of Joash the son of Ahaziah, king of Judah, Jehoahaz the son of Jehu began to reign over Israel in Samaria, and he reigned seventeen years. [2]He did what was evil in the sight of the LORD, and followed the sins of Jeroboam the son of Nebat, which he made Israel to sin; he did not depart from them. [3]And the anger of the LORD was kindled against Israel, and he gave them continually into the hand of Hazael king of Syria and into the hand of Ben-hadad the son of Hazael. [4]Then Jehoahaz besought the LORD, and the LORD hearkened to him; for he saw the oppression of Israel, how the king of Syria oppressed them. [5](Therefore the LORD gave Israel a savior, so that they escaped from the hand of the Syrians; and the people of Israel dwelt in their homes as formerly. [6]Nevertheless they did not depart from the sins of the house of Jeroboam, which he made Israel to sin, but walked in them; and the Asherah also remained in Samaria.) [7]For there was not left to Jehoahaz an army of more than fifty horsemen and ten chariots and ten thousand footmen; for the king of Syria had destroyed them and made them like the dust at threshing. [8]Now the rest of the acts of Jehoahaz and all that he did, and his might, are they not written in the Book of the Chronicles of the Kings of Israel? [9]So Jehoahaz slept with his fathers, and they buried him in Samaria; and Joash his son reigned in his stead.

134 The Reign of Jehoash/Joash of Israel

II Kings 13:10–13

[10]In the thirty-seventh year of Joash king of Judah Jehoash the son of Jehoahaz began to reign over Israel in Samaria, and he reigned sixteen years. [11]He also did what was evil in the sight of the LORD; he did not depart from all the sins of Jeroboam the son of Nebat, which he made Israel to sin, but he walked in them. [12]Now the rest of the acts of Joash, and all that he did, and the might with which he fought against Amaziah king of Judah, are they not written in the Book of the Chronicles of the Kings of Israel? [13]So Joash slept with his fathers, and Jeroboam sat upon his throne; and Joash was buried in Samaria with the kings of Israel.

135 The Death of Elisha

II Kings 13:14–25

[14]Now when Elisha had fallen sick with the illness of which he was to die, Joash king of Israel went down to him, and wept before him, crying, "My father, my father!

The chariots of Israel and its horsemen!" (15)And Elisha said to him, "Take a bow and arrows"; so he took a bow and arrows. (16)Then he said to the king of Israel, "Draw the bow"; and he drew it. And Elisha laid his hands upon the king's hands. (17)And he said, "Open the window eastward"; and he opened it. Then Elisha said, "Shoot"; and he shot. And he said, "The LORD's arrow of victory, the arrow of victory over Syria! For you shall fight the Syrians in Aphek until you have made an end of them." (18)And he said, "Take the arrows"; and he took them. And he said to the king of Israel, "Strike the ground with them"; and he struck three times, and stopped. (19)Then the man of God was angry with him, and said, "You should have struck five or six times; then you would have struck down Syria until you had made an end of it, but now you will strike down Syria only three times."

(20)So Elisha died, and they buried him. Now bands of Moabites used to invade the land in the spring of the year. (21)And as a man was being buried, lo, a marauding band was seen and the man was cast into the grave of Elisha; and as soon as the man touched the bones of Elisha, he revived, and stood on his feet.

(22)Now Hazael king of Syria oppressed Israel all the days of Jehoahaz. (23)But the LORD was gracious to them and had compassion on them, and he turned toward them, because of his covenant with Abraham, Isaac, and Jacob, and would not destroy them; nor has he cast them from his presence until now.

(24)When Hazael king of Syria died, Ben-hadad his son became king in his stead. (25)Then Jehoash the son of Jehoahaz took again from Ben-hadad the son of Hazael the cities which he had taken from Jehoahaz his father in war. Three times Joash defeated him and recovered the cities of Israel.

136 The Reign of Amaziah

II Kings 14:1–20

II Chronicles 25:1–28

(1)In the second year of Joash the son of Joahaz, king of Israel, Amaziah the son of Joash, king of Judah, began to reign.
(2)He was twenty-five years old when he began to reign, and he reigned twenty-nine years in Jerusalem. His mother's name was Jeho-addin of Jerusalem. (3)And he did what was right in the eyes of the LORD, yet not like David his father;

he did in all things as Joash his father had done. (4)But the high places were not removed; the people still sacrificed and burned incense on the high places.
(5)And as soon as the royal power was

(1)Amaziah was twenty-five years old when he began to reign, and he reigned twenty-nine years in Jerusalem. His mother's name was Jeho-addan of Jerusalem. (2)And he did what was right in the eyes of the LORD, yet not

with a blameless heart.

(3)And as soon as the royal power was

firmly in his hand he killed his
servants who had slain the king his
father. (6)But he did not put
to death the children of the
murderers;
according to what is written in the
book of the law of Moses,
where the LORD commanded, "The
  fathers
shall not be put to death for the
children, or the children be put to
death for the fathers; but every man
shall die for his own sin."

firmly in his hand he killed his
servants who had slain the king his
father. (4)But he did not put
their children to death,

according to what is written in the
law, in the book of Moses,
where the LORD commanded, "The
  fathers
shall not be put to death for the
children, or the children be put to
death for the fathers; but every man
shall die for his own sin."
(5)Then Amaziah assembled the
men of Judah, and set them by fathers'
houses under commanders of thousands
and of hundreds for all Judah and
Benjamin. He mustered those twenty
years old and upward, and found that
they were three hundred thousand
picked men, fit for war, able to
handle spear and shield. (6)He hired
also a hundred thousand mighty men
of valor from Israel for a hundred
talents of silver. (7)But a man of
God came to him and said, "O king, do
not let the army of Israel go with
you, for the LORD is not with Israel,
with all these Ephraimites. (8)But
if you suppose that in this way you
will be strong for war, God will cast
you down before the enemy; for God has
power to help or to cast down."
(9)And Amaziah said to the man of
God, "But what shall we do about the
hundred talents which I have given to
the army of Israel?" The man of God
answered, "The LORD is able to give
you much more than this." (10)Then
Amaziah discharged the army that had
come to him from Ephraim, to go home
again. And they became very angry
with Judah, and returned home in
fierce anger. (11)But Amaziah took
courage, and led out his people,

(7)He killed ten thousand
Edomites in

the Valley of Salt
and took Sela by storm, and called
it Jokthe-el, which is its name to
this day.

and went to
the Valley of Salt

and smote ten thousand men of Seir.
(12)The men of Judah captured
another ten thousand alive, and took
them to the top of a rock and threw
them down from the top of the rock;
and they were all dashed to pieces.
(13)But the men of the army whom
Amaziah sent back, not letting them
go with him to battle, fell upon the
cities of Judah, from Samaria to
Beth-horon, and killed three thousand
people in them, and took much spoil.
(14)After Amaziah came from the
slaughter of the Edomites, he brought
the gods of the men of Seir, and set
them up as his gods, and worshiped
them, making offerings to them.
(15)Therefore the LORD was angry
with Amaziah and sent to him a
prophet, who said to him, "Why have
you resorted to the gods of a people,
which did not deliver their own people
from your hand?" (16)But as he was
speaking the king said to him, "Have
we made you a royal counselor? Stop!
Why should you be put to death?" So
the prophet stopped, but said, "I know
that God has determined to destroy
you, because you have done this and
have not listened to my counsel."

(8)Then Amaziah

(17)Then Amaziah
king of Judah
took counsel and

sent
messengers
to Jehoash the son of Jehoahaz, son
of Jehu, king of Israel, saying,
"Come, let us look one another in
the face." (9)And Jehoash king of
Israel sent word to Amaziah king of
Judah, "A thistle on Lebanon sent to a
cedar on Lebanon, saying, 'Give your

sent

to Joash the son of Jehoahaz, son
of Jehu, king of Israel, saying,
"Come, let us look one another in
the face." (18)And Joash the king of
Israel sent word to Amaziah king of
Judah, "A thistle on Lebanon sent to a
cedar on Lebanon, saying, 'Give your

daughter to my son for a wife'; and
a wild beast of Lebanon passed by and
trampled down the thistle.
(10)You have indeed

smitten Edom,
and your heart has lifted you up.

Be content with your glory, and

stay at home; for why should you
provoke trouble so that you fall,
you and Judah with you?"
(11)But Amaziah would not listen.

So Jehoash king of Israel went up,
and he and Amaziah king of Judah faced
one another in battle at Beth-shemesh,
which belongs to Judah.
(12)And Judah was defeated by Israel,
and every man fled to his home.
(13)And Jehoash king of Israel
captured Amaziah king of Judah, the
son of Jehoash, son of Ahaziah, at
Beth-shemesh, and came to
Jerusalem, and broke down the wall of
Jerusalem for four hundred cubits,
from the Ephraim Gate to the Corner
Gate. (14)And he seized all the gold
and silver, and all the vessels that
were found in the house of the LORD

and in the treasuries of the king's
house, also hostages, and he returned
to Samaria.
(15)Now the rest of the acts of
Jehoash which he did, and his might,
and how he fought with Amaziah king
of Judah, are they not written in the
Book of the Chronicles of the Kings
of Israel? (16)And Jehoash slept
with his fathers, and was buried in
Samaria with the kings of Israel; and
Jeroboam his son reigned in his stead.

daughter to my son for a wife'; and
a wild beast of Lebanon passed by and
trampled down the thistle.

(19)You say, 'See, I have
smitten Edom,'
and your heart has lifted you up
in boastfulness.

But now
stay at home; why should you
provoke trouble so that you fall,
you and Judah with you?"
(20)But Amaziah would not listen;
for it was of God, in order that he
might give them into the hand of their
enemies, because they had sought
the gods of Edom.
(21)So Joash king of Israel went up;
and he and Amaziah king of Judah faced
one another in battle at Beth-shemesh,
which belongs to Judah.
(22)And Judah was defeated by Israel,
and every man fled to his home.
(23)And Joash king of Israel
captured Amaziah king of Judah, the
son of Joash, son of Ahaziah, at
Beth-shemesh, and brought him to
Jerusalem, and broke down the wall of
Jerusalem for four hundred cubits,
from the Ephraim Gate to the Corner
Gate. (24)And he seized all the gold
and silver, and all the vessels that
were found in the house of God,
and Obed-edom with them;
he seized also
the treasuries of the king's
house, and hostages, and he returned
to Samaria.

204

⁽¹⁷⁾Amaziah the son of Joash,
king of Judah, lived fifteen years
after the death of Jehoash son of
Jehoahaz, king of Israel. ⁽¹⁸⁾Now
the rest of the deeds of Amaziah,

are they not written in the Book
of the Chronicles
of the Kings of Judah?

⁽¹⁹⁾And they made a conspiracy
against him in Jerusalem, and he
fled to Lachish. But they sent
after him to Lachish, and slew him
there. ⁽²⁰⁾And they brought him
upon horses; and he was buried
in Jerusalem
with his fathers
in the city of David.

/25/Amaziah the son of Joash,
king of Judah, lived fifteen years
after the death of Joash son of
Jehoahaz, king of Israel. ⁽²⁶⁾Now
the rest of the deeds of Amaziah,
from first to last,
are they not written in the Book   ⅹ

of the Kings of Judah and Israel?
⁽²⁷⁾From the time when he
turned away from the LORD
they made a conspiracy
against him in Jerusalem, and he
fled to Lachish. But they sent
after him to Lachish, and slew him
there. ⁽²⁸⁾And they brought him
upon horses; and he was buried

with his fathers
in the city of David.

137 The Reign of Azariah/Uzziah Begins

II Kings 14:21–22

⁽²¹⁾And all the people of Judah
took Azariah, who was sixteen years
old, and made him king instead of his
father Amaziah. ⁽²²⁾He built Elath
and restored it to Judah, after the
king slept with his fathers.

II Chronicles 26:1–2

⁽¹⁾And all the people of Judah
took Uzziah, who was sixteen years
old, and made him king instead of his
father Amaziah. ⁽²⁾He built Eloth
and restored it to Judah, after the
king slept with his fathers.

138 The Reign of Jeroboam II

II Kings 14:23–29

⁽²³⁾In the fifteenth year of Amaziah the son of Joash, king of Judah, Jeroboam the
son of Joash, king of Israel, began to reign in Samaria, and he reigned forty-one years.
⁽²⁴⁾And he did what was evil in the sight of the LORD; he did not depart from all the
sins of Jeroboam the son of Nebat, which he made Israel to sin. ⁽²⁵⁾He restored the
border of Israel from the entrance of Hamath as far as the Sea of the Arabah, according
to the word of the LORD, the God of Israel, which he spoke by his servant Jonah the
son of Amittai, the prophet, who was from Gath-hepher. ⁽²⁶⁾For the LORD saw that the
affliction of Israel was very bitter, for there was none left, bond or free, and there was
none to help Israel. ⁽²⁷⁾But the LORD had not said that he would blot out the name of
Israel from under heaven, so he saved them by the hand of Jeroboam the son of Joash.

(28)Now the rest of the acts of Jeroboam, and all that he did, and his might, how he fought, and how he recovered for Israel Damascus and Hamath, which had belonged to Judah, are they not written in the Book of the Chronicles of the Kings of Israel? (29)And Jeroboam slept with his fathers, the kings of Israel, and Zechariah his son reigned in his stead.

139 The Reign of Azariah/Uzziah Continues

II Kings 15:1–3

(1)In the twenty-seventh year of Jeroboam king of Israel Azariah the son of Amaziah, king of Judah, began to reign. (2)He was sixteen years old when he began to reign, and he reigned fifty-two years in Jerusalem. His mother's name was Jecoliah of Jerusalem. (3)And he did what was right in the eyes of the LORD, according to all that his father Amaziah had done.

II Chronicles 26:3–5

(3)Uzziah was sixteen years old when he began to reign, and he reigned fifty-two years in Jerusalem. His mother's name was Jecoliah of Jerusalem. (4)And he did what was right in the eyes of the LORD, according to all that his father Amaziah had done. (5)He set himself to seek God in the days of Zechariah, who instructed him in the fear of God; and as long as he sought the LORD, God made him prosper.

140 The Military Accomplishments of Azariah/Uzziah

II Chronicles 26:6–15

(6)He went out and made war against the Philistines, and broke down the wall of Gath and the wall of Jabneh and the wall of Ashdod; and he built cities in the territory of Ashdod and elsewhere among the Philistines. (7)God helped him against the Philistines, and against the Arabs that dwelt in Gurbaal, and against the Me-unites. (8)The Ammonites paid tribute to Uzziah, and his fame spread even to the border of Egypt, for he became very strong. (9)Moreover Uzziah built towers in Jerusalem at the Corner Gate and at the Valley Gate and at the Angle, and fortified them. (10)And he built towers in the wilderness, and hewed out many cisterns, for he had large herds, both in the Shephelah and in the plain, and he had farmers and vinedressers in the hills and in the fertile lands, for he loved the soil. (11)Moreover Uzziah had an army of soldiers, fit for war, in divisions according to the numbers in the muster made by Je-iel the secretary and Ma-aseiah the officer, under the direction of Hananiah, one of the king's commanders. (12)The whole number of the heads of fathers' houses of mighty men of valor was two thousand six hundred. (13)Under their command was an army of three hundred and seven thousand five hundred, who could make war with mighty power, to help the king against the enemy. (14)And Uzziah prepared for all the army shields, spears, helmets, coats of mail, bows, and stones for slinging. (15)In Jerusalem he made engines, invented by skilful men, to be on the towers and the corners, to shoot arrows and great stones. And his fame spread far, for he was marvelously helped, till he was strong.

141 The Leprosy and Death of Azariah/Uzziah

II Kings 15:4–7

II Chronicles 26:16–23

(4)Nevertheless the high places were not taken away; the people still sacrificed and burned incense on the high places.

(16)But when he was strong he grew proud, to his destruction. For he was false to the LORD his God, and entered the temple of the LORD to burn incense on the altar of incense. (17)But Azariah the priest went in after him, with eighty priests of the LORD who were men of valor; (18)and they withstood King Uzziah, and said to him, "It is not for you, Uzziah, to burn incense to the LORD, but for the priests the sons of Aaron, who are consecrated to burn incense. Go out of the sanctuary; for you have done wrong, and it will bring you no honor from the LORD God." (19)Then Uzziah was angry. Now he had a censer in his hand to burn incense, and when he became angry with the priests leprosy broke out on his forehead, in the presence of the priests in the house of the LORD, by the altar of incense. (20)And Azariah the chief priest, and all the priests, looked at him, and behold, he was leprous in his forehead! And they thrust him out quickly, and he himself hastened to go out, because

(5)And the LORD smote the king, so that he was a leper to the day of his death, and

the LORD had smitten him. (21)And King Uzziah was a leper to the day of his death, and

	being a leper
he dwelt in a separate house.	dwelt in a separate house,
	for he was excluded from the
	house of the LORD.
And Jotham the king's son was over	And Jotham his son was over
the household, governing the	the king's household, governing the
people of the land.	people of the land.
⌐ (6)Now the rest of the acts of	(22)Now the rest of the acts of
Azariah,	Uzziah,
and all that he did,	
	from first to last,
✱ are they not written in the Book of	
the Chronicles of the Kings of Judah?	
	Isaiah the prophet the son of Amoz
∟	wrote.
(7)And Azariah slept with his	(23)And Uzziah slept with his
fathers, and they buried him with	fathers, and they buried him with
his fathers in the	his fathers in the
city of David,	
	burial field which belonged to the
	kings, for they said, "He is a leper."
and Jotham his son reigned in his	And Jotham his son reigned in his
stead.	stead.

142 The Final Kings of Israel

II Kings 15:8–31

(8)In the thirty-eighth year of Azariah king of Judah Zechariah the son of Jeroboam reigned over Israel in Samaria six months. (9)And he did what was evil in the sight of the LORD, as his fathers had done. He did not depart from the sins of Jeroboam the son of Nebat, which he made Israel to sin. (10)Shallum the son of Jabesh conspired against him, and struck him down at Ibleam, and killed him, and reigned in his stead. (11)Now the rest of the deeds of Zechariah, behold, they are written in the Book of the Chronicles of the Kings of Israel. (12)(This was the promise of the LORD which he gave to Jehu, "Your sons shall sit upon the throne of Israel to the fourth generation." And so it came to pass.)

(13)Shallum the son of Jabesh began to reign in the thirty-ninth year of Uzziah king of Judah, and he reigned one month in Samaria. (14)Then Menahem the son of Gadi came up from Tirzah and came to Samaria, and he struck down Shallum the son of Jabesh in Samaria and slew him, and reigned in his stead. (15)Now the rest of the deeds of Shallum, and the conspiracy which he made, behold, they are written in the Book of the Chronicles of the Kings of Israel. (16)At that time Menahem sacked Tappuah and all who were in it and its territory from Tirzah on; because they did not open it to him, therefore he sacked it, and he ripped up all the women in it who were with child.

(17)In the thirty-ninth year of Azariah king of Judah Menahem the son of Gadi began to reign over Israel, and he reigned ten years in Samaria. (18)And he did what was evil in the sight of the LORD; he did not depart all his days from all the sins of Jeroboam the son of Nebat, which he made Israel to sin. (19)Pul the king of Assyria came against the land; and Menahem gave Pul a thousand talents of silver, that he might help him to confirm his hold of the royal power. (20)Menahem exacted the money from Israel, that is, from all the wealthy men, fifty shekels of silver from every man, to give to the king of Assyria. So the king of Assyria turned back, and did not stay there in the land. (21)Now the rest of the deeds of Menahem, and all that he did, are they not written in the Book of the Chronicles of the Kings of Israel? (22)And Menahem slept with his father, and Pekahiah his son reigned in his stead.

(23)In the fiftieth year of Azariah king of Judah Pekahiah the son of Menahem began to reign over Israel in Samaria, and he reigned two years. (24)And he did what was evil in the sight of the LORD; he did not turn away from the sins of Jeroboam the son of Nebat, which he made Israel to sin. (25)And Pekah the son of Remaliah, his captain, conspired against him with fifty men of the Gileadites, and slew him in Samaria, in the citadel of the king's house; he slew him, and reigned in his stead. (26)Now the rest of the deeds of Pekahiah, and all that he did, behold, they are written in the Book of the Chronicles of the Kings of Israel.

(27)In the fifty-second year of Azariah king of Judah Pekah the son of Remaliah began to reign over Israel in Samaria, and reigned twenty years. (28)And he did what was evil in the sight of the LORD; he did not depart from the sins of Jeroboam the son of Nebat, which he made Israel to sin.

(29)In the days of Pekah king of Israel Tiglath-pileser king of Assyria came and captured Ijon, Abel-beth-maacah, Janoah, Kedesh, Hazor, Gilead, and Galilee, all the land of Naphtali; and he carried the people captive to Assyria. (30)Then Hoshea the son of Elah made a conspiracy against Pekah the son of Remaliah, and struck him down, and slew him, and reigned in his stead, in the twentieth year of Jotham the son of Uzziah. (31)Now the rest of the acts of Pekah, and all that he did, behold, they are written in the Book of the Chronicles of the Kings of Israel.

143 The Reign of Jotham

II Kings 15:32–38

(32)In the second year of Pekah the son of Remaliah, king of Israel, Jotham the son of Uzziah, king of Judah, began to reign.
(33)He was twenty-five years old when he began to reign, and he reigned sixteen years in Jerusalem. His mother's name was Jerusha the daughter of Zadok. (34)And he did what was right in the eyes of the LORD, according to all that his father Uzziah had done.
(35)Nevertheless the high places were not removed;

II Chronicles 27:1–9

(1)Jotham was twenty-five years old when he began to reign, and he reigned sixteen years in Jerusalem. His mother's name was Jerushah the daughter of Zadok. (2)And he did what was right in the eyes of the LORD according to all that his father Uzziah had done—

the people still
sacrificed and burned incense on
the high places.

He built the upper gate of the
house of the LORD.

only he did not invade the temple
of the LORD. But
the people still

followed corrupt practices.
(3)He built the upper gate of the
house of the LORD,
and did much building on the wall of
Ophel. (4)Moreover he built cities
in the hill country of Judah, and
forts and towers on the wooded hills.
(5)He fought with the king of the
Ammonites and prevailed against them.
And the Ammonites gave him that year
a hundred talents of silver, and ten
thousand cors of wheat and ten
thousand of barley. The Ammonites
paid him the same amount in the
second and the third years. (6)So Jotham
became mighty, because he ordered his
ways before the LORD his God.
(7)Now the rest of the acts of
Jotham, and all

(36)Now the rest of the acts of
Jotham, and all
that he did,

are they not written in the Book of
the Chronicles
of the Kings of Judah?
(37)In those days the LORD began to
send Rezin the king of Syria and Pekah
the son of Remaliah against Judah.

his wars, and his ways, behold,
they are written in the Book of

the Kings of Israel and Judah.

(8)He was twenty-five years old when
he began to reign, and he reigned
sixteen years in Jerusalem.*
(9)And Jotham slept with his fathers,
and they buried him

(38)Jotham slept with his fathers,
and was buried
with his fathers
in the city of David his father;
and Ahaz his son reigned in his stead.

in the city of David;
and Ahaz his son reigned in his stead.

144 The Reign of Ahaz Begins

II Kings 16:1–5

II Chronicles 28:1–7

(1)In the seventeenth year of
Pekah the son of Remaliah, Ahaz the

*Cf. II Kings 15:33.

son of Jotham, king of Judah, began
to reign.
(2)Ahaz was twenty years old when
he began to reign, and he reigned
sixteen years in Jerusalem. And he
did not do what was right in the eyes
of the LORD his God, as his father
David had done, (3)but he walked in
the way of the kings of Israel.

He even burned his son as an offering,
according to the abominable practices
of the nations whom the LORD drove
out before the people of Israel.
(4)And he sacrificed and burned
incense on the high places, and on
the hills, and under every green tree.

(5)Then Rezin
king of Syria

and Pekah the son of Remaliah,
king of Israel,
came up to wage war on Jerusalem, and
they besieged Ahaz but could not
conquer him.

/1/Ahaz was twenty years old when
he began to reign, and he reigned
sixteen years in Jerusalem. And he
did not do what was right in the eyes
of the LORD, as his father
David had done, (2)but he walked in
the ways of the kings of Israel.
He even made molten images for the
Baals; (3)and he burned incense
in the valley of the son of Hinnom,
and burned his sons as an offering,
according to the abominable practices
of the nations whom the LORD drove
out before the people of Israel.
(4)And he sacrificed and burned
incense on the high places, and on
the hills, and under every green tree.
(5)Therefore the LORD his God
gave him into the hand of the

king of Syria,
who defeated him and took captive a
great number of his people and brought
them to Damascus. He was also given
into the hand of the

king of Israel,

who defeated him with great slaughter.
(6)For Pekah the son of Remaliah slew
a hundred and twenty thousand in Judah
in one day, all of them men of valor,
because they had forsaken the LORD,
the God of their fathers. (7)And
Zichri, a mighty man of Ephraim, slew
Ma-aseiah the king's son and Azrikam
the commander of the palace and
Elkanah the next in authority to the
king.

145 The Story of the Prophet Oded

II Chronicles 28:8-15

(8)The men of Israel took captive two hundred thousand of their kinsfolk, women, sons, and daughters; they also took much spoil from them and brought the spoil to Samaria. (9)But a prophet of the LORD was there, whose name was Oded; and he went out to meet the army that came to Samaria, and said to them, "Behold, because the LORD, the God of your fathers, was angry with Judah, he gave them into your hand, but you have slain them in a rage which has reached up to heaven. (10)And now you intend to subjugate the people of Judah and Jerusalem, male and female, as your slaves. Have you not sins of your own against the LORD your God? (11)Now hear me, and send back the captives from your kinsfolk whom you have taken, for the fierce wrath of the LORD is upon you." (12)Certain chiefs also of the men of Ephraim, Azariah the son of Johanan, Berechiah the son of Meshillemoth, Jehizkiah the son of Shallum, and Amasa the son of Hadlai, stood up against those who were coming from the war, (13)and said to them, "You shall not bring the captives in here, for you propose to bring upon us guilt against the LORD in addition to our present sins and guilt. For our guilt is already great, and there is fierce wrath against Israel." (14)So the armed men left the captives and the spoil before the princes and all the assembly. (15)And the men who have been mentioned by name rose and took the captives, and with the spoil they clothed all that were naked among them; they clothed them, gave them sandals, provided them with food and drink, and anointed them; and carrying all the feeble among them on asses, they brought them to their kinsfolk at Jericho, the city of palm trees. Then they returned to Samaria.

146 The Reign of Ahaz Concludes

✗ ✗ ⌐

II Kings 16:6-20

(6)At that time
the king of Edom recovered Elath for
Edom, and drove the men of Judah from
Elath; and the Edomites came to Elath,
where they dwell to this day. (7)So
Ahaz sent
messengers to Tiglath-pileser
king of Assyria,

saying, "I am your servant and your
son. Come up, and rescue me from the
hand of the king of Syria and from the
hand of the king of Israel, who are
attacking me." (8)Ahaz also took the
silver and gold that was found in the
house of the LORD and in the treasures
of the king's house, and sent a
present to the king of Assyria.

II Chronicles 28:16-27

(16)At that time

King Ahaz sent to

the kings of Assyria
for help.

(17)For the Edomites had again invaded
and defeated Judah, and carried away
captives. (18)And the Philistines
had made raids on the cities in the
Shephelah and the Negeb of Judah, and
had taken Beth-shemesh, Aijalon,
Gederoth, Soco with its villages,
Timnah with its villages, and Gimzo
with its villages; and they settled
there. (19)For the LORD brought
Judah low because of Ahaz king of
Israel, for he had dealt wantonly in
Judah and had been faithless to the
LORD. (20)So Tilgath-pilneser
king of Assyria

(9)And the king of Assyria
hearkened to him; the king of Assyria
marched up against Damascus, and took
it, carrying its people captive to
Kir, and he killed Rezin.

came against him, and afflicted him
instead of strengthening him.
(21)For Ahaz took from the house
of the LORD and the house of the king
and of the princes, and gave tribute
to the king of Assyria; but it did
not help him.
(22)In the time of his distress
he became yet more faithless to the
LORD—this same King Ahaz.

(10)When King Ahaz went to
Damascus to meet Tiglath-pileser king
of Assyria, he saw the altar that was
at Damascus. And King Ahaz sent to
Uriah the priest a model of the altar,
and its pattern, exact in all its
details. (11)And Uriah the priest
built the altar; in accordance with
all that King Ahaz had sent from
Damascus, so Uriah the priest made
it, before King Ahaz arrived from
Damascus. (12)And when the king
came from Damascus, the king viewed
the altar. Then the king drew near
to the altar, and went up on it,
(13)and burned his burnt offering
and his cereal offering, and poured
his drink offering, and threw the

blood of his peace offerings upon
the altar.

(23)For he sacrificed to the gods of
Damascus which had defeated him, and
said, "Because the gods of the kings
of Syria helped them, I will sacrifice
to them that they may help me." But
they were the ruin of him, and of all
Israel.

(14)And the bronze altar which was
before the LORD he removed from the
front of the house, from the place
between his altar and the house of
the LORD, and put it on the north
side of his altar. (15)And King
Ahaz commanded Uriah the priest,
saying, "Upon the great altar burn
the morning burnt offering, and the
evening cereal offering, and the
king's burnt offering, and his cereal
offering, with the burnt offering of
all the people of the land, and their
cereal offering, and their drink
offering; and throw upon it all the
blood of the burnt offering, and all
the blood of the sacrifice; but the
bronze altar shall be for me to
inquire by." (16)Uriah the priest
did all this, as King Ahaz commanded.
(17)And King Ahaz cut off the
frames of the stands, and removed
the laver from them, and he took down
the sea from off the bronze oxen that
were under it, and put it upon a
pediment of stone. (18)And the
covered way for the sabbath which had
been built inside the palace, and the
outer entrance for the king he removed
from the house of the LORD, because
of the king of Assyria.

(24)And Ahaz gathered together the
vessels of the house of God and cut in
pieces the vessels of the house of
God, and he shut up the doors of the
house of the LORD; and he made himself
altars in every corner of Jerusalem.
(25)In every city of Judah he made

high places to burn incense to other
gods, provoking to anger the LORD, the
God of his fathers.

(19)Now the rest of the acts of Ahaz
which he did,

(26)Now the rest of his acts

and all his ways, from first to last,
behold,

are they not written in the Book of
the Chronicles of
the Kings of Judah?

they are written in the Book of

(20)And Ahaz slept with his fathers,
and was buried
with his fathers
in the city of David;

the Kings of Judah and Israel.
(27)And Ahaz slept with his fathers,
and they buried him

in the city,
in Jerusalem,
for they did not bring him into the
tombs of the kings of Israel.

and Hezekiah his son reigned in
his stead.

And Hezekiah his son reigned in
his stead.

147 The Fall of Israel, I

II Kings 17:1–41

(1)In the twelfth year of Ahaz king of Judah Hoshea the son of Elah began to reign
in Samaria over Israel, and he reigned nine years. (2)And he did what was evil in the
sight of the LORD, yet not as the kings of Israel who were before him. (3)Against him
came up Shalmaneser king of Assyria; and Hoshea became his vassal, and paid him
tribute. (4)But the king of Assyria found treachery in Hoshea; for he had sent messengers
to So, king of Egypt, and offered no tribute to the king of Assyria, as he had done year
by year; therefore the king of Assyria shut him up, and bound him in prison. (5)Then
the king of Assyria invaded all the land and came to Samaria, and for three years he
besieged it. (6)In the ninth year of Hoshea the king of Assyria captured Samaria, and
he carried the Israelites away to Assyria, and placed them in Halah, and on the Habor,
the river of Gozan, and in the cities of the Medes.

(7)And this was so, because the people of Israel had sinned against the LORD their
God, who had brought them up out of the land of Egypt from under the hand of Pharaoh
king of Egypt, and had feared other gods (8)and walked in the customs of the nations
whom the LORD drove out before the people of Israel, and in the customs which the
kings of Israel had introduced. (9)And the people of Israel did secretly against the LORD
their God things that were not right. They built for themselves high places at all their
towns, from watchtower to fortified city; (10)they set up for themselves pillars and
Asherim on every high hill and under every green tree; (11)and there they burned incense
on all the high places, as the nations did whom the LORD carried away before them.
And they did wicked things, provoking the LORD to anger, (12)and they served idols, of
which the LORD had said to them, "You shall not do this." (13)Yet the LORD warned
Israel and Judah by every prophet and every seer, saying, "Turn from your evil ways

215

and keep my commandments and my statutes, in accordance with all the law which I commanded your fathers, and which I sent to you by my servants the prophets." (14)But they would not listen, but were stubborn, as their fathers had been, who did not believe in the LORD their God. (15)They despised his statutes, and his covenant that he made with their fathers, and the warnings which he gave them. They went after false idols, and became false, and they followed the nations that were round about them, concerning whom the LORD had commanded them that they should not do like them. (16)And they forsook all the commandments of the LORD their God, and made for themselves molten images of two calves; and they made an Asherah, and worshiped all the host of heaven, and served Baal. (17)And they burned their sons and their daughters as offerings, and used divination and sorcery, and sold themselves to do evil in the sight of the LORD, provoking him to anger. (18)Therefore the LORD was very angry with Israel, and removed them out of his sight; none was left but the tribe of Judah only.

(19)Judah also did not keep the commandments of the LORD their God, but walked in the customs which Israel had introduced. (20)And the LORD rejected all the descendants of Israel, and afflicted them, and gave them into the hand of spoilers, until he had cast them out of his sight.

(21)When he had torn Israel from the house of David they made Jeroboam the son of Nebat king. And Jeroboam drove Israel from following the LORD and made them commit great sin. (22)The people of Israel walked in all the sins which Jeroboam did; they did not depart from them, (23)until the LORD removed Israel out of his sight, as he had spoken by all his servants the prophets. So Israel was exiled from their own land to Assyria until this day.

(24)And the king of Assyria brought people from Babylon, Cuthah, Avva, Hamath, and Sepharvaim, and placed them in the cities of Samaria instead of the people of Israel; and they took possession of Samaria, and dwelt in its cities. (25)And at the beginning of their dwelling there, they did not fear the LORD; therefore the LORD sent lions among them, which killed some of them. (26)So the king of Assyria was told, "The nations which you have carried away and placed in the cities of Samaria do not know the law of the god of the land; therefore he has sent lions among them, and behold, they are killing them, because they do not know the law of the god of the land." (27)Then the king of Assyria commanded, "Send there one of the priests whom you carried away thence; and let him go and dwell there, and teach them the law of the god of the land." (28)So one of the priests whom they had carried away from Samaria came and dwelt in Bethel, and taught them how they should fear the LORD.

(29)But every nation still made gods of its own, and put them in the shrines of the high places which the Samaritans had made, every nation in the cities in which they dwelt; (30)the men of Babylon made Succoth-benoth, the men of Cuth made Nergal, the men of Hamath made Ashima, (31)and the Avvites made Nibhaz and Tartak; and the Sepharvites burned their children in the fire to Adrammelech and Anammelech, the gods of Sepharvaim. (32)They also feared the LORD, and appointed from among themselves all sorts of people as priests of the high places, who sacrificed for them in the shrines of the high places. (33)So they feared the LORD but also served their own gods, after the manner of the nations from among whom they had been carried away. (34)To this day they do according to the former manner.

They do not fear the LORD, and they do not follow the statutes or the ordinances or the law or the commandment which the LORD commanded the children of Jacob, whom he named Israel. [35]The LORD made a covenant with them, and commanded them, "You shall not fear other gods or bow yourselves to them or serve them or sacrifice to them; [36]but you shall fear the LORD, who brought you out of the land of Egypt with great power and with an outstretched arm; you shall bow yourselves to him, and to him you shall sacrifice. [37]And the statutes and the ordinances and the law and the commandment which he wrote for you, you shall always be careful to do. You shall not fear other gods, [38]and you shall not forget the covenant that I have made with you. You shall not fear other gods, [39]but you shall fear the LORD your God, and he will deliver you out of the hand of all your enemies." [40]However they would not listen, but they did according to their former manner.

[41]So these nations feared the LORD, and also served their graven images; their children likewise, and their children's children—as their fathers did, so they do to this day.

148 Hezekiah's Reign Begins

II Kings 18:1–3	*II Chronicles 29:1–2*
[1]In the third year of Hoshea son of Elah, king of Israel, Hezekiah	[1]Hezekiah
the son of Ahaz, king of Judah, began to reign.	began to reign when
[2]He was twenty-five years old when he began to reign,	he was twenty-five years old,
and he reigned twenty-nine years in Jerusalem. His mother's name was Abi the daughter of Zechariah.	and he reigned twenty-nine years in Jerusalem. His mother's name was Abijah the daughter of Zechariah.
[3]And he did what was right in the eyes of the LORD, according to all that David his father had done.	[2]And he did what was right in the eyes of the LORD, according to all that David his father had done.

149 Hezekiah Purifies the Cult

II Chronicles 29:3–36

[3]In the first year of his reign, in the first month, he opened the doors of the house of the LORD, and repaired them. [4]He brought in the priests and the Levites, and assembled them in the square on the east, [5]and said to them, "Hear me, Levites! Now sanctify yourselves, and sanctify the house of the LORD, the God of your fathers, and carry out the filth from the holy place. [6]For our fathers have been unfaithful and have done what was evil in the sight of the LORD our God; they have forsaken him, and have turned away their faces from the habitation of the LORD, and turned their backs. [7]They also shut the doors of the vestibule and put out the lamps, and have not burned incense or offered burnt offerings in the holy place to the God of Israel. [8]Therefore the wrath of the LORD came on Judah and Jerusalem, and he has made them an object of horror,

of astonishment, and of hissing, as you see with your own eyes. (9)For lo, our fathers have fallen by the sword and our sons and our daughters and our wives are in captivity for this. (10)Now it is in my heart to make a covenant with the LORD, the God of Israel, that his fierce anger may turn away from us. (11)My sons, do not now be negligent, for the LORD has chosen you to stand in his presence, to minister to him, and to be his ministers and burn incense to him."

(12)Then the Levites arose, Mahath the son of Amasai, and Joel the son of Azariah, of the sons of the Kohathites; and of the sons of Merari, Kish the son of Abdi, and Azariah the son of Jehallelel; and of the Gershonites, Joah the son of Zimmah, and Eden the son of Joah; (13)and of the sons of Elizaphan, Shimri and Jeuel; and of the sons of Asaph, Zechariah and Mattaniah; (14)and of the sons of Heman, Jehuel and Shime-i; and of the sons of Jeduthun, Shemaiah and Uzziel. (15)They gathered their brethren, and sanctified themselves, and went in as the king had commanded, by the words of the LORD, to cleanse the house of the LORD. (16)The priests went into the inner part of the house of the LORD to cleanse it, and they brought out all the uncleanness that they found in the temple of the LORD into the court of the house of the LORD; and the Levites took it and carried it out to the brook Kidron. (17)They began to sanctify on the first day of the first month, and on the eighth day of the month they came to the vestibule of the LORD; then for eight days they sanctified the house of the LORD, and on the sixteenth day of the first month they finished. (18)Then they went in to Hezekiah the king and said, "We have cleansed all the house of the LORD, the altar of burnt offering and all its utensils, and the table for the showbread and all its utensils. (19)All the utensils which King Ahaz discarded in his reign when he was faithless, we have made ready and sanctified; and behold, they are before the altar of the LORD."

(20)Then Hezekiah the king rose early and gathered the officials of the city, and went up to the house of the LORD. (21)And they brought seven bulls, seven rams, seven lambs, and seven he-goats for a sin offering for the kingdom and for the sanctuary and for Judah. And he commanded the priests the sons of Aaron to offer them on the altar of the LORD. (22)So they killed the bulls, and the priests received the blood and threw it against the altar; and they killed the rams and their blood was thrown against the altar; and they killed the lambs and their blood was thrown against the altar. (23)Then the he-goats for the sin offering were brought to the king and the assembly, and they laid their hands upon them, (24)and the priests killed them and made a sin offering with their blood on the altar, to make atonement for all Israel. For the king commanded that the burnt offering and the sin offering should be made for all Israel.

(25)And he stationed the Levites in the house of the LORD with cymbals, harps, and lyres, according to the commandment of David and of Gad the king's seer and of Nathan the prophet; for the commandment was from the LORD through his prophets. (26)The Levites stood with the instruments of David, and the priests with the trumpets. (27)Then Hezekiah commanded that the burnt offering be offered on the altar. And when the burnt offering began, the song to the LORD began also, and the trumpets, accompanied by the instruments of David king of Israel. (28)The whole assembly worshiped, and the singers sang, and the trumpeters sounded; all this continued until the burnt offering was finished. (29)When the offering was finished, the king and all who were present with him bowed themselves and worshiped. (30)And Hezekiah the king and the princes commanded the Levites to sing praises to the LORD with the words of David and of Asaph the seer. And they sang praises with gladness, and they bowed down and worshiped.

(31)Then Hezekiah said, "You have now consecrated yourselves to the LORD; come near, bring sacrifices and thank offerings to the house of the LORD." And the assembly brought sacrifices and thank offerings; and all who were of a willing heart brought burnt offerings. (32)The number of the burnt offerings which the assembly brought was seventy bulls, a hundred rams, and two hundred lambs; all these were for a burnt offering to the LORD. (33)And the consecrated offerings were six hundred bulls and three thousand sheep. (34)But the priests were too few and could not flay all the burnt offerings, so until other priests had sanctified themselves their brethren the Levites helped them, until the work was finished—for the Levites were more upright in heart than the priests in sanctifying themselves. (35)Besides the great number of burnt offerings there was the fat of the peace offerings, and there were the libations for the burnt offerings. Thus the service of the house of the LORD was restored. (36)And Hezekiah and all the people rejoiced because of what God had done for the people; for the thing came about suddenly.

150 The Passover Renewed

II Chronicles 30:1–27

(1)Hezekiah sent to all Israel and Judah, and wrote letters also to Ephraim and Manasseh, that they should come to the house of the LORD at Jerusalem, to keep the passover to the LORD the God of Israel. (2)For the king and his princes and all the assembly in Jerusalem had taken counsel to keep the passover in the second month— (3)for they could not keep it in its time because the priests had not sanctified themselves in sufficient number, nor had the people assembled in Jerusalem—(4)and the plan seemed right to the king and all the assembly. (5)So they decreed to make a proclamation throughout all Israel, from Beer-sheba to Dan, that the people should come and keep the passover to the LORD the God of Israel, at Jerusalem; for they had not kept it in great numbers as prescribed. (6)So couriers went throughout all Israel and Judah with letters from the king and his princes, as the king had commanded, saying, "O people of Israel, return to the LORD, the God of Abraham, Isaac, and Israel, that he may turn again to the remnant of you who have escaped from the hand of the kings of Assyria. (7)Do not be like your fathers and your brethren, who were faithless to the LORD God of their fathers, so that he made them a desolation, as you see. (8)Do not now be stiff-necked as your fathers were, but yield yourselves to the LORD, and come to his sanctuary, which he has sanctified for ever, and serve the LORD your God, that his fierce anger may turn away from you. (9)For if you return to the LORD, your brethren and your children will find compassion with their captors, and return to this land. For the LORD your God is gracious and merciful, and will not turn away his face from you, if you return to him."

(10)So the couriers went from city to city through the country of Ephraim and Manasseh, and as far as Zebulun; but they laughed them to scorn, and mocked them. (11)Only a few men of Asher, of Manasseh, and of Zebulun humbled themselves and came to Jerusalem. (12)The hand of God was also upon Judah to give them one heart to do what the king and the princes commanded by the word of the LORD.

(13)And many people came together in Jerusalem to keep the feast of unleavened bread in the second month, a very great assembly. (14)They set to work and removed the altars that were in Jerusalem, and all the altars for burning incense they took away and threw into the Kidron valley. (15)And they killed the passover lamb on the fourteenth day of the second month. And the priests and the Levites were put to shame, so that they sanctified themselves, and brought burnt offerings into the house of the LORD. (16)They took their accustomed posts according to the law of Moses the man of God; the priests sprinkled the blood which they received from the hand of the Levites. (17)For there were many in the assembly who had not sanctified themselves; therefore the Levites had to kill the passover lamb for every one who was not clean, to make it holy to the LORD. (18)For a multitude of the people, many of them from Ephraim, Manasseh, Issachar, and Zebulun, had not cleansed themselves, yet they ate the passover otherwise than as prescribed. For Hezekiah had prayed for them, saying, "The good LORD pardon every one (19)who sets his heart to seek God, the LORD the God of his fathers, even though not according to the sanctuary's rules of cleanness." (20)And the LORD heard Hezekiah, and healed the people. (21)And the people of Israel that were present at Jerusalem kept the feast of unleavened bread seven days with great gladness; and the Levites and the priests praised the LORD day by day, singing with all their might to the LORD. (22)And Hezekiah spoke encouragingly to all the Levites who showed good skill in the service of the LORD. So the people ate the food of the festival for seven days, sacrificing peace offerings and giving thanks to the LORD the God of their fathers.

(23)Then the whole assembly agreed together to keep the feast for another seven days; so they kept it for another seven days with gladness. (24)For Hezekiah king of Judah gave the assembly a thousand bulls and seven thousand sheep for offerings, and the princes gave the assembly a thousand bulls and ten thousand sheep. And the priests sanctified themselves in great numbers. (25)The whole assembly of Judah, and the priests and the Levites, and the whole assembly that came out of Israel, and the sojourners who came out of the land of Israel, and the sojourners who dwelt in Judah, rejoiced. (26)So there was great joy in Jerusalem, for since the time of Solomon the son of David king of Israel there had been nothing like this in Jerusalem. (27)Then the priests and the Levites arose and blessed the people, and their voice was heard, and their prayer came to his holy habitation in heaven.

151 Places of Idolatry Destroyed

II Kings 18:4–8

II Chronicles 31:1

(1)Now when all this was finished, all Israel who were present went out to the cities of Judah

(4)He removed the high places, and broke the pillars, and cut down the Asherah.

and broke in pieces the pillars and hewed down the Asherim and broke down the high places and the altars throughout all Judah and Benjamin, and in Ephraim and Manasseh, until they had destroyed them all. Then all the people of Israel returned to their cities, every man to his possession.

And he broke in pieces the bronze
serpent that Moses had made, for until
those days the people of Israel had
burned incense to it; it was called
Nahushtan. (5)He trusted in the
LORD the God of Israel; so that there
was none like him among all the kings
of Judah after him, nor among those
who were before him. (6)For he held
fast to the LORD; he did not depart
from following him, but kept the
commandments which the LORD
commanded Moses.
(7)And the LORD was with
him; wherever he went forth, he
prospered. He rebelled against the
king of Assyria, and would not serve
him. (8)He smote the Philistines
as far as Gaza and its territory,
from watchtower to fortified city.

152 Additional Reforms of Worship

II Chronicles 31:2–21

(2)And Hezekiah appointed the divisions of the priests and of the Levites, division
by division, each according to his service, the priests and the Levites, for burnt offerings
and peace offerings, to minister in the gates of the camp of the LORD and to give thanks
and praise. (3)The contribution of the king from his own possessions was for the burnt
offerings: the burnt offerings of morning and evening, and the burnt offerings for the
sabbaths, the new moons, and the appointed feasts, as it is written in the law of the
LORD. (4)And he commanded the people who lived in Jerusalem to give the portion due
to the priests and the Levites, that they might give themselves to the law of the LORD.
(5)As soon as the command was spread abroad, the people of Israel gave in abundance
the first fruits of grain, wine, oil, honey, and of all the produce of the field; and they
brought in abundantly the tithe of everything. (6)And the people of Israel and Judah
who lived in the cities of Judah also brought in the tithe of cattle and sheep, and the
dedicated things which had been consecrated to the LORD their God, and laid them in
heaps. (7)In the third month they began to pile up the heaps, and finished them in the
seventh month. (8)When Hezekiah and the princes came and saw the heaps, they blessed
the LORD and his people Israel. (9)And Hezekiah questioned the priests and the Levites
about the heaps. (10)Azariah the chief priest, who was of the house of Zadok, answered
him, "Since they began to bring the contributions into the house of the LORD we have
eaten and had enough and have plenty left; for the LORD has blessed his people, so that
we have this great store left."
(11)Then Hezekiah commanded them to prepare chambers in the house of the LORD;
and they prepared them. (12)And they faithfully brought in the contributions, the tithes
and the dedicated things. The chief officer in charge of them was Conaniah the Levite,

with Shime-i his brother as second; [13]while Jehiel, Azaziah, Nahath, Asahel, Jerimoth, Jozabad, Eliel, Ismachiah, Mahath, and Benaiah were overseers assisting Conaniah and Shime-i his brother, by the appointment of Hezekiah the king and Azariah the chief officer of the house of God. [14]And Kore the son of Imnah the Levite, keeper of the east gate, was over the freewill offerings to God, to apportion the contribution reserved for the LORD and the most holy offerings. [15]Eden, Miniamin, Jeshua, Shemaiah, Amariah, and Shecaniah were faithfully assisting him in the cities of the priests, to distribute the portions to their brethren, old and young alike, by divisions, [16]except those enrolled by genealogy, males from three years old and upwards, all who entered the house of the LORD as the duty of each day required, for their service according to their offices, by their divisions. [17]The enrollment of the priests was according to their fathers' houses; that of the Levites from twenty years old and upwards was according to their offices, by their divisions. [18]The priests were enrolled with all their little children, their wives, their sons, and their daughters, the whole multitude; for they were faithful in keeping themselves holy. [19]And for the sons of Aaron, the priests, who were in the fields of common land belonging to their cities, there were men in the several cities who were designated by name to distribute portions to every male among the priests and to every one among the Levites who was enrolled.

[20]Thus Hezekiah did throughout all Judah; and he did what was good and right and faithful before the LORD his God. [21]And every work that he undertook in the service of the house of God and in accordance with the law and the commandments, seeking his God, he did with all his heart, and prospered.

153 The Fall of Israel, II*

II Kings 18:9–12	*II Kings 17:5–6*
[9]In the fourth year of King Hezekiah, which was the seventh year of Hoshea son of Elah, king of Israel, Shalmaneser king of Assyria came up	
against Samaria and	[5]Then the king of Assyria invaded all the land and came to Samaria, and for three years
besieged it [10]and at the end of three years he took it. In the sixth year of Hezekiah, which was the ninth year of Hoshea king of Israel,	he besieged it.
Samaria was taken. [11]The king of Assyria carried the Israelites away to Assyria,	[6]In the ninth year of Hoshea the king of Assyria captured Samaria, and he carried the Israelites away to Assyria,

*See also 147 The Fall of Israel, I, p. 214.

and <u>put them</u> in Halah, and on the Habor, the river of Gozan, and in the cities of the Medes, ⁽¹²⁾because they did not obey the voice of the LORD their God but transgressed his covenant, even all that Moses the servant of the LORD commanded; they neither listened nor obeyed.	and <u>placed them</u> in Halah, and on the Habor, the river of Gozan, and in the cities of the Medes.

154 The Invasion of Sennacherib

II Kings 18:13–37; Isaiah 36:1–22; II Chronicles 32:1–19

II Kings 18:13	*Isaiah 36:1*	*II Chronicles 32:1*
		⁽¹⁾After these things and these acts of faithfulness
⁽¹³⁾In the fourteenth year of King Hezekiah Sennacherib king of Assyria came <u>up</u>	⁽¹⁾In the fourteenth year of King Hezekiah, Sennacherib king of Assyria came up	Sennacherib king of Assyria came and <u>invaded Judah and encamped</u>
against <u>all</u> the fortified cities of Judah and took	against all the fortified cities of Judah and took	against the fortified cities,
them.	them.	<u>thinking to win</u> them <u>for himself.</u>

II Chronicles 32:2–8

⁽²⁾And when Hezekiah saw that Sennacherib had come and intended to fight against Jerusalem, ⁽³⁾he planned with his officers and his mighty men to stop the water of the springs that were outside the city; and they helped him. ⁽⁴⁾A great many people were gathered, and they stopped all the springs and the brook that flowed through the land, saying, "Why should the kings of Assyria come and find much water?" ⁽⁵⁾He set to work resolutely and built up all the wall that was broken down, and raised towers upon it, and outside it he built another wall; and he strengthened the Millo in the city of David. He also made weapons and shields in abundance. ⁽⁶⁾And he set combat commanders over the people, and gathered them together to him in the square at the gate of the city and spoke encouragingly to them, saying, ⁽⁷⁾"Be strong and of good courage. Do not be afraid or dismayed before the king of Assyria and all the horde that is with him; for there is one greater with us than with him. ⁽⁸⁾With him is an arm of flesh; but with us is the LORD our God, to help us and to fight our battles." And the people took confidence from the words of Hezekiah king of Judah.

II Kings 18:14–22

(14)And Hezekiah king
of Judah sent to the
king of Assyria at
Lachish, saying, "I
have done wrong;
withdraw from me;
whatever you impose on
me I will bear." And
the king of Assyria
required of Hezekiah
king of Judah three
hundred talents of
silver and thirty
talents of gold.
(15)And Hezekiah gave
him all the silver that
was found in the house
of the LORD, and in the
treasuries of the king's
house. (16)At that time
Hezekiah stripped the
gold from the doors of
the temple of the LORD,
and from the doorposts
which Hezekiah king of
Judah had overlaid and
gave it to the king of
Assyria.

II Chronicles 32:9–12

(9)After this
Sennacherib

Isaiah 36:2–7

(17)And the   (2)And the
king of Assyria   king of Assyria,
                               who was beseiging
                               Lachish with all his
                               forces,

sent   sent   sent
the Tartan,
the Rabsaris, and
the Rabshakeh   the Rabshakeh
with a great army

                                                       his servants to

from Lachish to   from Lachish to

224

		Jerusalem to Hezekiah king of Judah
King Hezekiah at Jerusalem.	King Hezekiah at Jerusalem, with a great army.	
		and to all the people of Judah that were in Jerusalem,
And they went up and came to		
Jerusalem. When they arrived, they came and stood by the conduit of the upper pool, which is on the highway to the Fuller's Field.	And he stood by the conduit of the upper pool on the highway to the Fuller's Field.	
(18)And when they called for the king, there came out to them Eliakim the son of Hilkiah, who was over the household, and Shebnah the secretary, and Joah the son of Asaph, the recorder.	(3)And there came out to him Eliakim the son of Hilkiah, who was over the household, and Shebna the secretary, and Joah the son of Asaph, the recorder.	
(19)And the Rabshakeh said to them, "Say to Hezekiah, 'Thus says the great king,	(4)And the Rabshakeh said to them, "Say to Hezekiah, 'Thus says the great king,	saying, (10)"Thus says
the king of Assyria: On what do you rest this confidence of yours?	the king of Assyria: On what do you rest this confidence of yours?	Sennacherib king of Assyria, 'On what are you relying, that you stand siege in Jerusalem?
(20)Do you think that mere words are strategy and power for war? On whom do you now rely, that you have rebelled against me? (21)Behold, you are relying now on Egypt, that broken reed	(5)Do you think that mere words are strategy and power for war? On whom do you now rely, that you have rebelled against me? (6)Behold, you are relying on Egypt, that broken reed	

225

of a staff, which will
pierce the hand of any
man who leans on it.
Such is Pharaoh king of
Egypt to all who rely on
him.

of a staff, which will
pierce the hand of any
man who leans on it.
Such is Pharaoh king of
Egypt to all who rely on
him.

(11)Is not Hezekiah
misleading you,* that he
may give you over to die
by famine and by thirst,
when he tells you,

(22)But if you say to
me, "We rely on
the LORD our God,"

(7)But if you say to
me, "We rely on
the LORD our God,"

"The LORD our God
will deliver us from
the hand of the king
of Assyria?"

is it not he whose
high places and altars

is it not he whose
high places and altars

/12/Has not this same
Hezekiah removed
his high places and
his altars,

Hezekiah has removed,

Hezekiah has removed,

saying to Judah and to
Jerusalem, "You shall
worship before this
altar in Jerusalem"?

saying to Judah and to
Jerusalem, "You shall
worship before this
altar"?

saying to Judah and to
Jerusalem, "You shall
worship before one
altar,
and upon it you shall
burn your sacrifices"?

II Kings 18:23–32

(23)Come now, make a wager with
my master the king of Assyria:
I will give you two thousand
horses, if you are able on your
part to set riders upon them.
(24)How then can you repulse
a single captain among the least
of my master's servants,
when you rely on Egypt for chariots
and for horsemen?
(25)Moreover, is it without the
LORD that I have come up against

Isaiah 36:8–18a

(8)Come now, make a wager with
my master the king of Assyria:
I will give you two thousand
horses, if you are able on your
part to set riders upon them.
(9)How then can you repulse
a single captain among the least
of my master's servants,
when you rely on Egypt for chariots
and for horsemen?
(10)Moreover, is it without the
LORD that I have come up against

*Cf. II Kings 18:32; Isa. 36:18.

this place to destroy it? The LORD
said to me, Go up against this
land, and destroy it.' "
(26)Then Eliakim
the son of Hilkiah,
and Shebnah, and Joah, said to the
Rabshakeh, "Pray, speak to your
servants in the Aramaic language
for we understand it; do not
speak to us in the language
of Judah within the hearing of
the people who are on the wall."
(27)But the Rabshakeh said to them,
"Has my master sent me to speak
these words to your master and to you,
and not to the men sitting on
the wall, who are doomed with you
to eat their own dung and to
drink their own urine?"
(28)Then the Rabshakeh stood and
called out in a loud voice in the
language of Judah: "Hear the word
of the great king, the king
of Assyria! (29)Thus says the king:
'Do not let Hezekiah deceive you,
for he will not be able to deliver
you out of my hand.
/30/Do not let Hezekiah make you rely
on the LORD by saying, The LORD
will surely deliver us, and this city
will not be given into the hand
of the king of Assyria.' (31)Do not
listen to Hezekiah; for thus says
the king of Assyria: 'Make your
peace with me and come out to me;
then every one of you will eat of
his own vine, and every one of
his own fig tree, and every one
of you will drink the water of his
own cistern; (32)until I come and
take you away to a land like your own
land, a land of grain and wine,
a land of bread and vineyards,

this land to destroy it? The LORD
said to me, Go up against this
land, and destroy it.' "
/11/Then Eliakim,

and Shebna, and Joah, said to the
Rabshakeh, "Pray, speak to your
servants in the Aramaic language
for we understand it; do not
speak to us in the language
of Judah within the hearing of
the people who are on the wall."
/12/But the Rabshakeh said,
"Has my master sent me to speak
these words to your master and to you,
and not to the men sitting on
the wall, who are doomed with you
to eat their own dung and to
drink their own urine?"
(13)Then the Rabshakeh stood and
called out in a loud voice in the
language of Judah*: "Hear the word
of the great king, the king
of Assyria! (14)Thus says the king:
'Do not let Hezekiah deceive you,
for he will not be able to deliver
you.†
/15/Do not let Hezekiah make you rely
on the LORD by saying, The LORD
will surely deliver us, this city
will not be given into the hand
of the king of Assyria.' /16/Do not
listen to Hezekiah; for thus says
the king of Assyria: 'Make your
peace with me and come out to me;
then every one of you will eat of
his own vine, and every one of
his own fig tree, and every one
of you will drink the water of his
own cistern; /17/until I come and
take you away to a land like your own
land, a land of grain and wine,
a land of bread and vineyards.

*Cf. II Chron. 32:18.
†Cf. II Chron. 32:15.

a land of olive trees and honey,
that you may live, and not die. And
do not listen to

	/18/Beware lest

Hezekiah when he misleads you by
saying, The Lord will deliver us.

Hezekiah mislead you by
saying,* The Lord will deliver us.

II Chronicles 32:13–19

(13)Do you not know what
I and my fathers have
done to all the peoples
of other lands?

II Kings 18:33–37

(33)Has any of the gods
of the nations

Isaiah 36:18b–22

Has any of the gods
of the nations

Were the gods
of the nations
of those lands
at all able to deliver

ever delivered
his land out of
the hand of
the king of Assyria?
(34)Where are the gods
of Hamath and Arpad?
Where are the gods of
Sepharvaim,
Hena, and Ivvah?
Have they delivered
Samaria out of my hand?
(35)Who among all the
gods of the countries

delivered
his land out of
the hand of
the king of Assyria?
(19)Where are the gods
of Hamath and Arpad?
Where are the gods of
Sepharvaim?

Have they delivered
Samaria out of my hand?
(20)Who among all the
gods of these countries

their lands out of
my hand?

/14/Who among all the
gods of these nations
which my fathers utterly
destroyed was able
to deliver his

have delivered their
countries out of my
hand, that the Lord
should
deliver Jerusalem
out of my hand?' "

have delivered their
countries out of my
hand, that the Lord
should
deliver Jerusalem
out of my hand?' "

people out of my
hand, that your God
should be able
to deliver you
out of my hand?
(15)Now therefore do
not let Hezekiah deceive
you or mislead you in
this fashion, and do not

*Cf. II Chron. 32:11.

believe him, for no god
of any nation or kingdom
has been able to deliver
his people from my hand
or from the hand of my
fathers. How much less
will your God deliver
you out of my hand!' "*
     (16)And his
servants said still more
against the LORD God and
against his servant
Hezekiah. (17)And he
wrote letters to cast
contempt on the LORD
the God of Israel and to
speak against him,
saying, "Like the gods
of the nations of the
lands who have not
delivered their people
from my hands, so the
God of Hezekiah will not
deliver his people from
my hand."†
/18/And they called
out with a loud voice in
the language of Judah to
the people of Jerusalem
who were upon the wall,
to frighten and terrify
them, in order that they
might take the city.‡
     (19)And they spoke of
the God of Jerusalem as
they spoke of the gods
of the peoples of the
earth, which are the
work of men's hands.

(36)But the people   (21)But they
were silent and answered   were silent and answered
him not a word, for the   him not a word, for the

*Cf. II Kings 18:29; Isa. 36:14.
†Cf. II Kings 19:14; Isa. 37:14.
‡Cf. II Kings 18:28; Isa. 36:13.

229

king's command was, "Do
not answer him."
(37)Then Eliakim the
son of Hilkiah, who was
over the household, and
Shebna the secretary,
and Joah the son of
Asaph, the recorder,
came to Hezekiah with
their clothes rent, and
told him the words of
the Rabshakeh.

king's command was, "Do
not answer him."
(22)Then Eliakim the
son of Hilkiah, who was
over the household, and
Shebna the secretary,
and Joah the son of
Asaph, the recorder,
came to Hezekiah with
their clothes rent, and
told him the words of
the Rabshakeh.

L

155 Hezekiah's Appeal

II Kings 19:1–34; Isaiah 37:1–35; II Chronicles 32:20

II Kings 19:1–13

(1)When King Hezekiah heard it,
he rent his clothes, and covered
himself with sackcloth, and went
into the house of the LORD.
(2)And he sent Eliakim, who was
over the household, and Shebna the
secretary, and the senior priests,
covered with sackcloth, to the
prophet Isaiah the son of Amoz.
(3)They said to him, "Thus says
Hezekiah, This day is a day of
distress, of rebuke, and of
disgrace; children have come to the
birth, and there is no strength to
bring them forth. (4)It may be
that the LORD your God heard all the
words of the Rabshakeh, whom his
master the king of Assyria has sent
to mock the living God, and will
rebuke the words which the LORD your
God has heard; therefore lift up
your prayer for the remnant that is
left." (5)When the servants of
King Hezekiah came to Isaiah,
(6)Isaiah said to them, "Say to
your master, 'Thus says the LORD:
Do not be afraid because of the
words that you have heard, with

Isaiah 37:1–13

(1)When King Hezekiah heard it,
he rent his clothes, and covered
himself with sackcloth, and went
into the house of the LORD.
(2)And he sent Eliakim, who was
over the household, and Shebna the
secretary, and the senior priests,
clothed with sackcloth, to the
prophet Isaiah the son of Amoz.
(3)They said to him, "Thus says
Hezekiah, 'This day is a day of
distress, of rebuke, and of
disgrace; children have come to the
birth, and there is no strength to
bring them forth. (4)It may be
that the LORD your God heard the
words of the Rabshakeh, whom his
master the king of Assyria has sent
to mock the living God, and will
rebuke the words which the LORD your
God has heard; therefore lift up
your prayer for the remnant that is
left.' " (5)When the servants of
King Hezekiah came to Isaiah,
(6)Isaiah said to them, "Say to
your master, 'Thus says the LORD:
Do not be afraid because of the
words that you have heard, with

which the servants of the king of
Assyria have reviled me. (7)Behold,
I will put a spirit in him, so that
he shall hear a rumor and return to
his own land; and I will cause him
to fall by the sword in his own
land.' "

(8)The Rabshakeh returned,
and found the king of Assyria fighting
against Libnah; for he heard that the
king had left Lachish. (9)And when
the king heard concerning Tirhakah
king of Ethiopia, "Behold, he has set
out to fight against you,"

he sent messengers again to Hezekiah,
saying, (10)"Thus shall you speak to
Hezekiah king of Judah: 'Do not let
your God on whom you rely deceive you
by promising that Jerusalem will not
be given into the hand of the king of
Assyria. (11)Behold, you have heard
what the kings of Assyria have done to
all lands, destroying them utterly.
And shall you be delivered? (12)Have
the gods of the nations delivered
them, the nations which my fathers
destroyed, Gozan, Haran, Rezeph, and
the people of Eden who were in
Tel-assar? (13)Where is the king of
Hamath, the king of Arpad, the king of
the city of Sepharvaim, the king of
Hena, or the king of Ivvah?' "

which the servants of the king of
Assyria have reviled me. /7/Behold,
I will put a spirit in him, so that
he shall hear a rumor, and return to
his own land; and I will cause him
to fall by the sword in his own
land.' "

(8)The Rabshakeh returned,
and found the king of Assyria fighting
against Libnah; for he had heard that the
king had left Lachish. (9)Now
the king heard concerning Tirhakah
king of Ethiopia, "He has set
out to fight against you."

And when he heard it,
he sent messengers to Hezekiah,
saying, (10)"Thus shall you speak to
Hezekiah king of Judah: 'Do not let
your God on whom you rely deceive you
by promising that Jerusalem will not
be given into the hand of the king of
Assyria. (11)Behold, you have heard
what the kings of Assyria have done to
all lands, destroying them utterly.
And shall you be delivered? (12)Have
the gods of the nations delivered
them, the nations which my fathers
destroyed, Gozan, Haran, Rezeph, and
the people of Eden who were in
Telassar? (13)Where is the king of
Hamath, the king of Arpad, the king of
the city of Sepharvaim, the king of
Hena, or the king of Ivvah?' "

II Kings 19:14–15a	*Isaiah 37:14–15*	*II Chronicles 32:20*
(14)Hezekiah received the letter from the hand of the messengers, and read it; and Hezekiah went up to the house of the LORD, and spread it before the LORD. (15)And Hezekiah	(14)Hezekiah received the letter from the hand of the messengers, and read it; and Hezekiah went up to the house of the LORD, and spread it before the LORD.* /15/And Hezekiah	(20)And Hezekiah the king and Isaiah the

*Cf. II Chron. 32:17.

II Kings		II Chronicles
		prophet, the son of Amoz,
prayed	prayed	prayed
before the LORD,	before the LORD,	because of this
and said:	and said:	and cried to heaven.

II Kings 19:15b–34	*Isaiah 37:16–35*
"O LORD	(16)"O LORD of hosts,
the God of Israel, who art enthroned	God of Israel, who art enthroned
above the cherubim, thou art the God,	above the cherubim, thou art the God,
thou alone, of all the kingdoms of the	thou alone, of all the kingdoms of the
earth; thou hast made heaven and	earth; thou hast made heaven and
earth. (16)Incline thy ear, O LORD,	earth. (17)Incline thy ear, O LORD,
and hear; open thy eyes, O LORD, and	and hear; open thy eyes, O LORD, and
see; and hear the words of	see; and hear all the words of
Sennacherib, which he has sent to mock	Sennacherib, which he has sent to mock
the living God. (17)Of a truth,	the living God. (18)Of a truth,
O LORD, the kings of Assyria have laid	O LORD, the kings of Assyria have laid
waste the nations and their lands,	waste all the nations and their lands,
(18)and have cast their gods into	(19)and have cast their gods into
the fire; for they were no gods, but	the fire; for they were no gods, but
the work of men's hands, wood and	the work of men's hands, wood and
stone; therefore they were destroyed.	stone; therefore they were destroyed.
(19)So now, O LORD our God, save us,	(20)So now, O LORD our God, save us
I beseech thee,	
from his hand, that all the kingdoms	from his hand, that all the kingdoms
of the earth may know that thou,	of the earth may know that thou
O LORD,	
art God alone."	alone art
	the LORD."
(20)Then Isaiah the son of Amoz	(21)Then Isaiah the son of Amoz
sent to Hezekiah, saying, "Thus says	sent to Hezekiah, saying, "Thus says
the LORD, the God of Israel:	the LORD, the God of Israel:
Your prayer to me	Because you have prayed to me
about	concerning
Sennacherib king of Assyria	Sennacherib king of Assyria,
I have heard.	
(21)This is the word that the LORD	/22/this is the word that the LORD
has spoken concerning him:	has spoken concerning him:
"She despises you, she scorns	'She despises you, she scorns
you—	you—
the virgin daughter of Zion;	the virgin daughter of Zion;
she wags her head behind you—	she wags her head behind you—
the daughter of Jerusalem.	the daughter of Jerusalem.

⁽²²⁾"Whom have you mocked and reviled?
    Against whom have you raised
      your voice
  and haughtily lifted your eyes?
    Against the Holy One of Israel!
⁽²³⁾By your messengers you have mocked
    the Lord,
    and you have said, 'With my many
      chariots
  I have gone up the heights of the
      mountains,
    to the far recesses of Lebanon;
  I felled its tallest cedars,
    its choicest cypresses;
  I entered its farthest retreat,
    its densest forest.
⁽²⁴⁾I dug wells
    and drank foreign waters,
  and I dried up with the sole
    of my foot
  all the streams of Egypt.'

⁽²⁵⁾"Have you not heard
    that I determined it long ago?
  I planned from days of old
    what now I bring to pass,
  that you should turn fortified
    cities
    into heaps of ruins,
⁽²⁶⁾while their inhabitants, shorn
    of strength,
    are dismayed and confounded,
  and have become like plants of the
    field,
    and like tender grass,
  like grass on the housetops;
    blighted before it is grown.

⁽²⁷⁾"But I know your sitting down
    and your going out and
      coming in,
    and your raging against me.
⁽²⁸⁾Because you have raged against me
    and your arrogance has come
      into my ears,
  I will put my hook in your nose
    and my bit in your mouth,

/23/ 'Whom have you mocked and reviled?
    Against whom have you raised
      your voice
  and haughtily lifted your eyes?
    Against the Holy One of Israel!
/24/ By your servants you have mocked
    the Lord,
    and you have said, With my many
      chariots
  I have gone up the heights of the
      mountains,
    to the far recesses of Lebanon;
  I felled its tallest cedars,
    its choicest cypresses;
  I came to its remotest height,
    its densest forest.
/25/ I dug wells
    and drank waters,
  and I dried up with the sole
    of my foot
  all the streams of Egypt.

/26/ 'Have you not heard
    that I determined it long ago?
  I planned from days of old
    what now I bring to pass,
  that you should make fortified
    cities
    crash into heaps of ruins,
/27/ while their inhabitants, shorn
    of strength,
    are dismayed and confounded,
  and have become like plants of the
    field
    and like tender grass,
  like grass on the housetops,
    a field before it is grown.

/28/ 'But I know your sitting down
    and your going out and
      coming in,
    and your raging against me.
/29/ Because you have raged against me
    and your arrogance has come
      into my ears,
  I will put my hook in your nose
    and my bit in your mouth,

and I will turn you back on the
way
by which you came.

(29)"And this shall be the sign
for you: this year you shall eat what
grows of itself, and in the second
year what springs of the same; then
in the third year sow, and reap, and
plant vineyards, and eat their fruit.
(30)And the surviving remnant of the
house of Judah shall again take root
downward, and bear fruit upward;
(31)for out of Jerusalem shall go
forth a remnant, and out of Mount
Zion a band of survivors. The zeal
of the LORD
will do this.
(32)"Therefore thus says the
LORD concerning the king of Assyria,
He shall not come into this city or
shoot an arrow there, or come before
it with a shield or cast up a siege
mound against it. (33)By the way
that he came, by the same he shall
return, and he shall not come into
this city, says the LORD. (34)For
I will defend this city to save it,
for my own sake and for the sake
of my servant David."

and I will turn you back on the
way
by which you came.'

/30/"And this shall be the sign
for you: this year you shall eat what
grows of itself, and in the second
year what springs of the same; then
in the third year sow, and reap, and
plant vineyards, and eat their fruit.
(31)And the surviving remnant of the
house of Judah shall again take root
downward, and bear fruit upward;
/32/for out of Jerusalem shall go
forth a remnant, and out of Mount
Zion a band of survivors. The zeal
of the LORD of hosts
will do this.
/33/"Therefore thus says the
LORD concerning the king of Assyria,
He shall not come into this city or
shoot an arrow there, or come before
it with a shield or cast up a siege
mound against it. (34)By the way
that he came, by the same he shall
return, and he shall not come into
this city, says the LORD. (35)For
I will defend this city to save it,
for my own sake and for the sake
of my servant David."

156 The Angel of Death

II Kings 19:35–37	*Isaiah 37:36–38*	*II Chronicles 32:21–23*
(35)And that night	(36)And	(21)And the LORD sent an angel,
the angel of the LORD went forth, and slew a hundred and eighty-five thousand	the angel of the LORD went forth, and slew a hundred and eighty-five thousand	
		who cut off all the mighty warriors and commanders and officers
in the camp of the Assyrians; and when men arose early	in the camp of the Assyrians; and when men arose early	in the camp of the king of Assyria.

234

in the morning, behold, these were all dead bodies.	in the morning, behold, these were all dead bodies.	
(36)Then Sennacherib king of Assyria departed, and went home, and dwelt at Nineveh.	(37)Then Sennacherib king of Assyria departed, and went home and dwelt at Nineveh.	So he returned with shame of face to his own land.
(37)And as he was worshiping in	(38)And as he was worshiping in	And when he came into the house of his god,
the house of Nisroch his god, Adrammelech and Sharezer,	the house of Nisroch his god, Adrammelech and Sharezer,	some of his own sons
his sons, slew him	his sons, slew him	struck him down there with the sword.
with the sword, and escaped into the land of Ararat. And Esarhaddon his son reigned in his stead.	with the sword, and escaped into the land of Ararat. And Esar-haddon his son reigned in his stead.	

(22)So the LORD saved Hezekiah and the inhabitants of Jerusalem from the hand of Sennacherib king of Assyria and from the hand of all his enemies; and he gave them rest on every side. (23)And many brought gifts to the LORD to Jerusalem and precious things to Hezekiah king of Judah, so that he was exalted in the sight of all nations from that time onward.

157 Hezekiah's Illness

II Kings 20:1–11	*Isaiah 38:1–8, 21–22*	*II Chronicles 32:24–26*
	Isaiah 38:1–6	

(1)In those days Hezekiah became sick and was at the point of death. And Isaiah the prophet the son of Amoz came to him, and said to him, "Thus says the LORD, 'Set your house in order; for you shall die, you shall not recover.' " (2)Then Hezekiah turned his face to the wall, and prayed to the LORD, saying, (3)"Remember now, O LORD, I beseech thee, how I have walked before thee in faithfulness and with a whole heart, and have done what is good in thy sight." And Hezekiah wept bitterly. (4)And before Isaiah had gone out of the middle court, the word of the LORD came to him: (5)"Turn back, and say to Hezekiah the prince of my people, Thus says the LORD, the God of David your father: I have heard your prayer, I have seen your tears; behold, I will heal you; on the third day you shall go up to the house of the LORD. (6)And I will add fifteen years

(1)In those days Hezekiah became sick and was at the point of death. And Isaiah the prophet the son of Amoz came to him, and said to him, "Thus says the LORD: Set your house in order; for you shall die, you shall not recover." (2)Then Hezekiah turned his face to the wall, and prayed to the LORD, (3)and said, "Remember now, O LORD, I beseech thee, how I have walked before thee in faithfulness and with a whole heart, and have done what is good in thy sight." And Hezekiah wept bitterly. (4)Then

the word of the LORD came to Isaiah: (5)"Go and say to Hezekiah,

Thus says the LORD, the God of David your father: I have heard your prayer, I have seen your tears; behold, I

will add fifteen years

(24)In those days Hezekiah became sick and was at the point of death,

and he

prayed to the LORD;

to your life. I will
deliver you and this
city out of the hand of
the king of Assyria, and
I will defend this city
for my own sake and for
my servant David's
sake."

(7)And Isaiah said,
"Bring a cake of
figs.
And let them take and
lay it on the boil,
that he may recover."
    (8)And Hezekiah said
to Isaiah,
"What shall be the sign
that the LORD will heal
me, and
that I shall go up to
the house of the LORD
on the third day?"

(9)And Isaiah said,

"This is the
sign
to you from the LORD,
that the LORD will do
the thing that he has
promised:
shall the shadow go
forward ten steps, or go
back ten steps?"
(10)And Hezekiah
answered, "It is an easy
thing for the shadow to
lengthen ten steps;
rather let the shadow
go back ten steps."
(11)And Isaiah the
prophet cried to the
LORD;

---

to your life. /6/I will
deliver you and this
city out of the hand of
the king of Assyria, and
I will defend this city.

Isaiah 38:21–22
/21/And Isaiah said,
"Let them take a cake of
figs,
and
apply it to the boil,
that he may recover."
/22/And Hezekiah said,

"What shall be the sign

that I shall go up to
the house of the LORD?"

Isaiah 38:7–8
    (7)"This is the
sign
to you from the LORD,
that the LORD will do
this thing that he has
promised:

---

and he answered him and
gave him a

sign.

and he brought	(8)Behold, I will make
the shadow	the shadow
	cast by the declining
	sun on the dial of Ahaz
	turn
back ten steps,	back ten steps."
	So the sun turned back
	on the dial the ten
	steps
by which the sun had	by which it had
declined	declined.
on the dial of Ahaz.	

(25)But Hezekiah did not make return according to the benefit done to him, for his heart was proud. Therefore wrath came upon him and Judah and Jerusalem. (26)But Hezekiah humbled himself for the pride of his heart, both he and the inhabitants of Jerusalem, so that the wrath of the LORD did not come upon them in the days of Hezekiah.

158 Hezekiah's Wealth

II Chronicles 32:27–30

(27)And Hezekiah had very great riches and honor; and he made for himself treasuries for silver, for gold, for precious stones, for spices, for shields, and for all kinds of costly vessels; (28)storehouses also for the yield of grain, wine, and oil; and stalls for all kinds of cattle, and sheepfolds. (29)He likewise provided cities for himself, and flocks and herds in abundance; for God had given him very great possessions. (30)This same Hezekiah closed the upper outlet of the waters of Gihon and directed them down to the west side of the city of David. And Hezekiah prospered in all his works.

159 The Embassy From Babylon

II Kings 20:12–19; Isaiah 39:1–8; II Chronicles 32:31

II Kings 20:12	Isaiah 39:1	II Chronicles 32:31
(12)At that time	(1)At that time	
Merodach-baladan the son	Merodach-baladan the son	

of Baladan, king of
Babylon, sent

of Baladan, king of
Babylon, sent

(31)And so in the
matter of the
envoys
of the princes of
Babylon,

envoys

envoys

with letters and a
present to Hezekiah; for
he heard that Hezekiah
had been sick.

with letters and a
present to Hezekiah; for
he heard that he
had been sick
and had recovered.

who had been sent to him
to inquire about the
sign that had been done
in the land, God left
him to himself, in order
to try him and to know
all that was in his
heart.

II Kings 20:13–19

(13)And Hezekiah
welcomed them, and he
showed them all his treasure
house, the silver, the
gold, the spices, the
precious oil, his
armory, all that
was found in his
storehouses; there was
nothing in his house or
in all his realm that
Hezekiah did not show
them. (14)Then Isaiah
the prophet came to King
Hezekiah, and said to
him, "What did these men
say? And whence did
they come to you?" And
Hezekiah said, "They
have come from a far
country, from Babylon."
(15)He said, "What have
they seen in your
house?" And Hezekiah
answered, "They have

Isaiah 39:2–8

(2)And Hezekiah
welcomed them; and he
showed them his treasure
house, the silver, the
gold, the spices, the
precious oil, his
whole armory, all that
was found in his
storehouses. There was
nothing in his house or
in all his realm that
Hezekiah did not show
them. (3)Then Isaiah
the prophet came to King
Hezekiah, and said to
him, "What did these men
say? And whence did
they come to you?"
Hezekiah said, "They
have come to me from a far
country, from Babylon."
/4/He said, "What have
they seen in your
house?" and Hezekiah
answered, "They have

seen all that is in my
house; there is nothing
in my storehouses that
I did not show them."
(16)Then Isaiah said
to Hezekiah, "Hear the
word of the LORD:

(17)Behold, the days are
coming, when all that is
in your house, and that
which your fathers have
stored up till this day,
shall be carried to
Babylon; nothing shall
be left, says the LORD.
(18)And some of your
own sons, who are born
to you, shall be taken
away; and they shall be
eunuchs in the palace of
the king of Babylon."
(19)Then said Hezekiah
to Isaiah, "The word of
the LORD which you have
spoken is good." For he
thought, "Why not, if
there will be peace and
security in my days?"

seen all that is in my
house; there is nothing
in my storehouses that
I did not show them."
(5)Then Isaiah said
to Hezekiah, "Hear the
word of the LORD
of hosts:

(6)Behold, the days are
coming, when all that is
in your house, and that
which your fathers have
stored up till this day,
shall be carried to
Babylon; nothing shall
be left, says the LORD.
(7)And some of your
own sons, who are born
to you, shall be taken
away; and they shall be
eunuchs in the palace of
the king of Babylon."
(8)Then said Hezekiah
to Isaiah, "The word of
the LORD which you have
spoken is good." For he
thought,
"There will be peace and
security in my days?"

160 The Death of Hezekiah

II Kings 20:20–21   *II Chronicles 32:32–33*

/20/Now the rest of the
acts of Hezekiah, and
all his might,

and how he made the pool and the
conduit and brought water into the
city,
are they not written in

the Book of the
Chronicles of the

(32)Now the rest of the
acts of Hezekiah, and

his good deeds, behold,

they are written in
the vision of Isaiah the prophet
the son of Amoz, in
the Book of the

240

Kings of Judah? (21)And Hezekiah slept with his fathers;	Kings of Judah and Israel. (33)And Hezekiah slept with his fathers, and they buried him in the ascent of the tombs of the sons of David; and all Judah and the inhabitants of Jerusalem did him honor at his death.
and Manasseh his son reigned in his stead.	And Manasseh his son reigned in his stead.

161 The Reign of Manasseh

II Kings 21:1–18	*II Chronicles 33:1–20*
(1)Manasseh was twelve years old when he began to reign, and he reigned fifty-five years in Jerusalem. His mother's name was Hephzibah. (2)And he did what was evil in the sight of the LORD, according to the abominable practices of the nations whom the LORD drove out before the people of Israel. (3)For he rebuilt the high places which Hezekiah his father had destroyed; and he erected altars for Baal, and made an Asherah, as Ahab king of Israel had done, and worshiped all the host of heaven, and served them. (4)And he built altars in the house of the LORD, of which the LORD had said, "In Jerusalem will I put my name." (5)And he built altars for all the host of heaven in the two courts of the house of the LORD. (6)And he burned his son as an offering,	(1)Manasseh was twelve years old when he began to reign, and he reigned fifty-five years in Jerusalem. (2)He did what was evil in the sight of the LORD, according to the abominable practices of the nations whom the LORD drove out before the people of Israel. /3/For he rebuilt the high places which Hezekiah his father had broken down, and erected altars to the Baals, and made Asherahs, and worshiped all the host of heaven, and served them. (4)And he built altars in the house of the LORD, of which the LORD had said, "In Jerusalem shall my name be for ever." (5)And he built altars for all the host of heaven in the two courts of the house of the LORD. (6)And he burned his sons as an offering in the valley of the son of Hinnom,
and practiced soothsaying and augury, and dealt with mediums and with wizards. He did much evil in the sight of the LORD, provoking him to anger. (7)And the graven image of Asherah that he had made he set in the house	and practiced soothsaying and augury and sorcery, and dealt with mediums and with wizards. He did much evil in the sight of the LORD, provoking him to anger. (7)And the image of the idol that he had made he set in the house

241

of which the LORD said to David and to
Solomon his son, "In this house, and
in Jerusalem, which I have chosen out
of all the tribes of Israel, I will
put my name for ever; (8)and I will
not cause the feet of Israel
to wander any more
out of the land which I gave
to their fathers, if only they will
be careful to do according to all that
I have commanded them, and
according to all the law

that my servant Moses
commanded them."
(9)But they did not listen,
and Manasseh seduced them

to do more evil than the nations
had done
whom the LORD destroyed before the
people of Israel.
(10)And the LORD said

by his servants the prophets,
(11)"Because Manasseh king of Judah
has committed these abominations, and
has done things more wicked than all
that the Amorites did, who were before
him, and has made Judah also to sin
with his idols; (12)therefore thus
says the LORD, the God of Israel,
Behold, I am bringing upon Jerusalem
and Judah such evil that the ears of
every one who hears of it will tingle.
(13)And I will stretch over Jerusalem
the measuring line of Samaria, and the
plummet of the house of Ahab; and I
will wipe Jerusalem as one wipes a
dish, wiping it and turning it upside
down. (14)And I will cast off the
remnant of my heritage, and give them
into the hand of their enemies, and
they shall become a prey and a spoil
to all their enemies, (15)because they

of God,
of which God said to David and to
Solomon his son, "In this house, and
in Jerusalem, which I have chosen out
of all the tribes of Israel, I will
put my name for ever; (8)and I will
no more remove the foot of Israel

from the land which I appointed
for your fathers, if only they will
be careful to do all that
I have commanded them,
all the law,
the statutes, and the ordinances
given through
Moses."

(9)Manasseh seduced Judah and the
inhabitants of Jerusalem, so that they
did more evil than the nations

whom the LORD destroyed before the
people of Israel.
(10)The LORD spoke
to Manasseh and to his people,

have done what is evil in my sight
and have provoked me to anger, since
the day their fathers came out of
Egypt, even to this day."

(16)Moreover Manasseh shed very
much innocent blood, till he had
filled Jerusalem from one end to
another, besides the sin which he made
Judah to sin so that they did what
was evil in the sight of the LORD.

but they gave no heed.

(11)Therefore the LORD brought
upon them the commanders of the army
of the king of Assyria, who took
Manasseh with hooks and bound him
with fetters of bronze and brought
him to Babylon. (12)And when he was
in distress he entreated the favor of
the LORD his God and humbled
himself greatly before the God of his
fathers. (13)He prayed to him, and
God received his entreaty and heard
his supplication and brought him again
to Jerusalem into his kingdom. Then
Manasseh knew that the LORD was God.
(14)Afterwards he built an outer
wall for the city of David west of
Gihon, in the valley, and for the
entrance into the Fish Gate, and
carried it round Ophel, and raised
it to a very great height; he also
put commanders of the army in all
the fortified cities in Judah.
(15)And he took away the foreign
gods and the idol from the house of
the LORD, and all the altars that he
had built on the mountain of the house
of the LORD and in Jerusalem, and he
threw them outside of the city.
(16)He also restored the altar of
the LORD and offered upon it
sacrifices of peace offerings and of
thanksgiving; and he commanded Judah
to serve the LORD the God of Israel.
(17)Nevertheless the people still
sacrificed at the high places, but

(17)Now the rest of the acts
of Manasseh,
and all that he did,
and the sin that he committed,

are they not written in the Book of
the Chronicles of the Kings of Judah?

(18)And Manasseh slept with his
fathers,
and was buried in
the garden of
his house,
in the garden of Uzza;
and Amon his son reigned in
his stead.

only to the LORD their God.
(18)Now the rest of the acts
of Manasseh,

and his prayer to his God, and the
words of the seers who spoke to him
in the name of the LORD the God of
Israel, behold,
they are in
the Chronicles of the Kings of Israel.
(19)And his prayer, and how God
received his entreaty, and all his
sin and his faithlessness, and the
sites on which he built high places
and set up the Asherim and the images,
before he humbled himself, behold,
they are written in the Chronicles
of the Seers.
(20)And Manasseh slept with his
fathers,
and they buried him in

his house;

and Amon his son reigned in
his stead.

162 The Reign of Amon

II Kings 21:19–26

II Chronicles 33:21–25

(19)Amon was twenty-two years
old when he began to reign, and he
reigned two years in Jerusalem.
His mother's name was Meshullemeth
the daughter of Haruz of Jotbah.
(20)And he did what was evil in
the sight of the LORD, as Manasseh
his father had done.
(21)He walked in all the way in
which

his father
walked,

(21)Amon was twenty-two years
old when he began to reign, and he
reigned two years in Jerusalem.

(22)And he did what was evil in
the sight of the LORD, as Manasseh
his father had done.

Amon sacrificed to all the images
that Manasseh
his father

and served
the idols that his father
served,
and worshiped
them;
(22)he forsook the LORD, the God of
his fathers, and did not walk in the
way of the LORD.

(23)And the servants of Amon conspired
against him, and killed the king in his
house. (24)But the people of the land
slew all those who had conspired
against King Amon, and the people of
the land made Josiah his son king in
his stead.
(25)Now the rest of the acts of Amon
which he did, are they not written in
the Book of the Chronicles of the
Kings of Judah? (26)And he was
buried in his tomb in the garden of
Uzza; and Josiah his son reigned in
his stead.

had made,
and served

them.

(23)And he did not humble himself
before the LORD, as Manasseh his
father had humbled himself, but this
Amon incurred guilt more and more.
(24)And his servants conspired
against him and killed him in his
house. (25)But the people of the land
slew all those who had conspired
against King Amon; and the people of
the land made Josiah his son king in
his stead.

163 The Reign of Josiah Begins, the Book of the Law Found

II Kings 22:1–20

(1)Josiah was eight years old
when he began to reign, and he reigned
thirty-one years in Jerusalem.
His mother's name was Jedidah the
daughter of Adaiah of Bozkath.
(2)And he did what was right in the
eyes of the LORD, and walked in all
the way of David his father, and he
did not turn aside to the right hand
or to the left.

II Chronicles 34:1–3, 8–28

II Chronicles 34:1–3

(1)Josiah was eight years old
when he began to reign, and he reigned
thirty-one years in Jerusalem.

(2)He did what was right in the
eyes of the LORD, and walked in
the ways of David his father; and he
did not turn aside to the right
or to the left.
(3)For in the eighth year of his
reign, while he was yet a boy, he
began to seek the God of David his

245

father; and in the twelfth year he
began to purge Judah and Jerusalem
of the high places, the Asherim, and
the graven and the molten images.

II Chronicles 34:8-28

(3)In the eighteenth year of
King Josiah,

(8)Now in the eighteenth year of
his reign,
when he had purged the land and the
house,
he sent Shaphan the son of
Azaliah,

the king sent Shaphan the son of
Azaliah, son of Meshullam, the
secretary,

and Ma-aseiah the governor of the
city, and Joah the son of Joahaz, the
recorder,

to
the house of the LORD,
saying,
(4)"Go up to Hilkiah the high
priest,
that he may reckon the amount of the

to repair
the house of the LORD his God.

(9)They came to Hilkiah the high
priest

money which has been brought into the
house of the LORD, which

and delivered the
money that had been brought into the
house of God, which
the Levites,

the keepers of the threshold
have collected from
the people;

the keepers of the threshold,
had collected from
Manasseh and Ephraim and from all the
remnant of Israel and from all Judah
and Benjamin and from the inhabitants
of Jerusalem.

(5)and let it be given into
the hand of the workmen who have the
oversight of the house of the LORD;
and

(10)They delivered it to
the workmen who had the
oversight of the house of the LORD;
and the workmen who were working in
the house of the LORD
gave it for

let them give it to
the workmen who are at the house
of the LORD,
repairing the house,
(6)that is,

repairing and restoring the house.

(11)They gave it
to the carpenters and the builders

to the carpenters, and to the builders,
and to the masons,
as well as for buying timber and
quarried stone

to buy
quarried stone,

and timber
for binders and beams and for the
buildings which the kings of Judah
had let go to ruin.

to repair the house.
(7)But no accounting shall be asked
from them for the money which is
delivered into their hand,
for they deal honestly."

(12)And the men did the work
faithfully. Over them were set Jahath
and Obadiah the Levites, of the sons
of Merari, and Zechariah and
Meshullam, of the sons of the
Kohathites, to have oversight. The
Levites, all who were skilful with
instruments of music, (13)were over
the burden bearers and directed all
who did work in every kind of service;
and some of the Levites were scribes,
and officials, and gatekeepers.
(14)While they were bringing out
the money that had been brought into
the house of the LORD, Hilkiah the
priest found the book of the law of
the LORD given through Moses.

(8)And Hilkiah the high priest said
to Shaphan the secretary, "I have
found the book of the law in the house
of the LORD." And Hilkiah gave the
book to Shaphan,
and he read it.
(9)And Shaphan the secretary came

to the king, and reported to the king,

"Your servants

have emptied out the money that was
found in the house,
and have delivered it into the hand
of the workmen who have
the oversight

of the house of the LORD."
(10)Then Shaphan the secretary told

(15)Then Hilkiah said
to Shaphan the secretary, "I have
found the book of the law in the house
of the LORD"; and Hilkiah gave the
book to Shaphan.

Cf. 2Chr 34:8

(16)Shaphan brought
the book
to the king, and further reported to the
king,
"All that was committed to
your servants
they are doing. (17)They
have emptied out the money that was
found in the house of the LORD
and have delivered it into the hand
of the
overseers and
the workmen."

(18)Then Shaphan the secretary told

247

the king, "Hilkiah the priest has
given me a book." And Shaphan read it
before the king.
⁽¹¹⁾And when the king heard
the words of the book of the law,
he rent his clothes. ⁽¹²⁾And the
king commanded Hilkiah the priest, and
Ahikam the son of Shaphan, and
Achbor the son of Micaiah, and
Shaphan the secretary, and Asaiah
the king's servant, saying, ⁽¹³⁾"Go,
inquire of the LORD for me, and for
the people, and
for all Judah,
concerning the words of this book that
has been found; for great is the wrath
of the LORD that is kindled against
us, because our fathers have not
obeyed the words of this book, to do
according to all that is written
concerning us."

⁽¹⁴⁾So Hilkiah the priest,
and Ahikam, and Achbor, and Shaphan,
and Asaiah
went to Huldah the prophetess, the
wife of Shallum the son of Tikvah,
son of Harhas, keeper of the wardrobe
(now she dwelt in Jerusalem in the
Second Quarter); and they talked with
her.

⁽¹⁵⁾And she said to them, "Thus says
the LORD, the God of Israel:
'Tell the man who sent you to me,
⁽¹⁶⁾Thus says the LORD, Behold, I will
bring evil upon this place and upon
its inhabitants, all the
words

of the book which the king of Judah
has read.
⁽¹⁷⁾Because they have forsaken me
and have burned incense to other gods,
that they might provoke me to anger
with all the work of their hands,
therefore my wrath will be kindled

248

the king, "Hilkiah the priest has
given me a book." And Shaphan read it
before the king.
⁽¹⁹⁾When the king heard
the words of the law,
he rent his clothes. ⁽²⁰⁾And the
king commanded Hilkiah,
Ahikam the son of Shaphan,
Abdon the son of Micah,
Shaphan the secretary, and Asaiah
the king's servant, saying, ⁽²¹⁾"Go,
inquire of the LORD for me and for
those who are left in Israel and
in Judah,
concerning the words of the book that
has been found; for great is the wrath
of the LORD that is poured out on
us, because our fathers have not
kept the word of the LORD, to do
according to all that is written

in this book."
^[22]So Hilkiah
and those whom the king*

went to Huldah the prophetess, the
wife of Shallum the son of Tokhath,
son of Hasrah, keeper of the wardrobe
(now she dwelt in Jerusalem in the
Second Quarter); and they talked with
her
to that effect.
⁽²³⁾And she said to them, "Thus says
the LORD, the God of Israel:
'Tell the man who sent you to me,
⁽²⁴⁾Thus says the LORD, Behold, I will
bring evil upon this place and upon
its inhabitants, all the

curses that are written
in the book which was read before the
king of Judah.
⁽²⁵⁾Because they have forsaken me
and have burned incense to other gods,
that they might provoke me to anger
with all the works of their hands,
therefore my wrath will be poured out

*Hebrews lacks "had sent"

against this place, and it will not be
quenched. [18]But as to the king of
Judah, who sent you to inquire of the
LORD, thus shall you say to him, Thus
says the LORD, the God of Israel:
Regarding the words which you have
heard, [19]because your heart was
penitent, and you humbled yourself
before the LORD, when you heard
how I spoke against this place, and
against its inhabitants,
that they should become a desolation
and a curse, and

you have rent your clothes and wept
before me, I also have heard you,
says the LORD.
[20]Therefore,
behold, I will gather you to your
fathers, and you shall be gathered
to your grave in peace, and your
eyes shall not see all the evil
which I will bring upon this
place.' "
And they brought back word
to the king.

upon this place and will not be
quenched. [26]But to the king of
Judah, who sent you to inquire of the
LORD, thus shall you say to him, Thus
says the LORD, the God of Israel:
Regarding the words which you have
heard, [27]because your heart was
penitent, and you humbled yourself
before God, when you heard
his words against this place, and
against its inhabitants,

and you have humbled yourself before
me, and
you have rent your clothes and wept
before me, I also have heard you,
says the LORD.

[28]Behold, I will gather you to your
fathers, and you shall be gathered
to your grave in peace, and your
eyes shall not see all the evil
which I will bring upon this
place and its inhabitants.' "
And they brought back word
to the king.

164 Josiah Purifies the Cult

II Kings 23:1–20   II Chronicles 34:29–33, 4–7

II Kings 23:1–6

[1]Then the king sent, and
all the elders of Judah and Jerusalem
were gathered to him.
[2]And the king went up to the
house of the LORD, and with him all
the men of Judah and all the
inhabitants of Jerusalem, and
the priests and
the prophets,

all the people, both small and great;
and he read in their hearing all the

II Chronicles 34:29–33

[29]Then the king sent and
gathered together
all the elders of Judah and Jerusalem.
[30]And the king went up to the
house of the LORD, with all
the men of Judah and the
inhabitants of Jerusalem and
the priests and

the Levites,
all the people both great and small;
and he read in their hearing all the

words of the book of the covenant
which had been found in the house of
the LORD. (3)And the king stood
by the pillar

and made a covenant before the LORD,
to walk after the LORD and to keep his
commandments and his testimonies and
his statutes, with all his heart and
all his soul, to perform the words
of this covenant that were written
in this book;
and all the people joined in the
covenant.

words of the book of the covenant
which had been found in the house of
the LORD. (31)And the king stood

in his place
and made a covenant before the LORD,
to walk after the LORD and to keep his
commandments and his testimonies and
his statutes, with all his heart and
all his soul, to perform the words
of the covenant that were written
in this book.

(32)Then he made all who were present
in Jerusalem and in Benjamin stand to
it. And the inhabitants of Jerusalem
did according to the covenant of God,
the God of their fathers. (33)And
Josiah took away all the abominations
from all the territory that belonged
to the people of Israel, and made all
who were in Israel serve the LORD
their God. All his days they did not
turn away from following the LORD the
God of their fathers.

(4)And the king commanded Hilkiah,
the high priest, and the priests of
the second order, and the keepers of
the threshold, to bring out of the
temple of the LORD all the vessels
made for Baal, for Asherah, and for
all the host of heaven; he burned them
outside Jerusalem in the fields of the
Kidron, and carried their ashes to
Bethel. (5)And he deposed the
idolatrous priests whom the kings of
Judah had ordained to burn incense
in the high places at the cities of
Judah and round about Jerusalem; those
also who burned incense to Baal, to
the sun, and the moon, and the
constellations, and all the host of
the heavens.

II Chronicles 34:4

(4)And they broke down the altars of
the Baals in his presence; and he

hewed down the incense altars which
stood above them; and he broke in
pieces

(6)And he brought out
the Asherah

the Asherim
and the graven and the molten images,

from the house of the LORD, outside
Jerusalem, to the brook Kidron, and
burned it at the brook Kidron,
and beat it to dust and
cast the dust of it upon the graves
of the common people.

and he made dust of them and
strewed it over the graves

of those who had sacrificed to them.

II Kings 23:7–16a

(7)And he broke down the houses of the male cult prostitutes which were in the house
of the LORD, where the women wove hangings for the Asherah. (8)And he brought all
the priests out of the cities of Judah, and defiled the high places where the priests had
burned incense, from Geba to Beer-sheba; and he broke down the high places of the
gates that were at the entrance of the gate of Joshua the governor of the city, which
were on one's left at the gate of the city. (9)However, the priests of the high places did
not come up to the altar of the LORD in Jerusalem, but they ate unleavened bread among
their brethren. (10)And he defiled Topheth, which is in the valley of the sons of Hinnom,
that no one might burn his son or his daughter as an offering to Molech. (11)And he
removed the horses that the kings of Judah had dedicated to the sun, at the entrance
to the house of the LORD, by the chamber of Nathan-melech the chamberlain, which
was in the precincts; and he burned the chariots of the sun with fire. (12)And the altars
on the roof of the upper chamber of Ahaz, which the kings of Judah had made, and the
altars which Manasseh had made in the two courts of the house of the LORD, he pulled
down and broke in pieces, and cast the dust of them into the brook Kidron. (13)And the
king defiled the high places that were east of Jerusalem, to the south of the mount of
corruption, which Solomon the king of Israel had built for Ashtoreth the abomination
of the Sidonians, and for Chemosh the abomination of Moab, and for Milcom the
abomination of the Ammonites. (14)And he broke in pieces the pillars, and cut down the
Asherim, and filled their places with the bones of men.

(15)Moreover the altar at Bethel, the high place erected by Jeroboam the son of
Nebat, who made Israel to sin, that altar with the high place he pulled down and he
broke in pieces its stones, crushing them to dust; also he burned the Asherah. (16)And
as Josiah turned, he saw the tombs there on the mount; and he sent and took

II Kings 23:16b–20

the bones
out of the tombs, and
burned them
upon the altar,
and defiled it, according to the word

II Chronicles 34:5–7

(5)He also burned
the bones of the priests

on their altars,

of the LORD which the man of God
proclaimed, who had predicted these
things. (17)Then he said, "What is
yonder monument that I see?" And the
men of the city told him, "It is the
tomb of the man of God who came from
Judah and predicted these things which
you have done against the altar at
Bethel." (18)And he said, "Let him
be; let no man move his bones." So
they let his bones alone, with the
bones of the prophet who came out of
Samaria.

(19)And all the shrines also of the
high places that were
in the cities
of Samaria,

and purged Judah and Jerusalem.
(6)And

in the cities

of Manasseh, Ephraim, and Simeon,
and as far as Naphtali, in their
ruins round about,

which kings of Israel had made,
provoking the LORD to anger, Josiah
removed; he did to them according to
all that he had done at Bethel.

(7)he broke down the altars, and
beat the Asherim and the images into
powder, and hewed down all the incense
altars throughout all the land of
Israel.

(20)And he slew all the priests of
the high places who were there, upon
the altars, and burned the bones of
men upon them.
Then he returned to Jerusalem.

Then he returned to Jerusalem.

165 The Passover Renewed, Other Reforms
II Kings 23:21–27; II Chronicles 35:1–19

II Kings 23:21

(21)And the king
commanded all the people,
"Keep the passover to the LORD
your God,

as it is written in this book of
the covenant."

II Chronicles 35:1a

(1)Josiah

kept a passover to the LORD

in Jerusalem;

II Chronicles 35:1b–17

and they killed the passover lamb on the fourteenth day of the first month. ⁽²⁾He appointed the priests to their offices and encouraged them in the service of the house of the LORD. ⁽³⁾And he said to the Levites who taught all Israel and who were holy to the LORD, "Put the holy ark in the house which Solomon the son of David, king of Israel, built; you need no longer carry it upon your shoulders. Now serve the LORD your God and his people Israel. ⁽⁴⁾Prepare yourselves according to your fathers' houses by your divisions, following the directions of David king of Israel and the directions of Solomon his son. ⁽⁵⁾And stand in the holy place according to the groupings of the fathers' houses of your brethren the lay people, and let there be for each a part of a father's house of the Levites. ⁽⁶⁾And kill the passover lamb, and sanctify yourselves, and prepare for your brethren, to do according to the word of the LORD by Moses."

⁽⁷⁾Then Josiah contributed to the lay people, as passover offerings for all that were present, lambs and kids from the flock to the number of thirty thousand, and three thousand bulls; these were from the king's possessions. ⁽⁸⁾And his princes contributed willingly to the people, to the priests, and to the Levites. Hilkiah, Zechariah, and Jehiel, the chief officers of the house of God, gave to the priests for the passover offerings two thousand six hundred lambs and kids and three hundred bulls. ⁽⁹⁾Conaniah also, and Shemaiah and Nethanel his brothers, and Hashabiah and Je-iel and Jozabad, the chiefs of the Levites, gave to the Levites for the passover offerings five thousand lambs and kids and five hundred bulls.

⁽¹⁰⁾When the service had been prepared for, the priests stood in their place, and the Levites in their divisions according to the king's command. ⁽¹¹⁾And they killed the passover lamb, and the priests sprinkled the blood which they received from them while the Levites flayed the victims. ⁽¹²⁾And they set aside the burnt offerings that they might distribute them according to the groupings of the fathers' houses of the lay people, to offer to the LORD, as it is written in the book of Moses. And so they did with the bulls. ⁽¹³⁾And they roasted the passover lamb with fire according to the ordinance; and they boiled the holy offerings in pots, in caldrons, and in pans, and carried them quickly to all the lay people. ⁽¹⁴⁾And afterward they prepared for themselves and for the priests, because the priests the sons of Aaron were busied in offering the burnt offerings and the fat parts until night; so the Levites prepared for themselves and for the priests the sons of Aaron. ⁽¹⁵⁾The singers, the sons of Asaph, were in their place according to the command of David, and Asaph, and Heman, and Jeduthun the king's seer; and the gatekeepers were at each gate; they did not need to depart from their service, for their brethren the Levites prepared for them.

⁽¹⁶⁾So all the service of the LORD was prepared that day, to keep the passover and to offer burnt offerings on the altar of the LORD, according to the command of King Josiah. ⁽¹⁷⁾And the people of Israel who were present kept the passover at that time, and the feast of unleavened bread seven days.

II Kings 23:22–27	*II Chronicles 35:18–19*
⁽²²⁾For no such passover had been kept since the days of the judges who judged Israel,	⁽¹⁸⁾No passover like it had been kept in Israel since the days of
	Samuel the prophet;
or during all the days of	

the kings of Israel
or of the kings of Judah;

none of the kings of Israel

had kept such a passover as was kept
by Josiah, and the priests and the
Levites, and all Judah and Israel who
were present, and the inhabitants of
Jerusalem.

(23)but in the eighteenth year of
King Josiah this passover
was kept
to the LORD in Jerusalem.

(19)In the eighteenth year of
the reign of Josiah this passover
was kept.

(24)Moreover Josiah put away the
mediums and the wizards and the
teraphim and the idols and all the
abominations that were seen in the
land of Judah and in Jerusalem, that
he might establish the words of the
law which were written in the book
that Hilkiah the priest found in the
house of the LORD. (25)Before him
there was no king like him, who turned
to the LORD with all his heart and
with all his soul and with all his
might, according to all the law of
Moses; not did any like him arise
after him.

(26)Still the LORD did not turn
from the fierceness of his great
wrath, by which his anger was kindled
against Judah, because of all the
provocations with which Manasseh had
provoked him. (27)And the LORD
said, "I will remove Judah also out
of my sight, as I have removed
Israel, and I will cast off this
city which I have chosen, Jerusalem,
and the house of which I said, My
name shall be there."

166 The Death of Josiah

II Kings 23:28–30a   *II Chronicles 35:20–27*

(28)Now the rest of the acts of
Josiah, and all that he did, are they
not written in the Book of the

254

Chronicles of the Kings of Judah?*
(29)In his days

(20)After all this, when Josiah
had prepared the temple,
Neco king of Egypt went up

Pharaoh Neco king of Egypt went up
to the king of Assyria

to fight at Carchemish
on the Euphrates and
Josiah went out against him.

to the river Euphrates.
King Josiah went to meet him;

(21)But he sent envoys to him, saying,
"What have we to do with each other,
king of Judah? I am not coming
against you this day, but against the
house with which I am at war; and God
has commanded me to make haste.
Cease opposing God, who is with me,
lest he destroy you." (22)Nevertheless
Josiah would not turn away from him,
but disguised himself in order to
fight with him. He did not listen to
the words of Neco from the mouth of
God, but joined battle in the
plain of

and Pharaoh Neco slew him at
Megiddo,
when he saw him.

Megiddo.

(23)And the archers shot King
Josiah; and the king said to his
servants, "Take me away, for I am
badly wounded."
(24)So his servants

(30a)And his servants

took him out of the chariot and

carried him dead in a chariot
from Megiddo,
and brought him to Jerusalem,

carried him in his second chariot

and brought him to Jerusalem.
And he died,

and buried him
in his own tomb.

and was buried
in the tombs of his fathers.
All Judah and Jerusalem mourned for
Josiah. (25)Jeremiah also uttered
a lament for Josiah; and all the
singing men and singing women have
spoken of Josiah in their laments
to this day. They made these an
ordinance in Israel; behold, they are
written in the Laments.

*Cf. II Chron. 35:26–27.

(26)Now the rest of the acts of
Josiah, and his good deeds according
to what is written in the law of the
LORD, (27)and his acts, first and
last, behold, they are written in the
Book of the Kings of Israel
and Judah.*

L

167 The Reign of Jehoahaz of Judah

II Kings 23:30b–34

(30b)And the people of the land
took Jehoahaz the son of Josiah, and
anointed him, and
made him king in his father's stead.

(31)Jehoahaz was twenty-three
years old when he began to reign, and
he reigned three months in Jerusalem.
His mother's name was Hamutal the
daughter of Jeremiah of Libnah.
(32)And he did what was evil in the
sight of the LORD, according to all
that his fathers had done.
(33)And Pharaoh Neco
put him in bonds at Riblah in the land
of Hamath, that he might not reign

in Jerusalem, and laid upon the land
a tribute of a hundred talents of
silver and a talent of gold. (34)And
Pharaoh Neco made Eliakim
the son of Josiah king
in the place of Josiah his father,

and changed his name to Jehoiakim.
But he took Jehoahaz away;
and he came to Egypt,
and died there.

II Chronicles 36:1–4

(1)The people of the land
took Jehoahaz the son of Josiah and

made him king in his father's stead
in Jerusalem.
(2)Jehoahaz was twenty-three
years old when he began to reign; and
he reigned three months in Jerusalem.

(3)Then the king of Egypt

deposed him
in Jerusalem and laid upon the land
a tribute of a hundred talents of
silver and a talent of gold. (4)And
the king of Egypt made Eliakim
his brother king

over Judah and Jerusalem,
and changed his name to Jehoiakim;
but Neco took Jehoahaz his brother
and carried him to Egypt.

*Cf. II Kings 23:28.

168 The Reign of Jehoiakim

<table>
<tr><td>II Kings 23:35–24:7</td><td>II Chronicles 36:5–8</td></tr>
</table>

(35)And Jehoiakim gave the silver
and the gold to Pharaoh, but he taxed
the land to give the money according
to the command of Pharaoh. He exacted
the silver and the gold of the people
of the land, from every one according
to his assessment, to give it to
Pharaoh Neco.

(36)Jehoiakim was twenty-five
years old when he began to reign, and
he reigned eleven years in Jerusalem.
His mother's name was Zebidah the
daughter of Pedaiah of Rumah.

/5/Jehoiakim was twenty-five
years old when he began to reign, and
he reigned eleven years in Jerusalem.

(37)And he did what was evil in the sight
of the LORD,
according to all that his fathers
had done.

And he did what was evil in the sight
of the LORD his God.

(24:1)In his days

Nebuchadnezzar king of Babylon came
up,
and Jehoiakim became his servant
three years;

(6)Against him
came up Nebuchadnezzar king of
Babylon,

and bound him in fetters to take him
to Babylon.

then he turned and rebelled against
him. (2)And the LORD sent against
him bands of the Chaldeans, and bands
of the Syrians, and bands of the
Moabites, and bands of the Ammonites,
and sent them against Judah to destroy
it, according to the word of the LORD
which he spoke by his servants the
prophets. (3)Surely this came upon
Judah at the command of the LORD, to
remove them out of his sight, for the
sins of Manasseh, according to all
that he had done, (4)and also for
the innocent blood that he had shed;
for he filled Jerusalem with innocent
blood, and the LORD would not pardon.

(7)Nebuchadnezzar also carried part
of the vessels of the house of the

LORD to Babylon and put them in his palace at Babylon.

/8/Now the rest of the deeds of Jehoiakim, and

(5)Now the rest of the deeds of Jehoiakim, and
all

the abominations

that he did,

that he did,
and what was found against him, behold,

are they not written in the Book of the Chronicles
of the Kings of Judah?

they are written in the Book

of the Kings of Israel and Judah;

(6)So Jehoiakim slept with his fathers,
and Jehoiachin his son reigned in his stead.

and Jehoiachin his son reigned in his stead.

(7)And the king of Egypt did not come again out of his land, for the king of Babylon had taken all that belonged to the king of Egypt from the brook of Egypt to the river Euphrates.

169 The Reign of Jehoiachin

II Kings 24:8–17

II Chronicles 36:9–10

/8/Jehoiachin was eighteen years old when he began to reign, and he reigned three months

/9/Jehoiachin was eight years old when he began to reign, and he reigned three months
and ten days

in Jerusalem.
His mother's name was Nahushta the daughter of Elnathan of Jerusalem.

in Jerusalem.

(9)And he did what was evil in the sight of the LORD,
according to all that his father had done.

And he did what was evil in the sight of the LORD.

(10)At that time the servants of

(10)In the spring of the year King Nebuchadnezzar

Nebuchadnezzar king of Babylon came up to Jerusalem, and the city was besieged. (11)And Nebuchadnezzar king of Babylon came to the city, while his servants were besieging it; (12)and Jehoiachin the king of Judah

gave himself up to the king of
Babylon, himself, and his mother, and
his servants, and his princes, and his
palace officials. The king of Babylon
took him prisoner in the eighth year
of his reign, (13)and carried off
all the treasures of the house of the
LORD,* and the treasures of the king's
house, and cut in pieces all the
vessels of gold in the temple of the
LORD, which Solomon king of Israel
had made, as the LORD had foretold.

(14)He carried away all Jerusalem,
and all the princes, and all the
mighty men of valor, ten thousand
captives, and all the craftsmen and
the smiths; none remained, except the
poorest people of the land.

(15)And he carried away Jehoiachin
to Babylon;

	sent and brought him
	to Babylon,
	with the precious vessels of the
	house of the LORD,†

the king's mother, the king's wives,
his officials, and the chief men of
the land, he took into captivity from
Jerusalem to Babylon. (16)And the
king of Babylon brought captive to
Babylon all the men of valor, seven
thousand, and the craftsmen and the
smiths, one thousand, all of them
strong and fit for war.

(17)And the king of Babylon made
Mattaniah,
Jehoiachin's uncle,

and made

his brother
Zedekiah

king
in his stead,

king

over Judah and Jerusalem.

and changed his name to Zedekiah.

---

*Cf. II Chron. 36:10b.   †Cf. II Kings 24:13a.

170 The Reign of Zedekiah Begins

II Kings 24:18–20	*Jeremiah 52:1–3*	*II Chronicles 36:11–21*
		II Chronicles 36:11–13a
/18/Zedekiah was twenty-one years old when he began to reign, and he reigned eleven years in Jerusalem. His mother's name was Hamutal the daughter of Jeremiah of Libnah. (19)And he did what was evil in the sight of the LORD, according to all that Jehoiakim had done.	/1/Zedekiah was twenty-one years old when he began to reign, and he reigned eleven years in Jerusalem. His mother's name was Hamutal the daughter of Jeremiah of Libnah. (2)And he did what was evil in the sight of the LORD, according to all that Jehoiakim had done.	(11)Zedekiah was twenty-one years old when he began to reign, and he reigned eleven years in Jerusalem. /12/And he did what was evil in the sight of the LORD his God. He did not humble himself before Jeremiah the prophet, who spoke from the mouth of the LORD.
/20/For because of the anger of the LORD it came to the point in Jerusalem and Judah that he cast them out from his presence. And Zedekiah rebelled against the king of Babylon.	/3/For because of the anger of the LORD* it came to the point in Jerusalem and Judah that he cast them out from his presence. And Zedekiah rebelled against the king of Babylon.	(13)He also rebelled against King Nebuchadnezzar,

II Chronicles 36:13b–21

who had made him swear by God; he stiffened his neck and hardened his heart against turning to the LORD, the God of Israel. (14)All the leading priests and the people likewise were exceedingly unfaithful, following all the abominations of the nations; and they polluted the house of the LORD which he had hallowed in Jerusalem.

(15)The LORD, the God of their fathers, sent persistently to them by his messengers, because he had compassion on his people and on his dwelling place; (16)but they kept mocking the messengers of God, despising his words, and scoffing at his prophets, till the wrath of the LORD† rose against his people, till there was no remedy.

(17)Therefore he brought up against them the king of the Chaldeans, who slew their

*Cf. II Chron. 36:16.
†Cf. II Kings 24:20; Jer. 52:2.

young men with the sword in the house of their sanctuary, and had no compassion on young man or virgin, old man or aged; he gave them all into his hand. (18)And all the vessels of the house of God, great and small, and the treasures of the house of the LORD, and the treasures of the king and of his princes, all these he brought to Babylon. (19)And they burned the house of God, and broke down the wall of Jerusalem, and burned all its palaces with fire, and destroyed all its precious vessels.* (20)He took into exile in Babylon those who had escaped from the sword,† and they became servants to him and to his sons until the establishment of the kingdom of Persia, (21)to fulfil the word of the LORD by the mouth of Jeremiah, until the land had enjoyed its sabbaths. All the days that it lay desolate it kept sabbath, to fulfil seventy years.

171 The Fall of Jerusalem

II Kings 25:1–12	*Jeremiah 39:1–10*	*Jeremiah 52:4–16*
(1)And in the ninth year of his reign,	(1)In the ninth year of Zedekiah king of Judah,	/4/And in the ninth year of his reign,
in the tenth month, on the tenth day of the month,	in the tenth month,	in the tenth month, on the tenth day of the month,
Nebuchadnezzar king of Babylon came	Nebuchadrezzar king of Babylon	Nebuchadrezzar king of Babylon came
and all his army	and all his army came	and all his army
against Jerusalem, and	against Jerusalem and	against Jerusalem, and they
laid siege to it; and they built siegeworks against it round about. (2)So the city was besieged till	besieged it;	laid siege to it; and they built siegeworks against it round about. (5)So the city was besieged till
the eleventh year of King Zedekiah.	(2)in the eleventh year of Zedekiah, in the fourth month,	the eleventh year of King Zedekiah.
(3)On the ninth day of the month, the famine was so severe in the city that there was no food for the people of the land.	on the ninth day of the month,	/6/In the fourth month on the ninth day of the month, the famine was so severe in the city that there was no food for the people of the land.
[4]Then a breach was made in the city;	a breach was made in the city;	/7/Then a breach was made in the city;

*Cf. II Kings 25:9; Jer. 39:8; 52:13.
†Cf. II Kings 25:11; Jer. 39:9; 52:15.

261

	/3/and all the princes of the king of Babylon came and sat in the middle gate: Nergal-sharezer, Samgar-nebo, Sarsechim the Rabsaris, Nergal-sharezer the Rabmag, with all the rest of the officers of the king of Babylon. /4/When Zedekiah king of Judah	
and all the soldiers	and all the soldiers saw them,	and all the soldiers
*	they fled	fled
	and went out	and went out
by night	by night from the city	from the city by night
by way of	by way of	by way of
the gate between the two walls,		the gate between the two walls,
by the king's garden,	the king's garden in the gate between the two walls.	by the king's garden,
though the Chaldeans were around the city. And they went in the direction of the Arabah. (5)But the army of the Chaldeans pursued the king,	And they went in the direction of the Arabah. (5)But the army of the Chaldeans pursued them,	though the Chaldeans were around the city. And they went in the direction of the Arabah. (8)But the army of the Chaldeans pursued the king,
and overtook him in the plains of Jericho; and all his army was scattered from him. /6/Then they captured the king, and brought him up to	and overtook Zedekiah in the plains of Jericho; and when they had taken him, they brought him up to Nebuchadrezzar	and overtook Zedekiah in the plains of Jericho; and all his army was scattered from him. (9)Then they captured the king, and brought him up to
the king of Babylon at Riblah,	king of Babylon, at Riblah, in the land of Hamath;	the king of Babylon at Riblah, in the land of Hamath;

*"fled" is missing.

and he passed sentence upon him.	and he passed sentence upon him.	and he passed sentence upon him.
(7)They slew the sons of Zedekiah	(6)The king of Babylon slew the sons of Zedekiah at Riblah	(10)The king of Babylon ⚹ slew the sons of Zedekiah
before his eyes,	before his eyes; and the king of Babylon slew all the nobles of Judah.	before his eyes, and also slew ⚹ all the princes of Judah at Riblah.
and put out the eyes of Zedekiah, and bound him in fetters, and	(7)He put out the eyes of Zedekiah, and bound him in fetters	(11)He put out the eyes ⚹ of Zedekiah, and bound him in fetters, and the king of Babylon
took him to Babylon.	to take him to Babylon.	took him to Babylon, and put him in prison till the day of his death.
(8)In the fifth month, on the seventh day of the month— which was the nineteenth year of King Nebuchadnezzar, king of Babylon— Nebuzaradan, the captain of the bodyguard, a servant of the king of Babylon, came to Jerusalem.		(12)In the fifth month, on the tenth ⚹ day of the month— which was the nineteenth year of King Nebuchadrezzar, king of Babylon— Nebuzaradan the captain of the bodyguard who served the king of Babylon, entered Jerusalem.
(9)And he burned the house of the LORD, and the king's house and all the houses of Jerusalem; every great house he burned down.	(8)The Chaldeans burned the king's house and the house of the people,	(13)And he burned the house of the LORD, and the king's house and all the houses of Jerusalem; every great house he burned down.
(10)And all the army of the Chaldeans, who were with the captain of the guard, broke down the walls around Jerusalem.	and broke down the walls of Jerusalem.	(14)And all the army of the Chaldeans, who were with the captain of the guard, broke down all the walls round about Jerusalem.
		/15/And some of the poorest of the people
(11)And the rest of the	/9/And the rest of the	and the rest of the

263

people who were left in
the city, and the
deserters who had
deserted to
the king of Babylon,
together with the rest
of the multitude,

Nebuzaradan the
captain of the guard
carried into exile.

(12)But

the captain of the guard
left

some of the poorest
of the land

to be vinedressers and
plowmen.

people who were left in
the city, and the
deserters who had
deserted to
him,
together with the rest

of the people who
remained

Nebuzaradan the
captain of the guard
carried into exile
to Babylon.

(10)Nebuzaradan
the captain of the guard
left
in the land of Judah
some of the poor people

who owned nothing,

and gave them vineyards
and fields at the same
time.

people who were left in
the city, and the
deserters who had
deserted to
the king of Babylon,
together with the rest

of the artisans
Nebuzaradan the
captain of the guard
carried into exile.

(16)But
Nebuzaradan
the captain of the guard
left

some of the poorest
of the land

to be vinedressers and
plowmen.

172 The Plundering of the Temple

II Kings 25:13–17

(13)And the pillars of bronze
that were in the house of the LORD,
and the stands and the bronze sea
that were in the house of the LORD,
the Chaldeans broke in pieces, and
carried the bronze to Babylon.
(14)And they took away the pots,
and the shovels, and the snuffers,

and the dishes for incense and all
the vessels of bronze used in the
temple service, (15)the
firepans also, and the bowls.

Jeremiah 52:17–23

(17)And the pillars of bronze
that were in the house of the LORD,
and the stands and the bronze sea
that were in the house of the LORD,
the Chaldeans broke in pieces, and
carried all the bronze to Babylon.
/18/And they took away the pots,
and the shovels, and the snuffers,
and the basins,
and the dishes for incense and all
the vessels of bronze used in the
temple service; (19)also
the small bowls, and the firepans,
and the basins, and the pots, and the
lampstands, and the dishes for

What was of gold the captain of the
guard took away as gold, and what
was of silver, as silver. (16)As
for the two pillars, the one sea,

and the stands, which Solomon

had made for the house of the LORD,
the bronze of all these vessels
was beyond weight.

(17)The height of the one pillar
was eighteen cubits,

and upon it was a capital of
bronze; the height of the capital
was three cubits; a network and
pomegranates, all of bronze, were
upon the capital round about. And
the second pillar had the like, with
the network.

incense, and the bowls for libation.
What was of gold the captain of the
guard took away as gold, and what
was of silver, as silver. /20/As
for the two pillars, the one sea,
the twelve bronze bulls which were
under*
and the stands, which Solomon
the king
had made for the house of the LORD,
the bronze of all these vessels
was beyond weight.
(21)As for the pillars,
the height of the one pillar
was eighteen cubits,
its circumference was twelve cubits,
and its thickness was four fingers,
and it was hollow.
(22)Upon it was a capital of
bronze; the height of the one capital
was five cubits; a network and
pomegranates, all of bronze, were
upon the capital round about. And
the second pillar had the like, with

pomegranates. (23)There were
ninety-six pomegranates on the sides;
all the pomegranates were a hundred
upon the network round about.

173 Additional Victims of the Babylonians

II Kings 25:18–21

(18)And the captain of the guard
took Seraiah the chief priest, and
Zephaniah the second priest, and the
three keepers of the threshold;
(19)and from the city he took an
officer who had been in command of
the men of war, and five men of the
king's council who were found in the
city; and the secretary of the
commander of the army who mustered

Jeremiah 52:24–27

(24)And the captain of the guard
took Seraiah the chief priest, and
Zephaniah the second priest, and the
three keepers of the threshold;
/25/and from the city he took an
officer who had been in command of
the men of war, and seven men of the
king's council who were found in the
city; and the secretary of the
commander of the army who mustered

*Hebrew lacks "the sea."

the people of the land; and sixty
men of the people of the land who
were found in the city. (20)And
Nebuzaradan the captain of the guard
took them, and brought them to the
king of Babylon at Riblah. (21)And
the king of Babylon smote them, and
put them to death at Riblah in the
land of Hamath. So Judah was taken
into exile out of its land.

the people of the land; and sixty
men of the people of the land who
were found in the city. (26)And
Nebuzaradan the captain of the guard
took them, and brought them to the
king of Babylon at Riblah. (27)And
the king of Babylon smote them, and
put them to death at Riblah in the
land of Hamath. So Judah was taken
into exile out of its land.

174 The Governorship of Gedaliah

II Kings 25:22–26

Jeremiah 52:28–30; 40:5–41:3

(52:28)This is the number of the
people whom Nebuchadrezzar carried
away captive; in the seventh year,
three thousand and twenty-three Jews;
(29)in the eighteenth year of
Nebuchadrezzar he carried away captive
from Jerusalem eight hundred and
thirty-two persons; (30)in the
twenty-third year of Nebuchadrezzar,
Nebuzaradan the captain of the guard
carried away captive of the Jews seven
hundred and forty-five persons; all
the persons were four thousand and six
hundred.
(40:5)"If you remain, then return to

(22)And over the people who
remained in the land of Judah, whom
Nebuchadnezzar king of Babylon had
left, he appointed
Gedaliah the son of Ahikam, son of
Shaphan,

governor.

Gedaliah the son of Ahikam, son of
Shaphan,
whom the king of Babylon appointed
governor
of the cities of Judah, and dwell with
him among the people; or go wherever
you think it right to go." So the
captain of the guard gave him an
allowance of food and a present, and
let him go. (6)Then Jeremiah went
to Gedaliah the son of Ahikam, at
Mizpah, and dwelt with him among the
people who were left in the land.

⁽²³⁾Now when all the captains
of the forces

and their men heard that the king of
Babylon had appointed Gedaliah

governor,

they came
with their men
to Gedaliah at Mizpah, namely,
Ishmael the son of Nethaniah, and
Johanan the son of Kareah, and
Seraiah the son of Tanhumeth

the Netophathite, and Ja-azaniah the
son of the Ma-acathite.

⁽²⁴⁾And Gedaliah

swore to them and their men, saying,
"Do not be afraid because

of the Chaldean
officials;
dwell in the land, and serve the king
of Babylon, and it shall be well with
you."

/7/Now when all the captains
of the forces
in the open country
and their men heard that the king of
Babylon had appointed Gedaliah
the son of Ahikam
governor in the land,
and had committed to him men, women,
and children, those of the poorest of
the land who had not been taken into
exile to Babylon,
/8/they came

to Gedaliah at Mizpah, namely
Ishmael the son of Nethaniah, and
Jonathan the son of Kareah, and
Seraiah the son of Tanhumeth, and
the sons of Ephai
the Netophathite, and Jezaniah the
son of the Ma-acathite,
they and their men.
/9/And Gedaliah
the son of Ahikam, son of Shaphan,
swore to them and their men, saying,
"Do not be afraid
to serve
the Chaldeans.

Dwell in the land, and serve the king
of Babylon, and it shall be well with
you.
⁽¹⁰⁾As for me, I will dwell at Mizpah,
to stand for you before the Chaldeans
who will come to us; but as for you,
gather wine and summer fruits and oil,
and store them in your vessels, and
dwell in your cities that you have
taken." ⁽¹¹⁾Likewise, when all the
Jews who were in Moab and among the
Ammonites and in Edom and in other
lands heard that the king of Babylon
had left a remnant in Judah and had
appointed Gedaliah the son of Ahikam,
son of Shaphan, as governor over them,
⁽¹²⁾then all the Jews returned
from all the places to which they had
been driven and came to the land of

267

Judah, to Gedaliah at Mizpah; and they gathered wine and summer fruits in great abundance.

(13)Now Johanan the son of Kareah and all the leaders of the forces in the open country came to Gedaliah at Mizpah (14)and said to him, "Do you know that Baalis the king of the Ammonites has sent Ishmael the son of Nethaniah to take your life?" But Gedaliah the son of Ahikam would not believe them. (15)Then Johanan the son of Kareah spoke secretly to Gedaliah at Mizpah, "Let me go and slay Ishmael the son of Nethaniah, and no one will know it. Why should he take your life, so that all the Jews who are gathered about you would be scattered, and the remnant of Judah would perish?" (16)But Gedaliah the son of Ahikam said to Johanan the son of Kareah, "You shall not do this thing, for you are speaking falsely of Ishmael."

/25/In the seventh month, Ishmael the son of Nethaniah, son of Elishama, of the royal family,	(41:1)In the seventh month, Ishmael the son of Nethaniah, son of Elishama, of the royal family, one of the chief officers of the king,
came with ten men,	came with ten men to Gedaliah the son of Ahikam, at Mizpah. As they ate bread together there at Mizpah, (2)Ishmael the son of Nethaniah and the ten men with him
and attacked	rose up and struck down Gedaliah the son of Ahikam, son of Shaphan, with the sword,
and killed Gedaliah	and killed him, whom the king of Babylon had appointed governor in the land. (3)Ishmael also slew
and the Jews and the Chaldeans who were with him at Mizpah.	all the Jews who were with Gedaliah at Mizpah, and the Chaldean soldiers who happened to be there.
(26)Then all the people, both small and great,	

and the captains of the forces arose,*
and went to Egypt;†
for they were afraid of the Chaldeans.‡

175 Jehoiachin Remembered

II Kings 25:27–30

(27)And in the thirty-seventh
year of the exile of Jehoiachin king
of Judah, in the twelfth month, on
the twenty-seventh day of the month,
Evil-merodach king of Babylon, in
the year that he began to reign,
graciously freed Jehoiachin king
of Judah
from prison;
(28)and he spoke kindly to him,
and gave him a seat above the seats
of the kings who were with him in
Babylon. (29)So Jehoiachin put off
his prison garments. And every day
of his life he dined regularly at
the king's table; (30)and for his
allowance, a regular allowance was
given him by the king,
every day a portion,

as long as he lived.

Jeremiah 52:31–34

/31/And in the thirty-seventh
year of the exile of Jehoiachin king
of Judah, in the twelfth month, on
the twenty-fifth day of the month,
Evil-merodach king of Babylon, in
the year that he became king,
graciously freed Jehoiachin king
of Judah
and brought him out of prison;
(32)and he spoke kindly to him,
and gave him a seat above the seats
of the kings who were with him in
Babylon. (33)So Jehoiachin put off
his prison garments. And every day
of his life he dined regularly at
the king's table; (34)and for his
allowance, a regular allowance was
given him by the king of Babylon,
every day a portion,
until the day of his death,
as long as he lived.

176 The End of the Exile

Ezra 1:1–4

(1)In the first year of Cyrus
king of Persia, that the word of the
LORD by the mouth of Jeremiah might
be accomplished, the LORD stirred up
the spirit of Cyrus king of Persia
so that he made a proclamation

II Chronicles 36:22–23

/22/In the first year of Cyrus
king of Persia, that the word of the
LORD by the mouth of Jeremiah might
be accomplished, the LORD stirred up
the spirit of Cyrus king of Persia
so that he made a proclamation

*Cf. Jer. 41:16.
†Cf. Jer. 41:17.
‡Cf. Jer. 41:18.

throughout all his kingdom and also put it in writing:

(2)"Thus says Cyrus king of Persia: The LORD, the God of heaven, has given me all the kingdoms of the earth, and he has charged me to build him a house at Jerusalem, which is in Judah. (3)Whoever is among you of all his people, may his God be with him, and let him go up to Jerusalem, which is in Judah, and rebuild the house of the LORD, the God of Israel—he is the God who is in Jerusalem; (4)and let each survivor, in whatever place he sojourns, be assisted by the men of his place with silver and gold, with goods and with beasts, besides freewill offerings for the house of God which is in Jerusalem."

throughout all his kingdom and also put it in writing:

/23/"Thus says Cyrus king of Persia: The LORD, the God of heaven, has given me all the kingdoms of the earth, and he has charged me to build him a house at Jerusalem, which is in Judah. Whoever is among you of all his people, may the LORD his God be with him, and let him go up."

Index of Passages in I and II Chronicles, Psalms, Isaiah, Jeremiah, and Ezra